Advance praise for
The California Snatch Racket

"A dark history that succeeds brilliantly as neo-noir crime writing, *The California Snatch Racket* is smart, enthusiastically detailed, and a damn good read!"

—**Ron Franscell**, bestselling author of *The Darkest Night*

"A fun and informative jaunt back in time to an era long forgotten. Many of the cases amazed me."

—**Kathryn Casey**, author of *Blood Lines* and *Singularity*

"Captures the flavor of the time and the impact of the events on the average guy, all with the urgency of an angry Tommy gun."

—**Pat Craig**, critic, Bay Area News Group

"True-crime readers will be fascinated by the meticulous research and case write-ups in this book detailing the era when kidnappings were so prevalent. *The California Snatch Racket* takes the reader into a world of coldhearted criminals, desperate family members, and determined law officers. Don't miss this one."

—**Sandie Kirkland**, Booksie's Blog

"A must read for anyone interested in the evolution of criminal activity or in the prohibition and depression eras in the United States."

—**Diane Fanning**, bestselling author of true-crime books, including *Mommies Little Girl*

"Smith and Rogers rip back the candy-coating on the land of sunshine, Hollywood dreams and beach parties, exposing the seedy underworld of gangsters and brutal kidnappings during prohibition and the depression. History buffs and true crime aficionados will relish this inside look into the Golden State's vicious past."

—**Kathleen Antrim**, bestselling author of *Capital Offense*

THE CALIFORNIA SNATCH RACKET

Kidnappings During the Prohibition and Depression Eras

by James R. Smith and W. Lane Rogers

CRAVEN STREET
B O O K S
Fresno, California

The California Snatch Racket
Copyright © 2010 by James R. Smith and W. Lane Rogers.
All rights reserved.

Published by Craven Street Books
an imprint of Linden Publishing
2006 South Mary, Fresno, California 93721
559-233-6633 / 800-345-4447
CravenStreetBooks.com

Craven Street Books and Colophon are trademarks of
Linden Publishing, Inc.

ISBN 978-1-884995-63-7

135798642

Printed in the United States of America
on acid-free paper.

Library of Congress Cataloging-in-Publication Data

Smith, James R.
  The California snatch racket : kidnappings during the Prohibition
and Depression eras / by James R. Smith and W. Lane Rogers.
     p. cm.
Includes bibliographical references and index.
  ISBN 978-1-884995-63-7 (pbk. : alk. paper)
  1. Kidnapping--California--Case studies. 2. Crime--California--
History--20th century. I. Rogers, W. Lane, 1944- II. Title.

  HV6601.C2S65 2010
  364.15'40979409042--dc22

                                        2010008593

Contents

This book is dedicated to my friend and co-author, the late W. Lane Rogers. May God bless and keep you.

Preface & Acknowledgments

Writing about crime in not unlike a criminal investigation. However, a significant advantage enjoyed over investigatory agencies is knowing the outcome at the beginning. Nevertheless, like any specialized area of history, crime research—in this instance, kidnapping—burdens its practitioners with problems and challenges unique to the genre.

In most instances, there exist no archived police reports to examine, no dust-laden files that reveal the twists and turns and minutiae of forgotten criminal investigations. Standardized police reporting is a relatively new phenomenon. Yet even after police reporting came into practice, long-term preservation of meticulously gathered information did not. During those pre-computer days, files were boxed and stacked in odd corners. When space requirements demanded removal of clutter, old records often were the first things to go. Consequently, a distressing amount of crime history was set ablaze in police department incinerators or mixed with discarded fish wrappers, watermelon rinds, and broken beer bottles in the tumblers of rumbling garbage trucks. Regrettably, many criminal trial transcripts were given the same treatment.

From its beginning, the FBI kept meticulous records. A small percentage of its files—meaningless when compared to total FBI holdings—are readily available to researchers. However, the overwhelming majority must be accessed through the Freedom of

Information Act, which demands a laborious, time consuming, costly effort. Then, more often than not, key sections of salient documents released to historians are obscured by heavy ink from black markers.

But never mind. FBI files are largely useless anyway. Rarely did Justice Department operatives play more than a peripheral role in local kidnappings during the 1920s and 1930s.

Consequently, newspapers cease to be secondary sources and become primary documents. In most instances, they are the only original documents available, and that very fact creates its own set of problems.

In 1921, a prisoner sat in the San Mateo county jail awaiting trial for the kidnapping and murder of a Colma priest. The *San Francisco Chronicle* penned an innocuous story in which the jailer left the prisoner unattended while he went to lunch. All was well when he returned. The *San Francisco Examiner* wrote an altogether different story. While the jailer was away, a large crowd congregated about the jail and boisterous threats of lynching shattered the noonday calm.

A writer has two choices: Based on the manner in which each newspaper covered the kidnapping and murder as a whole, a reasonable conclusion can be drawn about the accuracy of the reporting. Still, however, a "reasonable conclusion" falls short of a definitive conclusion and may, in fact, be dead wrong.

The second choice—a choice we have chosen with frequency in writing *The California Snatch Racket*—is to present each newspaper's story and let readers draw their own conclusion. By doing so, however, a third dimension is introduced into the narrative: The *Chronicle* and *Examiner* move beyond their roles as reporting entities and become an integral part of the story itself.

In fact, pitting one newspaper against another—editorial slugfests were common during the 1920s and 1930s—is an effective way to place the era into context and offer the reader a front row seat to a multiplicity of lively opinions from argumentative reporters and moody editors.

Radio was introduced to the American public in 1922, and the first network, NBC, invented itself in 1927. Practitioners of jazz, swing, and big band, and live broadcasts of outrageous comedies, dark mysteries, and heart-rending dramas dominated the airwaves. Not until the eve of World War II, did this newfangled medium become a reliable source for information and news reporting.

As early as World War I, Pathe newsreels were seen in the nation's motion picture theaters, and by the 1920s and 1930s most major studios produced their own product. Newsreels ran about ten minutes and competed as intermission fare with popcorn, restrooms, and Lucky Strikes. Stories given the most coverage were beauty pageants, baby contests, and weight lifting events. Fox Movietone even developed a category it called "Curiosities and Freaks." Newsreels had little news value and the medium never matured beyond being an entertainment venue.

If one sought a daily helping of news—and most folks did—newspapers were the single source.

During the first three decades of the twentieth century, newspapers—marginal as some were—flourished. Californians got their news in morning and evening doses and occasionally by extras hawked on street corners. So widely read was the printed word that even small towns often had two or three daily papers. It was a golden era of newspapering and giants of the industry—the *San Francisco Chronicle*, *Los Angeles Times*, *San Francisco Examiner*, *San Diego Union*, and *Los Angeles Herald*—wielded enormous power and influence, not always proportionate to their excellence.

The vagary of news reporting was evident in the early 1920s when a particularly loathsome kidnapping-murder commanded a 27-day front page run in California newspapers. In the blink of an eye, the story was relegated to the back pages of second sections when Fatty Arbuckle, one of the best known silent film comedians of the day, was arrested and charged with the brutal murder of a young starlet.

Simple arithmetic prevailed. The comedian's trouble with the law would sell more newspapers than the ongoing murder investigation of an obscure kidnap victim. Fatty got the headlines.

Manifestations of irresponsibility played out when newspapers thrust themselves into an investigation by playing amateur sleuth. Reporters poked around crime scenes and "found" valuable clues that less inventive police officers had overlooked. They tracked down elusive witnesses, extracted "exclusive" confessions, vindicated or condemned the accused, and otherwise muddied the waters of legitimate investigatory procedure. Rarely did the sleuthing produce anything more useful than self-serving headlines.

In 1933, a young San Jose department store heir was kidnapped and murdered. Two men who confessed to the crime were, themselves, kidnapped from the county jail and hanged in a local park. Every newspaper in California—and many around the world—gave front page coverage to the lynching. The reportage was sensational, garish, lurid, and, in some instances, ugly and obscene. Nevertheless, today's historian finds great value in the stories. Shocking as the coverage was, inflamed words scribbled by passionate reporters provide a lens through which to view the uniqueness of a place, an incident, a people, and the era in which they lived.

For that very reason, we conceived *The California Snatch Racket* as a book in which long-silent voices would speak anew. Wherever appropriate, portions of original newspaper reports are included in the narrative, allowing victims, perpetrators, law enforcement officers, witnesses, lawyers, judges, and reporters to speak for themselves.

They do, and in many instances they speak in a language as unique as the era itself. A married woman was a matron, a single woman a girl. Whether matron or girl, however, if someone close to them was kidnapped they were prostrated for days.

An automobile was a machine, a pistol a gat, an apartment a flat, a hat a bowler, and a hat store a toggery. A psychiatrist was an alienist, a juror a venireman.

If folks wanted by the law were on the loose, the city, county, state, or all three conducted the greatest manhunt in the history of the city, county, state, or all three. Any suspect who had at least two shady associates was a member of a notorious gang of hoodlums, and virtually all kidnappings were the most ruthless ever recorded in the annals of California crime.

Regardless of sensational reporting, outlandish exaggeration, and outrageous bias, early newspapers are a tremendous repository of historical information. The authors of *The California Snatch Racket* extend profound gratitude to the scores of reporters—men and women, most nameless, all deceased—who unknowingly contributed lively prose and tangy opinion to this narrative.

Examining newspaper microfilm is a tedious, often frustrating endeavor that demands a keen eye and dogged persistence. Warm thanks are due Liberty Smith, whose newspaper research contributed immeasurably to this volume.

We are grateful to the late George Mallman, who shared his expertise in state archive holdings and was helpful in ferreting out California prison records.

Appreciation is extended to the dedicated professionals in California's archival repositories, whose expertise was vital to our research effort. The San Francisco Main Library offered critical resources with the able support of Christina Moretta. The extensive collections at the California State Library in Sacramento were invaluable. Staff at the Dr. Martin Luther King, Jr. Library in San Jose was particularly helpful, especially Stacy Mueller, California Room Librarian, who shared the institution's photo archive. Linda Valdez at the Sutter County Library in Yuba City was generous in her assistance, as was volunteer Don Burtis, who contributed considerable research. The California State Archives provided photographs and documents of those incarcerated in California's state prisons, thanks to the research efforts of archivist Genevieve Troka.

Other repositories important to the research process were Special Collections at the University of Arizona Library and the Arizona

Historical Society in Tucson. Also, thanks go to Hayden Library at Arizona State University and the Arizona Department of Library, Archives and Public Records in Phoenix.

Within the University of Arizona South, thanks are given to Patricia F. Moreno, Esq., adjunct instructor in political science, for directing the authors to useful sources in immigration law. Teri Goral, Esq., adjunct professor of political science and counselor in the Cochise County Public Defenders Office, helped make sense of otherwise unintelligible legal language. A special debt of gratitude is owed Dr. Barbara Wiedemann Citera, assistant professor of history—always a reliable friend who lent her expertise in translating otherwise elusive documents from German to English. Thanks are due Dr. Todd O. Lutes, associate professor of political science and division chair-liberal studies, for his unintended contribution as a sounding board over countless cups of truck stop coffee.

Introduction

During the summer of 1874, four-year-old Charley Ross was kidnapped near his parents' home in Germantown, Pennsylvania. The perpetrators demanded $20,000 ransom—well over half a million dollars today—under the threat of death.

Christian Ross, the boy's father, was advised by police to stall for time and not pay the ransom. Doing so might encourage other abductions, authorities reasoned. Ross did as advised. He communicated with the culprits through newspaper personal columns, while the kidnappers wrote him more than two dozen letters. Each was more threatening than the last.

Charley was never seen again.

However, "sightings," fatuous as they were, occurred around the country. As time wore on—months, then years—a crop of teenage boys claimed to be Charley. None were. Circus impresario P. T. Barnum, attuned to the kidnapping's publicity value, offered a personal reward of $10,000 for the lad's return. He got the publicity he sought, but not the boy.

A clever glass manufacturer produced souvenir bottles bearing Charley's name and likeness. The trinkets enjoyed brisk sales across the nation. The boy's father wrote a book, *The Father's Story of Charley Ross, the Kidnapped Child*. It, too, sold well.

In time, a presumption of murder prevailed. Nonetheless, Charley's name was kept alive well into the 1880s. Each year, the anniversary of his kidnapping was marked in the press and his story retold.

The abduction was 65-years-old when, in 1939, a 69-year-old man filed suit in superior court in Phoenix, Arizona, in an attempt to establish his identity as the kidnapped boy—grown old. The effort failed.

Historians have cited the Ross case as the first reported ransom kidnapping in America. Perhaps it was. However, because kidnapping was rare, only a handful of jurisdictions nationwide acknowledged it as a specific crime. Yet, kidnapping, for myriad purposes, is as old as recorded history—and may be older.

The uniqueness of the Ross case exists in the fact that the nation's press embraced it as a cause cèlébre. Newspapers across the land devoted untold yards of column inches to the story, and they did so long after it ceased to be news. Publishers, business managers, and circulation directors had discovered a simple maxim: Sensational crime stories, especially kidnappings, sold newspapers in great numbers.

In the aftermath of the Ross excitement, a clergyman took to the pulpit and told congregates that he opposed capital punishment for murderers. Not so for "ransomers." The gallows and the electric chair ought to be reserved for kidnappers.

While ransom kidnapping became the most popular, other forms of the genre were at play as well. An early California case speaks to the multiplicity of motives that inspired abductions—and purposefully orchestrated disappearances made to look like abductions. In July 1902, Los Angeles attorney Adolphus Gustavus Hinckley, appearing none the worse for the wear, popped in on his family after a two-month absence.

The lawyer's reappearance shed no light on his disappearance. "The story of my absence is as strange as any that ever has been told by the most fanciful writer of fiction," said Hinckley with a straight face, "but it is impossible for me to relate any of the details [without exposing] me to loss of life."

With skepticism dripping from its pen, the *Los Angeles Times* wrote, "It may have been a band of mountain brigands hankering for a golden ransom; a crowd of expert thieves intent on filtching from him a large amount of money…or it may have been a small-pox quarantine. Huh!"

What Hinckley was up to during his two-month absence is anyone's guess. Presumably, the wily lawyer carried his secret to the grave. His disappearance, however, demonstrated that a kind of romantic mythology associated with the insidious crime of kidnapping could be used for personal benefit.

Despite nonsense and ballyhoo, kidnapping remained an isolated crime until the second decade of the twentieth century. Still, its ability to stir hearts, minds, and pocket books did not go unnoticed. During the early days of film, kidnapping was a popular subject. The flickering image of an Arabian knight galloping into the sunset clutching the bare midriff of a stolen maiden was a mainstay of silent films. Lurid depictions of kidnappings were so popular in Chicago's nickelodeons that police were compelled to confiscate films and outlaw the genre. Overt portrayals, it was feared, would incite the genuine act.

Shameless exploitation aside, kidnapping was dead serious business. For reasons long debated among historians and sociologists, ransom kidnapping entered its heyday at the close of World War I and the onset of the Jazz Age. It reached its apogee during the next two decades.

Certainly, Prohibition and the explosion of organized crime it engendered played a significant role in the emergence of kidnapping as a means of influencing events and, theoretically at least, acquiring a fat pile of money—fast.

During this era of bathtub gin and rumble seat sin, competition among Prohibition gangs was intense and ruthless. Bootlegging was a billion dollar business. In Detroit, for example, distilling and distributing illegal liquor was the city's second largest industry, surpassed only by the manufacture of automobiles. So pervasive was the demand for illicit booze, Prohibition spawned a generation of nouveau riche—and rich corpses.

Gun-point abductions between competing gangs became a means of achieving sundry ends. It was an efficient method of intimidation, persuasion, elimination, and disposal—now and again at a river's bottom with chunks of concrete affixed to a hoodlum's torso. Ransom kidnapping was not ignored and large sums of money passed between gang hierarchies.

Kidnapping was a cottage industry and its frequency sent reporters and headline writers scurrying for descriptive phrases. By the early 1920s, the "snatch racket" was coined by a clever pundit—and it stuck.

Not surprisingly, gangland snatchings made headlines and provoked copycat crimes. Abductions orchestrated by amateurs were risky propositions for both perpetrators and victims. Money-hungry improvisers lacked the patience employed by professionals. All too often, knee-jerk reactions to unanticipated events led to the death of the captive.

Now and then, aberrant minds joined the snatch racket. The 1924 abduction and murder of Bobby Franks in Chicago was a case in point. Homosexual lovers Richard Loeb and Nathan Leopold—both came from rich families and were strikingly intelligent—killed 14-year-old Franks in cold blood just for the thrill of it. William Edward Hickman—he was an outstanding scholar and popular student—did the same in Los Angeles in 1927. He murdered and dismembered a young girl for no other reason than to "test his capacity to deliberately take a human life under the most revolting conditions."

One of the most publicized kidnapping cases of the 1920s may have borrowed from Adolphus Gustavus Hinckley's cleverness, and it may not have been a kidnapping at all. In 1926, famed Los Angeles evangelist Aimee Semple McPherson disappeared from Venice Beach. Presumed drowned, she was resurrected a few weeks later in Douglas, Arizona, with a sermonized tale of kidnapping and torture in a Mexican shack. In fact, her disappearance may have taken her—and a lover—to a cabin by the sea at Carmel.

As the Jazz Age segued into the Great Depression, gangsterism gripped America and violence became a breakfast staple of morning newspaper readers. The incidence of ransom kidnappings, and the stakes demanded, increased exponentially as the nation's economic health declined. A disturbing phenomenon emerged when otherwise ordinary folks turned to kidnapping to assuage the sting of unemployment.

Neighbors were astonished when 65-year-old Mary Skeele was kidnapped by rank amateurs. The victim's husband was a University of Southern California music professor of modest means, and the $10,000 ransom demand was simply outrageous. The Depression was in full bloom, banks suffered diminished liquidity, mortgage foreclosures were common, a quarter of the nation's workforce was unemployed, and Professor Skeele was fortunate to bring home a reduced paycheck. The naive perpetrators of the crime were a ne'er-do-well ex-convict and an unemployed former music student in financial distress.

Charles Lindbergh, a tall, lanky air mail pilot was, arguably, the best known name in the world. In 1927, he flew non-stop from New York to Paris—the first aviator who challenged the treacherous Atlantic and won. Five years later, his life was reduced to seemingly endless days in a hot, muggy courtroom at Flemington, New Jersey. Bruno Richard Hauptman was on trial for kidnapping and murder.

What the press called the "crime of the century" occurred when Lindbergh's young son was snatched from his crib. Fifty-thousand dollars ransom was paid for his return, but to no good purpose.

Before this staggering sum of money was delivered, the child was murdered and his body discarded in a patch of weeds.

Hundreds of reporters, newsreel cameramen, and radio commentators converged on an otherwise obscure New Jersey town, and, for the duration of the trial, Flemington was the news capital of the world.

Convicted and sentenced to die by electrocution, four years dragged by before Hauptman's execution in 1936. By the time the killer met his fate, societal misfits, drooling over the $50,000 ransom paid to Hauptman, made the snatch racket something close to an American pastime.

The *San Francisco Chronicle* summed up the situation in a blistering editorial: "Kidnapping for ransom in the United States has grown to the proportions of an epidemic. Reports of men, women and children seized and carried off for ransom come in so fast that they have become almost routine."

Congress reacted to public outrage by passage of the Lindberg Act. The legislation made it a federal crime to transport anyone across state lines who had been "unlawfully seized, confined, inveigled, decoyed, kidnapped, abducted or carried away…and held for ransom or reward."

In 1934, the law's teeth were sharpened when the death penalty was added to the statute. At the same time, the FBI, a newly constituted federal police agency, stepped into the fray. The agency was mandated to enter kidnapping investigations after seven days, under the assumption that the victim had been taken out-of-state.

Yet another law passed the same year made it a federal offense for kidnappers to flee from one state to another to avoid prosecution. Not surprisingly, the new laws failed to stem the tide of kidnappings. It was business as usual in the snatch racket, and it seemed no one was safe.

When a plot to kidnap screen idol Mary Pickford was foiled, the attendant publicity inspired a string of uninspired copycats and they, too, were foiled. Regardless, the film colony was seized by a collective shudder. High walls, some topped with concertina wire, went up, and bars, some electrified, were placed on the windows of Hollywood mansions. Bodyguards were hired and some among the rich and famous armed themselves. When millionaire film star neighbor William F. Gettle was kidnapped and held for a ransom rivaling the Lindbergh sum, more than a few celluloid luminaries ordered moving vans.

Still, most kidnappings involved ordinary folks who may have had—or appeared to have had—more than their neighbors. The victims were not well known, and not fabulously wealthy. And many perished at the hands of their captors.

Behavioral psychologist Charles B. Fester once observed, "You either get wealth by inheriting it, by working for it, or by stealing it." During the Depression, when the gulf between rich and poor was excavated to new depths, ransom kidnapping appealed to deviate minds as a surefire scheme to eliminate the economic vagaries imposed by a failed economy. While, in fact, few kidnappers ever realized the ransoms they sought, visions of easy money led them into the snatch racket.

It is interesting to note that flagrant criminality indigenous to the second and third decades of the twentieth century proved transitory and largely situational. By the 1940s, when the nation's wartime economy boomed, kidnappings had all but disappeared from the American landscape. The snatch racket became a quaint term connoting an untidy, if not bloody, past.

The California Snatch Racket is by no means an analytical examination, but a lively telling of fifteen kidnappings that made headlines in the Golden State during the tumultuous 1920s and 1930s. A few of the cases are well known, but most are not. Each offers a compelling glimpse at a unique period in California history when the business of the snatch racket gripped the state with chilling frequency.

"I guess the snatch racket is not such a paying proposition as we thought."

—Roy Williams, after receiving a life sentence for kidnapping, May 1934

Chapter 1: Dark Days in San Jose

Brooke Hart was a fastidiously dressed young man, but on this day—Thursday, November 9, 1933—he labored over his appearance even more than usual. In the afternoon, the 22-year-old executive's schedule included a photography session in connection with a department managers' sale at his father's elegant San Jose store. It was incumbent upon him to project a stylish image that would reflect the kind of tone associated with the Hart Department Store.

Figure 1.1 Brooke Hart; photo taken on day of kidnapping.
San Jose Library, California Room

Unbeknownst to Brooke, the photograph would become part of the historical record. The black and white image portrayed a strikingly handsome fellow: tall, lean, with piercing eyes—they were blue—and wavy blond hair. He had dressed immaculately in a gray suit flecked with white, offset by a light gray shirt with narrow stripes, and a tie and pocket handkerchief of even lighter hue. His face appeared open and friendly, and his eyes seemed to twinkle for the camera.

Just prior to 6:00 P.M., about an hour-and-a-half after having his photo taken, Brooke left the store with a gray double-breasted camel hair topcoat slung over his arm and a gray felt hat atop his head. He walked the short distance to the parking lot and his sporty Studebaker roadster convertible. At about 6:05, the young man pulled out of the parking lot and into the early evening traffic. A few minutes later, store employee Mary Van Arsdale gave him a friendly wave when she spotted his auto at the intersection of Fourteenth and Santa Clara streets in downtown San Jose.

Brooke's failure to appear for dinner at the Hart mansion by seven o'clock caused no anxiety. His mother Nettie knew that he planned to meet his friend John O'Brien, to attend a public speaking class at the De Anza Hotel.

Alexander "Alex" J. Hart, Brooke's father, was away from home during the dinner hour. He had arrived at his private club at 6:15 for cocktails and later left for the San Jose Country Club to attend a banquet in honor of the incoming and outgoing directors of the Chamber of Commerce.

O'Brien was a bit miffed when his friend failed to appear at the De Anza by the appointed time. It was unlike Brooke to miss an engagement. Assuming Brooke was merely running late, O'Brien went into the speaking class alone. It was just before 9:00 when the session ended and, by then, O'Brien's annoyance had turned to concern. He left the hotel and drove to the Hart mansion on The Alameda, San Jose's most prestigious residential area, arriving there at 9:00 P.M.

Nettie was alarmed. Why was Brooke not with O'Brien? Where could he be? It would have been wholly out of character for her son to change his plans without having telephoned the family. Something was amiss. She put in a call to the San Jose Country Club and asked that Alex return home at once. He did, and because the elder Hart had never learned to drive an automobile, he came to the mansion in the company of friends.

Brooke's friends were called. None had seen or heard from him. Someone suggested calling the police. The family nixed that notion. Brooke was, after all, over 21 and it was not even ten o'clock. While reassuring one another that Brooke would walk through the door at any moment, they joked about their concern and offered one another plausible explanations for his absence. Nettie and Alex were determined to wait it out. Contacting the police department could result in needless embarrassment.

They would not wait long.

At 10:30, the telephone rang. Unbeknownst to Alex, his daughter, Elyse, answered an extension in another room. Alex picked up the telephone, only to hear the tail end of a message. What he heard was chilling. A strange man, soft spoken and seemingly well-educated, calmly told Elyse that Brooke had been kidnapped and was being held for ransom.

"We have your son," was the message, intended for Nettie and Alex. "We want $40,000. Don't go to the police or you'll never see your son alive again. We will phone you instructions tomorrow."

The unthinkable had occurred. Brooke had been kidnapped.

Horror, grief, confusion, and anger settled over the Hart residence. Despite the kidnapper's threat of death, there was little discussion, for Alex knew what he must do. He notified the police immediately.

As quick as the eye could blink, officers of the San Jose Police Department converged on the Hart estate. They were followed in short order by deputies of the Santa Clara Sheriff's Department, detectives from the San Francisco Police Department, investigators from other Bay Area law enforcement agencies, and what were loosely called "G-Men" from the Department of Justice. The officers and agents sealed off the estate and the compound took on the appearance of an armed camp.

Officers did what they could to respect the Harts' privacy. Still, it was impossible to keep the matter quiet given the sudden burst of activity surrounding the mansion and the widespread search pressed upon the streets of San Jose, the roadways of Santa Clara County, and throughout the Bay Area. Word leaked to the press. Before the night was over, law enforcement officials reluctantly acknowledged Brooke's kidnapping.

It was sensational news. The next day saw a bold splash of headlines on the front pages of virtually every daily newspaper in California and others across the nation.

From Brooke's friends came the unsettling story of what may have been an earlier kidnapping attempt. Three weeks prior, a trio of men in a large automobile tried to crowd Brooke's Studebaker to the curb. Unsuccessful, they followed him for several blocks until he was able to gain speed sufficient to outdistance them.

Brooke had given little thought to the incident, having supposed the men were intoxicated and out on a lark. Law enforcement officials, however, found it a telling story.

Strange as well were a number of telephone calls made recently to John O'Brien's home asking if "Brookie" was there. Told that he was not, the caller inquired about his whereabouts. Apparently, someone wanted to document the young man's habits. O'Brien was struck by the oddity of the calls but saw no cause for alarm.

At one o'clock Friday morning came the first break in the case. Brooke's Studebaker roadster was discovered a mile and a half east of Milpitas—two miles from the San Jose Country Club, seven miles from San Jose proper, and on a road leading to the hilly Calaveras Dam and Black Mountain region. Authorities took the automobile to San Jose and examined it for fingerprints.

At 7:15 on the previous Thursday evening, John Sepulveda, a rancher on the Evans road, had observed the car parked in the roadway with its lights on. A man stood beside it and appeared to be doing something with the headlights. Sepulveda thought nothing of it and went about his business. Not until hours later, after learning of the Hart kidnapping, did he notify authorities.

On the theory that the victim might be a prisoner in some isolated mountain cabin, scores of Hart Department Store employees
voluntarily took up the search for Brooke. Students from San Jose
State Teachers College, the institution from which the popular
young Hart had recently graduated, joined them in the hunt. With
marked generosity, concerned San Jose car dealers donated automobiles necessary to the search.

Brooke had been missing for some thirty-six hours when the *San
Francisco Chronicle* hit the newsstands Saturday morning, Novem-
ber 11, sporting a lurid headline: "Hundreds Hunt Kidnapped Heir
in Gangster Hideout." That was followed by subheads which read,
"Rich San Jose Youth Believed Held in Wilds; $40,000 Ransom
Asked," followed by "Gang Phone Call Traced to S.F. Speakeasy."

The newspaper was mistaken. The first ransom call was traced
to the Hotel Whitcomb in San Francisco, not to a speakeasy. Most
sensational in the *Chronicle*'s reporting, however, was the assertion
that the kidnapping was gangster related:

> The ominous suggestion that "Pretty Boy" Floyd, notorious
> Middle West desperado, was involved in the plot spurred the
> efforts of police, Sheriff's deputies and Department of Justice
> officials.
>
> But although the San Jose Police Chief professed the belief
> that local underworld figures were responsible for young Hart's
> disappearance, it was admitted that authorities were seriously
> looking into the possibility that "Pretty Boy" Floyd had a hand
> in the case.
>
> Floyd has been reported seen a dozen times during re-
> cent months at California points, including San Francisco,
> Modesto, Ventura, Salinas and Hollywood.
>
> The boldness of the crime, the speed and celerity with which
> it was perpetrated, have all the earmarks, investigators admit-
> ted, of professional kidnappers, most of whose operations have
> engaged the Eastern authorities.

Sensational theories involving a notable gangster made lively
copy, but they were largely the product of reporters' imaginations.

San Jose Police Chief J. N. Black had other ideas. He expressed the belief that the crime was the work of "local talent," former liquor racketeers now turned to kidnapping. He pointed out that the perpetrators of the crime had displayed great familiarity with Brooke's habits and an intimate knowledge of the countryside.

Meantime, the elder Hart busied himself at the Hart Department Store. He still waited for the telephone call the kidnappers promised to make the day following the abduction, but he had not received it. Shaken by fear and anxiety, he did his best to maintain a calm facade. It was no easy task.

Nettie, in seclusion at the Hart mansion, was prostrate with fear and under the care of a physician.

Brooke's younger brother Alex Jr., his younger sisters Elyse and Miriam, and his married half-sister Jeanette remained under twenty-four hour police guard.

Amid rumors and speculation, a substantial lead developed the same day. Brooke's wallet turned up on the guardrail of a fuel ship moored alongside the liner *Lurline* at Los Angeles Pier 32.

Police and Justice Department agents flew to Los Angeles. There they learned of "two suspicious characters" reported to have stowed away on the ship during its San Francisco to Los Angeles voyage.

The ship's officer related that two strange men, demanding to see friends among the passengers, had brushed by purser's protests. The men did not carry tickets and no one saw them leave the ship before it embarked from San Francisco early Friday afternoon.

Officers theorized that the wallet, embossed with Brooke's name, had been tossed from a porthole of the *Lurline*. Rather than hit the water, however, it landed propitiously on the guardrail of the fuel ship *Midway*.

The *Lurline* was detained and its passengers forbidden to disembark while authorities boarded the vessel and conducted a cabin-by-cabin search. The officers questioned each passenger, including a much-chagrined Babe Ruth, who was vacationing with his daughter.

It was all for naught. There was no trace of Brooke and no trace of the alleged stowaways. The disappointed officers flew back to San Francisco empty-handed.

Something seemed out of character in the Hart kidnapping case, and it nagged at investigators. The brief time that had elapsed between Brooke's disappearance and the receipt of the anonymous ransom call was most unusual. Invariably, a kidnapper's *modus operandi* was to wait a day or two before making extortion demands. By that time, the family of the victim would be so desperate they would often agree to the kidnapper's demands without police interference. In the Hart case, the ransom demand occurred within four hours of the kidnapping. It was, indeed, puzzling.

That same day, Brooke's father granted the press its first interview. His initial statement debunked what he called "an absolute fabrication" and "a damn lie" published by the *San Francisco Examiner*. The newspaper reported that the kidnappers had contacted him both by telephone and by letter after their November 9 ransom demand. Alex Hart stated: "The kidnappers have made absolutely no contact of any kind since Thursday night's anonymous telephone call from San Francisco."

That said, the elder Hart's attitude softened and he spoke to reporters about his son. The Associated Press (AP) quoted him as saying:

> Brooke's is an exceptional character. We have been wonderful pals. Why, many times the boy offered to take me to the football game instead of going with young friends.
>
> It was a high moment in my life when I took Brooke into the department store recently as vice president. My father had taken me into the business in the same way and we had looked forward to the day when Brooke would take an active part in the conduct of the store.

When he came into the business, Brooke did not want a large salary. He understood he was to be on his own.

Before coming into the store he had had a fairly liberal allowance. He does not gamble, and he was never drunk in his life.

At social gatherings I've seen him take one or two cocktails, perhaps. He always rejected a third cocktail.

Hart said Brooke carried only fifteen or twenty dollars on his person when kidnapped. He did not carry his checkbook and his bank account was "not large."

The interview did nothing to help locate Brooke. However, it did imprint on the public consciousness the young man's sterling qualities.

A new twist developed Monday morning when the *Chronicle* informed its readers that "Handsome Jack" Klutas was a prime suspect in the kidnapping. Klutas, a college graduate, was said to be the "head of a Chicago band of well-educated men accused of having collected $500,000 tribute in kidnap operations."

"Klutas, sought for seven years for major crimes," declared AP dispatches from Chicago, "was said to have recently been traced to California."

Mal Coghlan, assistant state's attorney, who claimed he was "convinced" Klutas "had a hand in the ... abduction," said:

The gang is not the typical underworld mob. All members are well educated and use three- and four-syllable words with facility. The leaders probably are the slickest in the United States. For seven years, authorities have been on the trail of Klutas, a name that hasn't reached the [newspapers] frequently because of the difficulty of connecting him with crimes.

The gang has money, plenty of it. Several times officers have been within a few minutes of arresting Klutas, but he has been quick-witted enough to escape, taking with him or destroying any incriminating evidence.

It was just a shot in the dark. Klutas was a most unpleasant man engaged in a despicable racket, but he had nothing whatever to do with Brooke's abduction.

Within a few days, however, police who sought to question him about the Hart kidnapping cornered one of his lieutenants, Russell Hughes, in a Peoria, Illinois, barbershop. Hughes "huddled behind a barber chair," reported the AP, "and blazed away with pistols in both hands until he fell [mortally injured] with seven bullet wounds."

Inadvertently, the Hart case had brought about the demise of a notorious criminal.

While speculation about the Klutas gang ran rampant, Alex Hart appealed to his son's kidnappers, using the media to relay his message:

"We are anxious for the return of our son, Brooke. We desire to negotiate for his return personally or through any intermediary who might be selected. When contact is made we will, of course, want evidence to prove that Brooke is held by you. All negotiations will be considered confidential by us and we will allow no interference from any outside source."

An unbalanced fellow, Oakland printer Burr W. Poole, emerged unexpectedly and momentarily stirred East Bay police. A former patient of the psychopathic ward at Highland Hospital, Burr telephoned the Oakland police and advised them to pick up a man at a specific location who "knew all about the Hart case." Poole gave the license number of his own vehicle and when police arrived, they found a disjointed note in his possession that read, "Contact Hart family. Phone Jack Klutas. Do not destroy."

"I thought it was a good idea at the time to write that note and phone the police," explained Poole after his arrest and incarceration in the Oakland city jail. "The idea, somehow, doesn't seem so good now," he concluded with remorse.

More important than Poole were two woodcutters, Vinton Ridley and Al Coley. They reported to Alameda County Undersheriff Frank Swayne that on the night of Brooke's disappearance that they had heard muffled cries for help coming from the bay below Dumbarton Bridge.

They could see nothing because of the dark, but they shouted for the man to "hang on." While they searched for a boat, they thought they heard the voice answer, "I can't hang on any longer."

The two were unable to find any trace of the man and did not immediately connect the incident with the Hart kidnapping.

"Pretty Boy" Floyd was again mentioned as a suspect when it was revealed that two men "obviously of the mobster type" visited O'Brien's soda fountain and cafe, a downtown San Jose landmark for some fifty years. The men sat at the soda fountain for some time and "carefully read an issue of the *Chronicle* bearing an account of developments in the Hart disappearance case.

"From time to time they studied young [John] O'Brien, who assists his father in managing the place ...." The report stated that in the cafe's "atmosphere of refinement" the men "struck a discordant note."

An employee, distrustful of their intentions, telephoned the police. By the time lawmen arrived, however, the mysterious duo had gone on their way, never to be heard from again.

It was an interesting tale, but yet another dead end.

On Wednesday, November 15, six days after the kidnapping, the elder Hart received what he believed was a legitimate communication from his son's abductors.

"... The Harts divulged they have received several communications from the supposed kidnappers," reported the *Chronicle*. "Some of the communications ... obviously were not from persons acting in good faith, but the family indicated others were considered bona fide."

Law enforcement officials felt certain they were dealing with professionals experienced in the snatch racket. Whether professional or not, however, Brooke's kidnappers failed to do their homework. In their latest missive, they demanded that the senior Hart drive alone in his car to a designated spot where he would deliver the ransom money.

It was a request impossible for him to honor. Alex had never driven an automobile, nor did he have the slightest notion of what made one go forward or backward. Unfortunately, he had no way of conveying that information to the kidnappers.

As was typical in kidnapping cases, sightings of Brooke were common. Witnesses reported seeing him more than once in San Francisco. A mother and daughter spoke with him in Ross. Someone spotted him eating with two burly Italians in a Los Angeles restaurant. The proprietress of a Hollywood dress shop gave him money. In Orland, he was observed with two men "of the gangster type." And on and on.

The sightings were nonsense. From the moment of his abduction, Brooke was not seen again. Nor would he ever be seen again. Brooke Hart was dead.

"KIDNAPPERS MURDER HART" read the fiery words emblazoned atop the front page of the *Chronicle*, Friday, November 17. "Rich San Jose Boy Tied, Slugged, Thrown in Bay," read the sub-head. Finally, in type slightly smaller, "Jailed Men Confess Slaying."

Neither "Pretty Boy" Floyd, "Handsome Jack" Klutas, or other "professionals" of the "gangster type" had anything to do with the kidnapping and brutal slaying of the young department store heir. A pair of mismatched misfits from San Jose accepted sole responsibility for the heinous crime. Societal dropout Thomas H. Thurmond, 28 years old and married with two children, and college dropout John M. Holmes, a 27-year-old bachelor, each admitted to the kidnapping. Holmes was thought to be the mastermind, while Thurmond was his unconscionable lackey.

Holmes and Thurmond were arrested after they walked into a clever but simple trap devised by Department of Justice operatives and sheriff's deputies. Utilizing relatively new technology that the kidnappers knew nothing about, officers installed a parallel telephone line into the Hart mansion that provided them with access to all incoming calls. They attached a rudimentary call-tracing system and federal agents monitored the line day and night.

Holmes and Thurmond were staying in San Francisco at the California Hotel on First Street. On Thursday evening, November 16, Holmes retired early. Thurmond, however, walked to the Plaza Garage on Market Street, just a few blocks from city hall, and placed a call to the Hart home. When Alex came on the line, Thurmond's warning to him was brief and grim: "You had better get a move on if you want to see your son alive."

The elder Hart stalled for time. How and where did the unidentified caller want the ransom money delivered? While Alex kept Thurmond on the line, Justice Department agents traced the call.

The ploy worked.

They notified San Jose authorities stationed in San Francisco and moments later, a group of heavily armed men hurriedly disembarked from an automobile and approached the garage owner.

"Have you a man in here using the telephone?" they asked.

"Yes, in there," replied the owner, indicating a telephone booth.

Seconds later, Thurmond found himself dragged from the booth and handcuffed. He was taken to the county jail, where they questioned him for more than six hours. Finally, at 2:00 A.M., he led officers to Holmes' room at the California Hotel.

"Knock on his door," the officers instructed Thurmond, as they approached Holmes' room. He did, and out poked his partner's head. In another moment Holmes, too, was in handcuffs. Both men were sped to San Jose and locked away in the Santa Clara county jail, carefully isolated from each other. Each man confessed, both insisting the other man was the ringleader and murderer.

Figure 1.2 San Francisco police escort team, San Francisco to San Jose.
San Francisco History Center, San Francisco Public Library

Despite the early morning hour, word of the arrests and confessions spread rapidly throughout San Jose and neighboring communities. Fearful of mob violence, Sheriff William J. Emig telephoned San Francisco authorities stating his desire to return his prisoners there for safekeeping. The San Francisco police agreed.

Just after 7:00 A.M., Holmes and Thurmond were smuggled under heavy guard out of the county jail—foiling the scrutiny of reporters, cameramen, and gawking citizens. They were whisked by automobile back to the city of their arrest. The murderers, for the time being at least, found themselves securely incarcerated.

In retrospect, the kidnapping of Brooke Hart was a deed more sinister than ever imagined. During seven days of agonized waiting, hoping, and praying, the Hart family and the public at-large were made to believe that Brooke was alive. But it was never the intention of his kidnappers to return Brooke to his family. Little more than an hour after his abduction, they left the young man for dead in San Francisco Bay.

In his confession, released to the public by San Jose district attorney Fred Thomas, Thurmond stated that he and Holmes plotted the kidnapping for "five or six weeks."

"The thing to do is snatch him—then kill him," Thurmond accused Holmes of telling him:

> Jack … and I had previously discussed just how we would
> kidnap … Hart. Jack … was to get in the [Hart] car as it approached Market Street. Jack … met the car … on the curb
> and opened the door with one hand and had the other in his
> pocket as though he had a gun.
>
> He forced … Hart to go away with him. I was parked in …
> Holmes' car on Market Street close to Post Street and I saw …
> Jack drive by in … Hart's roadster and according to directions
> I followed that car.
>
> … [When] I saw him pass me in … Hart's car I proceeded to
> Milpitas and waited for them at the Spangler garage.
>
> Shortly thereafter … Holmes and … Hart drove by in the
> latter's roadster and I followed it to a point on the Evans road
> ….
>
> … They both got out of the car and … Holmes told … Hart
> to get in the back of the car which I was driving.
>
> We then drove a short distance ahead when … Jack, who
> was now driving his own car, turned it around and headed
> back to Milpitas with … Hart in the back seat. I was sitting at
> the right of … Holmes, who was driving the car.
>
> We then turned north and drove through Irvington to
> Alvarado and then direct to the San Mateo Bridge. We stopped
> about half a mile out on the … bridge, at which time … Hart
> was ordered out of the car and … Holmes walked back of the
> car and hit him over the head with a brick which I had obtained at a cement company in San Jose before we started on
> this trip with … Hart.
>
> When … Holmes first hit … Hart over the head with the
> brick he hollered, "Help, help," but … Holmes hit him over the
> head again with the brick and knocked … Hart unconscious
> and then I took some bailing wire from the car which I had
> previously purchased on the [same] afternoon at a hardware
> store in Santa Clara for 55 cents and bound the arms of …
> Hart around his body up close to his shoulders.

... Holmes then told me to get hold of him. Holmes took hold of the upper part ... of Hart's body and I took hold of him from his knees down and together we lifted [him] onto the railing of the ... bridge and tossed him into the bay. I recall as we lifted him up onto the ... bridge he struggled slightly.

What Thurmond failed to reveal were the heavy concrete weights they had attached to Brooke's body.

On their way to the San Mateo Bridge, the men divested Brooke of his wallet, which contained a $5 bill and $2.50 in silver, and then they tossed the empty wallet into the bay. Or so they thought. The wallet, of course, landed on the guardrail of the fuel ship *Midway*, en route to Los Angeles—thus causing the authorities' initial confusion.

Holmes' confession was substantially the same as Thurmond's with the exception that Holmes characterized Thurmond as the mastermind. He said Thurmond first broached the kidnapping scheme some two days before the abduction, after the two had attended a movie.

The only other significant variation—and one to which Thurmond later admitted—was that while young Hart struggled in the water below the San Mateo Bridge, Thurmond emptied a pistol at the victim. "He said he thought he had hit him but wasn't sure," insisted Holmes. Later, Holmes claimed Thurmond told him, "I don't think he will ever come up again."

"My God—my God!" wailed Alex Hart when told of his son's hideous fate. With that, he fell to the floor in a faint.

The *Chronicle* reported: "A mansion filled with grief—that was the picture painted here today by the man to whom fell the sad duty of telling a family who had everything—[that] their son, their pride, their joy, was dead, the victim of fiends."

In a state of near collapse, Nettie refused to believe the news, insisting that she would not give up hope until there was positive proof that Brooke was dead.

Even officers of the law, men inured to tales of crime and blood-shed, found themselves shocked by the kidnapper's cold-blooded accounts of Brooke's killing.

Maurice P. Holmes, Jack Holmes' father, spent much of Thursday at the Santa Clara county jail. At almost hourly intervals, he asked to see Sheriff Emig, who was not there. On each visit, he noted the rapidly increasing size of the crowd, mostly men, gathering in the jail yard.

On his last visit—it was mid-afternoon and the crowd numbered some 500—he sidled through the jail door and cried to the jail attendants, "What is this crowd gathering for? What do they intend to do? Are they after my son?"

With considerable difficulty, jail officials at last convinced him that his son, in the company of Sheriff Emig, had been spirited away to San Francisco.

When reporters approached the nervous father, he shouted, "I will make no statement. No, not a word. Get away from me. Leave me alone." With that, he ran down the street and darted into a store.

The same day, Evelyn Holmes made it clear that she was unable to believe anything but good of her husband: "Oh, I know John never could have done this thing. He couldn't. Do they think that just because he was out of work he would become a kidnapper? Do they think he would murder? No! I cannot believe it. I will not!"

As tempers flared and tension mounted, the most important task before law enforcement officials was to find Brooke Hart's body—and to make certain his killers were meted out swift, sure judgment.

On Saturday, November 18, the *Chronicle* left no doubt about the hard-line position it had taken. A front page editorial stated:

> There is only one thing to do with the murderers of Brooke Hart.
>
> That is to hang them, legally but promptly. The forms of law must be followed, but in this case they are only forms.

The guilt of the culprits is unquestioned. They have confessed. There is no defense or mitigation. The crime was cold-blooded, premeditated, fiendish and sordid. It had not even the poor motive of anger or passion.

The first twelve persons called will be competent jurors; the plea should be guilty; the facts can be quickly presented, and there can be only one verdict and one sentence.

Then, without the law's needless delays, at the earliest legal date, the gallows should end two lives which have forfeited all rights except that to be executed by the law.

Something is owed to public feeling. The revulsion of horror of the whole people at the unexampled callousness of this crime will find its normal relief in the knowledge that its perpetrators are put promptly out of the way, with only such ceremony as regard for the law, not for them, requires.

What happens to the culprits themselves does not matter. They have no rights; least of all the right to live. Their death by the law will preserve the integrity of the law. Their death without delay will relieve the tension of public feeling. Then they can pass into oblivion.

What will remain will be the grief of a stricken family, the wrath of an outraged community and a sense of the futility of a time in which such things are possible.

Whether by design or accident, this inflammatory editorial added fuel to the fire of revenge burning in the hearts of San Jose's citizenry.

The following day, Brooke's gray felt hat was found in the mud-flats during low tide, 171 feet from the Alameda County shore and 976 feet north of the San Mateo Bridge. Meanwhile, police continued to drag the bay with grappling hooks in an effort to recover the body.

On Thursday morning, November 23, the *Chronicle* reported:

Bound for a city rife with threats of lynch law, the two confessed killers of Brooke Hart were spirited out of the San

Francisco City Prison at 10:45 o'clock last night and taken to San Jose under escort of an armed caravan.

The dozen officers that accompanied them were virtually "armed to the teeth" to resist any attempt by vigilantes to intercept them en route.

Each of the four cars contained a machine gun, shotguns and a supply of tear gas bombs, besides the sidearms of the officers.

After a short stop at Santa Clara, where Sheriff Emig telephoned his office to make sure the coast was clear, the motorcade arrived at San Jose shortly before midnight and the two shackled prisoners were locked in separate cells of the County Jail.

The return of the two kidnap-slayers … was expected to precipitate a crisis in the city.…

Every precaution was to be taken to prevent mob violence and the seizure of the … prisoners.

Two days later, as the search for Hart's body continued unabated, the *Chronicle* revealed that "An old-time California 'Vigilante Committee,' pledged to 'see justice done' in the Brooke Hart case, is being organized in San Jose.

"Already between 60 and 70 San Jose citizens have signed the secret agreement and stand ready to take 'adequate action' against the kidnappers and slayers of the San Jose youth."

In the same story, it was related:

The jail itself is a veritable arsenal of revolvers, rifles, shotguns, riot guns, tear gas bombs and other weapons.

The force of deputies on guard at the jail was trebled yesterday as the Sheriff stepped up the voltage of his protective system to meet the growing potential of the San Jose Citizens.

All day long, as they have done since Thurmond and Holmes were brought to the jail, a crowd paced back and forth in front of the jail.

In fact, the force of deputies guarding the jail was wholly inadequate to insure the safety of its charges and the sheriff apparently knew it. Moreover, if notions of taking the law into its own hands played on the minds of San Jose's citizenry, the newspaper's lurid reportage was a heady stimulant.

At last, on Sunday, November 26, San Francisco Bay gave up the body of Brooke Hart. It was found by two duck hunters, floating in five feet of water about a mile west of the Mt. Eden-Hayward shore, and a half mile south of the San Mateo Bridge.

The body was taken to a morgue at Hayward, where friends of the dead youth and executives of the Hart Department Store identified the rapidly decomposing corpse.

"Because of the condition of the body after 17 days in the water," wrote the *Chronicle*, "identification was established by the clothing, by a pearl handle knife found in the clothing ….The torso and head of the victim were practically a skeleton.

"The chance find terminated a search that had called into play all the agencies of four counties and the assistance of the government—a search employing divers, Coast Guard boats, airplanes and even a navy blimp."

Then it happened.

Twelve hours after the discovery of young Brooke's body, an incensed mob of some 10,000 men and women gathered around the Santa Clara county jail, a veritable fortress built a year after the Civil War ended.

It was shortly before 9:00 P.M. About a dozen officers—a ridiculously inadequate force—manned a barricade some 30 feet from the jail entrance. Little by little, the crowd pushed forward. Taunts and jeers turned ugly. Shouting became a communal drone. The sound emitted was akin to a deep, throaty growl—an ever-swelling growl.

All at once, the front line lunged. Police locked arms to hold them back, but at least a hundred angry people exerted pressure against them. The small contingent of officers was no match for the mob.

Police shouted orders, but no one listened. Then the sound of gunfire rent the air. "Shooting! Shooting! Shooting!" cried the mob.

A tear gas bomb exploded. From out of the jail poured another half dozen deputies, each armed with additional tear gas canisters. More bombs exploded with choking, blinding fury. However, the insurgents were not dissuaded. The first chants of "Lynch 'em, lynch 'em!" were heard, followed by "Brooke Hart! Brooke Hart! Brooke Hart!"

Tear gas bombs exploded repeatedly, filling the night air with blue acrid smoke. The crowd broke and ran, women and children screaming, men cursing and threatening. Then, for a moment, the area fronting the jail was deserted. Police drew in a collective sigh, thinking the threat had passed.

It had not.

The crowd took refuge next door to the jail, where a new post office was under construction. As smoke from tear gas bombs dissipated, police officers became easy targets for rocks. Loose tiles and bricks scattered about the construction site became convenient missiles. Glass was shattered and a steady tattoo of hurled debris smashing against the stone walls of the jail and against its steel doors resounded.

More than an hour had passed when it occurred to the unruly mob that rocks, tiles, and bricks were no match for the fortress-like jail, unbreached since its construction in 1866. Then someone spotted an iron pipe, some nine inches in diameter and weighing several hundred pounds. Instinctively, fifteen or twenty men lifted the massive pipe, and, forging through a constant barrage of tear gas explosions, they made their way to the jail's steel door.

The mob cheered each time the pipe—put into play as a battering ram—crashed against the door. "Get 'em! Get 'em! Get 'em!" roared the crowd. Then, "The cops are coming! The cops are coming!"

Word circulated among the rowdies that San Francisco and Oakland's inexhaustible supply of peace officers were speeding toward San Jose in automobiles and on motorcycles. Time was of the essence.

Figure 1.3 Mob breaks down jail door.
Underwood Archives

Disregarding the tear gas and officers armed with riot guns, the mob went about its work—ramming, ramming, ramming against its target. Then, with one great lunge of the battering ram, the double steel doors gave way with a tremendous crash. Into the corridor spilled the mob, carrying the pipe and screaming madly for vengeance.

Across the corridor was a heavy barred grating. In moments, the ram tore the grating from its moorings. There would be no stopping the mob. They ran through the jail and up the stairs. Jailers, who knew many of the unmasked perpetrators, refused to shoot. They stood by in helpless fear, knowing what was coming. The mob was in complete control.

Deputy Sheriff John Moore was one of twenty guards charged with the protection of Holmes and Thurmond as well as the other one hundred or so prisoners. Moore gave the following account of events inside the jail to the *San Jose Mercury News* and the *Oakland Tribune*:

Figure 1.4 Jail entryway following mob break-in. *Underwood Archives*

> I was on the second floor of the jail with Earl Hamilton, the undersheriff, and Howard M. Buffington, deputy. Sheriff Emig had given me his duplicate set of keys which opened the cells of Thurmond and Holmes, believing that the mob would search him but would not think of searching me.
>
> I backed into a corner when they advanced on me and held up my hands, telling them I didn't have the keys. A man with a mask over his face choked me. They threw me on the floor and trampled on me. Then they went through my pockets and found the keys. Meanwhile, Buffington had been hit over the head and the mob got his keys too.
>
> They opened Holmes' cell first on the second floor. And then they brought in a length of rope. There must have been 50 men who entered his cell. I stood outside.
>
> "Are you Holmes?" the man with the mask shouted at the prisoner cringing in the corner. "No, I'm not Holmes," he replied.
>
> "'You're a damned Liar: I know you," the masked lyncher cried and many hands drew the rope around Holmes' neck. He cried for mercy.
>
> "Spare me, spare me: Don't take me out, don't deliver me to that crazy mob," Holmes pleaded.

Fists crashed against his face. He went down on the floor, still crying for mercy. Then he was kicked and they spat on him. His head was knocked against the floor. Dragging him on the end of the rope, they pulled him headfirst downstairs. Then these 50 leaders came up against me and asked me if it was Holmes they had taken out.

When I told them I didn't know, they said: "You're a liar, Moore. You brought him from San Francisco and we know it." Once again I was choked and thrown on the floor.

Then the mob pushed upstairs and entered Thurmond's cell but they could not find him. They came back and demanded matches. With the aid of the matches and a candle, they searched the cell. In a small closet [toilet] adjoining the cell but still a part of it, they found Thurmond.

Like a human fly, he had crawled up the walls, bracing himself against the sides with his feet and hands to a height of 15 feet. It is an oddly-built closet and extends up to the roof. When they sighted him in the light of the matches, the most terrible blood-curdling cries of fiendish delight I have ever heard rang through the jail.

They pulled him down and he put up a fight. He fought like a demon for a minute but he was soon a mass of blood. They tied the rope around his neck and dragged him down to the second floor, where they asked me to identify him. I told them I didn't know him.

"It must be him," the masked leader said. Before they took Thurmond out, they demanded Antone Serpa, [in order] to lynch him with the other two men. Serpa was sentenced for manslaughter last week after killing a rancher. I tried to reason with them. I pleaded with them to play square, pointing out that Serpa was already sentenced and that a jury had found him guilty of nothing worse than manslaughter. They finally agreed to give up on the idea of lynching Serpa.

We were trapped in there like dogs. The gas that we shot out at the mob drifted back in on the wind. The inside of the jail was a hellish place to be. I'll never forget until my dying day what I saw and experienced that night.

Figure 1.5 Sketch of mob scene.
San Jose Library, California Room

By the time the mob reached the jail doors, Holmes had been stripped to nothing more than a tee shirt. The killers were half-dragged, half-carried out of the jail and into the alley. Without hesitation, the throng hauled the two men down the alley past the south side of the courthouse and across First Street to St. James Park.

No one attempted to stop them. Defeated, humiliated, and bewildered, the police simply wandered away, leaving the mob to its devices.

"String 'em up!" cried the thousands of people—men, women, and children—who were milling about. "String 'em up!"

And that is what they did. As related by the *Chronicle*:

> After a delay of almost fifteen minutes, ropes were produced, and Thurmond ... was the first man to be hanged. He was benumbed with fear and his crazed mutterings were without meaning.
>
> Thurmond was hanged to a low limb. As his body was slowly hoisted, the crowd broke into frantic cheering. Someone in that crowd must have had the technique of hangman's knots. Thurmond thrashed as he hung there, swaying to and fro, seeming to bend his body at the hips in a last spasm of life.

For perhaps three minutes he swayed there, his face blackening slowly, his tongue extended. Not satisfied, the screaming crowd tore off his trousers, saving the scraps of his garments as souvenirs. They struck at his swaying body, clapping and cheering as Thurmond twitched in his death throes.

Figure 1.6 Harold Thurmond strung up in St. James Park.
San Jose Public Library, California Room

Holmes' execution followed that of Thurmond but a few minutes. In a despairing voice, which was nevertheless clear, he kept denying that he was Holmes, but the crowd knew better....

Holmes, his bloody face turned on his captors, took death with more stamina than did Thurmond. As the rope was tossed over a limb, he begged, "Don't string me up, boys. Don't string me up."

Naked by the time the mob reached the park, Holmes fought furiously and his face was pounded to a bloody pulp. The noose was dropped over his head and about his neck, and with wild cheers from the crowd his body was flung into the air. Twice he thwarted the hanging by grasping the rope above the noose. Twice they lowered him down and beat him unmercifully until he was half-conscious. Then, lighted by flashlight beams, they jerked him back up. Holmes' neck was broken on the third attempt. Thurmond and Homes were dead. Still, the frenzied mob's blood lust had not been satiated.

Figure 1.7 Holmes strung up naked by crowd.
San Jose Public Library, California Room

As a kind of barometer of the hysteria prevalent, the *Chronicle* took special note of women in the crowd:

… [They] all but danced around the death trees. They hurled maledictions against the [dead] men. They clawed at their dangling bodies like avenging furies.

The scene was like the hell of Dante—the awful avenging hell of the New Testament— a hell peopled by women.

Impelled by the Biblical edict of "an eye for an eye, a tooth for a tooth," they cast their robes of femininity from them and roared their approval of the fate meted out ….

"God!" screamed one, "God, I'm excited."

The bodies dangled from limbs in St. James Park for almost an hour. Shortly before midnight, squads of San Francisco and Oakland police officers and federal agents arrived on the scene. Its work completed, the mob scattered. There was nothing left for the officers to do but cut down the bodies hanging from the trees.

But it was not over yet. The bodies were still warm when Governor James Rolph, Jr. told the world: "This is the best lesson that California has ever given the country. We've shown the country that the state is not going to tolerate kidnapping."

Figure 1.8 Harold Thurmond, hung and stripped by crowd.
San Jose Public Library, California Room

Should legal action be taken against any member of the mob, it was Rolph's intention to pardon "all persons who participated in the Holmes-Thurmond lynching ...."

Rolph added, "No kidnappers will ever be turned loose or pardoned while I am governor, but they'll learn they can't kidnap in this state and get away with it. Kidnappers will find they are not safe even in our penitentiaries....

"The aroused people of [San Jose] were so enraged at the slaying and kidnapping of this youth from their midst that it was only natural that as peaceful and as law abiding as they are, they arose in their might and meted out swift justice to those kidnappers."

In equal measure, praise and scorn followed the governor's pronouncement. The American Civil Liberties Union was furious. So was Roy Wilkins, assistant secretary of the NAACP. Earl Warren, future governor and chief justice of the United States Supreme Court, sympathized with Rolph. So did Henry Darlington, the well-known rector of New York's Church of the Heavenly Rest.

**Figure 1.9 California Governor James Rolph openly
condoned lynching in St. James Park.**
Bancroft Library, University of California, Berkeley

One man who vociferously disagreed with the California governor was former president Herbert Hoover, then living on an estate on the campus of Stanford University at Palo Alto. Speaking publicly for the first time since leaving the oval office, Hoover said, "The issue here is plain, and not to be obscured … The governor has been advocating lynch law. It is a subversion of the very spirit of organized society. It is un-American and is a reflection on the state of California."

The day after the lynching, Brooke Hart left home for the last time, his body removed from the Hart mansion where it had lain in state. His family laid Hart to rest at Oak Hill Memorial Park.

A few days later, city workers uprooted the hanging trees in St. James Park. They hauled them away in trucks and cut them up for firewood.

But for memories that would linger forever, the kidnapping and murder of Brooke Hart had come full circle.

Chapter 2: The Greased Chute of Justice

Shortly before six o'clock, Tuesday evening, January 25, 1921, a tall, gray-haired stranger rapped at the door of Elizabeth Warden's Hollywood bungalow. Was this the residence of Mrs. Gladys Witherell, he inquired? "No," she told him. He had knocked at 1841 Whitley Avenue, and the Witherells lived in the bungalow next door at 1843.

Before leaving, the stranger told Miss Warden that there had been a serious accident on "the boulevard." A badly injured woman was calling for Gladys to come to her.

That said, he bade her adieu and went next door.

"I was expecting my mother-in-law for dinner [that evening]," Gladys Witherell later recalled, "and the first thought that ran through my mind was that she was hurt. I did not stop to think about the man." Leaving her 18-month-old son, Jack, with his nanny, she put on her hat and coat and rushed off with the stranger. "He led me to the car, right in front of the house, and he and I got in the back seat. The other man was in front.

"As we turned onto Hollywood Boulevard we were nearly killed by a street car that dashed in our path. The automobile swerved and the gray-haired man swore at the driver. I kept on asking him if he was sure I was the woman they wanted, and he said, 'Yes, you can feel perfectly safe.' There was a premonition in my heart that something was wrong, however, and I asked him what kind of car it was that was wrecked. He said it was a large sedan. Then I knew something was wrong."

As Gladys discovered all too quickly, the gray-haired stranger and his accomplice behind the steering wheel were practitioners of the snatch racket. And she—wife of O. S. Witherell, manager of the Financial Loan and Investment Company, and daughter-in-law of A. J. Witherell, vice president of the Hollywood Savings Bank—was their carefully targeted victim. Gladys' recollection continued:

As I turned toward him I saw a handkerchief in his hand and I smelled something like medicine. A thought came that the man must have been hurt in this accident. We passed Santa Monica Boulevard then and I realized that the story was wrong. "Now I know there is something crooked about this," I called out and turned toward him. In the same instant his hand shot out for my head, and his arm crooked around my neck. The handkerchief came nearer my mouth and I smelled ether or chloroform. Then I fought.

I struggled like a wild cat. I made up my mind not to be gagged, and not to breathe. When he pressed the handkerchief to my mouth, I relaxed and pretended that I lost consciousness. He let go of me, and there I lay on the bottom of the car, hearing him give directions to the driver, telling him to go to the right and to the left, and straight ahead. I lay still, though I remember we passed West Adams, and then I made another attempt to free myself. It must have been somewhere near Thirty-Ninth and Vermont, and I began to fight.

I got hold of the robe rack and pulled it off the car. I bent the rod trying to strike at the man. I remember that the side curtains flew off when I kicked through them with my feet. The gray-haired man then jumped on top of me, put his knee on my chest and again pressed the drug-soaked handkerchief against my mouth. He was trying to force the handkerchief into my mouth, and I was holding it back with my tongue. During this part of the struggle I kicked one slipper off my foot. When I realized that he was overcoming me, I again pretended to be unconscious and lay still.

Frightened as she was, the plucky young woman did not give in to her abductors until all her energy was spent and further struggle useless.

We went a few blocks further and then a tire blew out. They stopped the car near some flats. I could see [a] white house, and the windows all lit up. I thought of all the people there, and no one to help me. They got out and started to jack up the car. Then, I thought, my chance to escape had come. I lifted my hand and quietly opened the door. Slowly working my hands from under me, I got them free, and was sliding out of the car when they discovered me. Then I pulled the gag out of my mouth and screamed. No one came. The gray-haired man was fighting me again. They got me back into the car and I tried to get out over the door. I got half way out, my back on the door, and just as I lurched backward and was about to fall head first, the man caught me by the feet and pulled me back into the car.

"Never mind the tire," I heard him say, and they threw the jack back into the car and drove away. We bumped over the road, the man's knees on my chest. Then the man said to me, "Why don't you stop fighting? We don't want to hurt you." I promised I would not scream if they did not harm me, and they said they would not. We drove on and suddenly, as I realized that I was being taken away from my husband and baby and my home and all I held dear, my nerves gave way and I screamed again.

Then the man … kicked me again and again. "This will fix you," I heard him growl, and he choked me [until] I lost consciousness. I recovered just in time to feel that he was putting a gag in my mouth. I again stuck my tongue between my teeth and kept the gag from going in. I dimly remember that he was tying my hands and feet, [and] I pulled my hands up so that when he tied them to my feet I had slack in the rope. The drug got into my brain, and I forgot everything.

When I recovered, there was a gag in my mouth, I smelled chloroform, and [a] robe was tied over me. My belt was strapped around me. I could breathe and I heard them talking.

"Is she dead? Will she come out [of it]?" asked the driver.

"Yes, she's alive. She'll be all right."

Then they got me to Huntington Park. I was semiconscious. I knew what was going on, but felt like I was paralyzed.

Somewhere along the route the car stopped. The driver got out and into another vehicle. The men tied Gladys securely to the seat and, with the second automobile following close behind, the gray-haired man took the wheel and off they sped—flat tire and all—to an unknown destination.

The journey ended at a white clapboard ranch house somewhere in the mountains. Gladys related: "They carried me out of the car … and dumped me on the bed. Floyd [the gray-haired man] lit an oil stove. 'We'll treat you like a sister,' he said. 'If some one treated your sister like [this], what would you do?' I asked him. 'We are forced to do this,' he replied. 'Don't be afraid. We want money, that's all,' Jack [the other man] added."

Thus it was that Gladys Witherell—devoted young wife and mother—was thrust into a terrifying abyss. If she kept her wits about her, she might emerge relatively unscathed. If she did not, she was certain to endure further pain and suffering, perhaps even death. Regardless of what she did—rationalize as she might—her fate rested in the hands of two ruthless, desperate men.

It was about 11 o'clock when we got to the ranch. They told me they wanted $30,000. I told them there wasn't that much money in our family. "Never you mind. Leave that to us. Maybe your daddy will come across." "But daddy hasn't got that much, either," I told them. I told them how O. S.—that's my husband—and I went through school together, how we were sweethearts, and how we were building up our home. We talked late and they told me of their plans to get the ransom.

That night Floyd—I later heard Jack call the gray-haired man that—went back to town. They lit a lamp and filled the oil stove for me. The blankets were filthy but the mattress was new. The furniture was new, it had price tags on it. Just before Floyd went to town he told me they had kidnapped two others before. "When people are in trouble the family will come through with the money," he said. "Don't you worry. There is no use of struggling. We want the money and we will take you back home when we get it."

They left the stove burning and after Floyd went away, Jack nailed my door [shut] and went to sleep.

I did not close my eyes all night long. I thought it all over, and after a fashion I became a little calmer. Next morning Floyd returned. He brought the papers to read.

What Gladys read was not encouraging.

"A police bulletin issued to every officer in the city," wrote the *Los Angeles Times*, "describes Mrs. Witherell as 25 years of age [she was 24 and looked younger], 5 feet, 1 inch tall [she was 5 feet, 3 inches tall], 112 pounds in weight [she weighed 115], and having brownish eyes [her eyes were hazel], black bobbed hair and a dark complexion. She is of medium build, has gold-filled upper and lower front teeth, and wore a three-fourths-length tan sport coat, black patent leather pumps, black silk stockings, white kid gloves and a small taupe velvet turban hat."

The description was only relatively close to the mark, but it had little value anyway. Gladys was, after all, a captive in a remote mountain cabin, far from public view.

She learned as well that her husband and father-in-law had posted a $500 reward for "any information as to her whereabouts."

John Carol Baldwin, a Harvard Military School student, told authorities that he had seen a young woman being carried away in a battered five-passenger Ford on Washington Street between Western and Vermont avenues on Tuesday evening. He said there were three men in the machine, two of whom were forcibly holding the woman down.

Whatever it was Baldwin saw, he did not see Gladys and her abductors.

J. E. Baumann, operator of a filling station at Thirty-Eighth Street and Hooper Avenue, reported to authorities that he saw a woman who looked like the published photo of Mrs. Witherell. He said she was in a Ford coupe that was broken down. There was a man with her who was repairing the car.

It was altogether possible that Baumann saw the kidnappers and their captive when the automobile in which they were riding suffered a blowout. However, the information was of little value. The man failed to record the vehicle's license number and Ford coupes dotted California roads.

"Friends of various clairvoyants," wrote the *Times*, "urged the Witherell family … to try occult means to locate the missing woman. Sundry 'seers' went into more or less complete 'trances,' but without notable result."

In a statement both optimistic and realistic, O. S., Gladys' husband, said, "I have no enemy, as far as I know, and Mrs. Witherell never at any time told me of anyone who might have become infatuated with her and taken such means to take her away from me. Our life ever since we were married in 1917, and when we were sweethearts in the Hollywood High School, has always been ideal. Never at any time has there been a word of difference. We have many friends, and they all have treated Mrs. Witherell with greatest respect. I do not believe that she has been taken for immoral purposes or by a degenerate. The manner in which she left does not indicate it. I am more inclined to think that I will soon hear from someone asking for money."

When Gladys awakened after her first night of captivity, her body was a mass of bruises. Her neck was swollen twice its normal size. Her chest was bruised and sore, and her legs were swollen, as well.

"I believe both men were osteopaths. They knew every bone in the human body," she quipped. "Floyd said he could relieve my pain, and he massaged my neck, getting the swelling down. Then he said he would treat my nervous system. He certainly seemed to know how to do it. I was soothed and quieted down, and the swelling and pain was gone somewhat. Floyd brought some bandages and some Unguentine for my bruises.

"I washed the dishes the first day and swept the room. It was filthy. There were cigarette butts all over the place."

Both men were good cooks, she said. They cooked big plank steaks for her, and "the best griddle cakes I ever ate. [And] they taught me how to play cribbage."

Gladys had been missing two days when O. S. and his father increased the reward for information about her whereabouts to $1,500. The police, meanwhile, told the press that she was first taken to a yellow house near Twenty-Third and Main streets—the first bit of "definite information" they had retrieved.

Mistaken, the police were grasping at straws.

As late as Wednesday—while Gladys was ensconced in the mountain ranch house—a taxi driver saw her in an old "battered Ford," being held by force on the back seat by "one or two other men." She appeared to be gagged by a white handkerchief. The car had no license plates.

While the story was rubbish, Ford Motor Company may have appreciated the ongoing publicity.

Most important, however, was a note found by O. S. in his screen door when he returned home about 10:30 Wednesday night: "Mr. Witherell—your wife is safe. Don't worry until you hear further from me. Have $50,000 cash ready for me as you will hear from me again soon. Don't notify police or detectives or all will be lost."

On January 29, the *Los Angeles Times* reported:

"Although [police] officers denied yesterday that any communication other than the typed note left at the Witherell home two days ago had been received from the kidnappers, rumors of a second note and a letter from the missing woman were afloat at Central Station. The second note demanded $20,000 in cash and stated where the money should be left, claimed the rumor. The kidnapper's letter is reported to have contained a note from Mrs. Witherell stating that she is unharmed, but in great danger and asking that the money be paid for her release."

In fact, the "rumor" about a second note was the first bit of reliable information the press was able to report. The ransom, for reasons known only to the kidnappers, had indeed been reduced by $30,000. Moreover, Gladys had enclosed with the note a letter to her husband. "Please help me to come home," she wrote. "If you don't I never will see you all again."

It was the first of three pleas penned by the young wife to her anxious husband.

In the same newspaper article, a perplexing sentence read, "No real motive for a kidnapping has been uncovered." It demands a generous stretch of imagination to accept the notion that ransom in five figures was not a motive.

Gladys had been sequestered in the mountain hideaway for five days when the Sunday *Times* announced that area churches would hold prayer services in askance of her speedy delivery from her abductors. Also noted was the sudden death of Charles Beverly, former partner of O. S. Witherell in the Financial Loan and Investment Company, and of Leda Tenney, the company's head stenographer. Both were crushed to death beneath the wreckage of Beverly's automobile when it collided with a streetcar.

Police officers had interviewed Beverly several times since the kidnapping and, at the time of his and Tenney's deaths, detectives were following his car.

It was an interesting twist, but neither Beverly nor Tenney had anything to do with Gladys' kidnapping.

Los Angeles residents awakened Monday morning to optimistic news from the *Times*: "The kidnapping of Mrs. Gladys Witherell may be cleared up before the day is over...." The story lauded search efforts by police officers and volunteer groups, but offered nothing substantial to justify its optimism.

However, it was not necessary. The newspaper's optimism was a fortuitous accident. Unbeknownst to the *Times*—a morning paper that went to press in the black of night while the city slept—unforeseeable events soon unfolded.

The day's heroes were not police officers, and not verbose reporters. The heroes were a quartet of keen-witted telephone operators, or "hello girls," as they were called then: Alma Bryant, Georgie Pond, Bessie Schaeffer, and Bertha Heere.

Technology necessary to place a simple trace on a telephone line did not exist in 1921. Ingenious improvisation, however, did exist. When dialing a call, it was necessary to go through an operator who could determine from what exchange a call originated and, if it originated from a pay station, determine the telephone's location.

After consultation with telephone engineers, law enforcement officials ordered two extensions placed on the Witherell line. One went to the telephone of Gladys' father, the other to the telephone of a neighbor. This established a triangle, monitored day and night by detectives.

"We came on duty Sunday night and were told by the day force of the arrangements for the watching of the wires," related Alma Bryant, night chief operator of the Hollywood exchange:

> Hundreds [of people] in Hollywood were searching the hills, and we talked it over, saying we hoped we could do something.
>
> At 10:23 P.M., Miss Bertha Heere received a call for Mr. Witherell's residence. She listened in long enough to hear the man on the downtown end of the line ask for O. S. Witherell and say, "This is the man who's got your wife." Then she called me.
>
> Working in a prearranged manner, I got Miss Georgie Pond [and told her] to hold the line and be ready to give us [the] location of a number as soon as possible.
>
> Miss Bessie Schaeffer got the detective bureau [on the phone] and told the officer there that a call was being made by the kidnapper, and that she would let him know from where the man was talking as soon as possible, asking him to stay on the line.

Miss Heere, in the meantime, got Chief Operator Moore at the main exchange and had her trace the call there. The main exchange said the call was being made from Main 1691. As I repeated the number, Miss Pond shouted it to the information operator, who immediately gave her the location [near the] A to Z drug store, [at] 200 East Fifth. Miss Pond repeated this aloud and Miss Schaeffer repeated this to the police headquarters. We did not get excited till it was all over. The girls worked like lightning and not a second was lost. We listened to the conversation and heard the man hang up the receiver without completing what he had to say. Then we knew he was caught.

Witherell had kept the kidnapper on the line fourteen minutes—enough time to determine that the call was being made from the Auto Bus Depot at Fifth and Los Angeles streets. Police officers leaped into a "fast machine" and sped to the depot, where they waited outside the phone booth.

"The stranger concluded his conversation," reported the *Times*, "and as he turned to leave the booth he faced three detectives.

"'Who were you talking to?' they demanded.

"The stranger, startled, hesitated a few moments and then replied meekly, 'Witherell.'"

It was 10:50 P.M. The wheels of justice were in motion. Under grueling examination at Central Station, the man told officers his name was Jack Carr. He denied knowledge of Gladys' whereabouts, insisting he was simply a "tool"—that he had kidnapped the woman on the instructions of someone "higher up." There were seven members in the gang, he said, and he had delivered Gladys to their headquarters in Bakersfield and from there to a destination some twenty-five miles distant—a destination he knew not where.

The more he talked, the less coherent was his tale. Carr's story was tangling into a snarl of contradictions. For reasons known only to the police department, they hastily transferred him from Central Station to Boyle Heights Station, where they questioned him further. Whether intimidated by new surroundings and new officers,

Figure 2.1 Processing Jack and Floyd Carr into the local jail.
San Francisco History Center, San Francisco Public Library

or simply worn out, the kidnapper's story soon broke down. He finally collapsed completely and agreed to make a confession.

The *Times* took up the story:

> He told how Mrs. Witherell was being held—and where, and offered to lead the officers to her. His cousin, Floyd Carr, was with her. The cousin was armed, he said, and would fire upon the first strange man who dared approach the hiding place. A battle seemed imminent and, to protect the detectives from being led into a trap prepared, possibly, by many desperadoes, an auto load of rifles, shotguns and ammunition was sent from Central Station. Reinforcements arrived quickly, and Jack Carr, displaying marks of a severe grueling at the hands of the police, was led, handcuffed, from the substation.
>
> Five automobiles, loaded with heavily armed men ... started on the long and anxious trip to the rendezvous of the kidnappers. None of the officers knew where they were headed ... but Carr, seated in the forward automobile, directed the route to

be followed. It was then 2 A.M. The way led over boulevards and dirt roads and through a driving rain.

For two hours the vigilante procession skidded over the wet roads, through towns and into Santa Ana Canyon, Orange County. It speeded through the canyon, up the grades, around dangerous curves at an excessive speed and then down into the valley. Corona was reached. A few miles beyond Corona, Carr guided his captors off the paved boulevard and into the hills.

Half a mile from [the house in which Carr claimed Gladys was being held], the autos were halted in the road and the lights were switched off while the men organized into combat groups preparatory to surrounding the house. Nine of the best crack shots of the posse climbed into the first car with Jack Carr. Each of the officers was armed with rifles and sawed-off shotguns. As the car moved silently forward through the protecting darkness, Carr sat calmly in the rear seat smoking a cigarette.

Then the clapboard house, once the home of a sheepherder, came into sight. Twenty-five heavily armed men left their vehicles and ran silently across plowed fields. The lead automobile, containing Carr, moved up to within a few feet of the dwelling. Officers took positions in the brush and awaited the signal to attack.

The *Times* reported:

The front door was locked, but the rear door had been left unlocked. [A deputy], clutching the handcuffed prisoner [Carr], kicked open the rear door and rushed into the darkened kitchen. The other officers followed. The door to a bedroom was evidently barred. Carr said it was held fast only by a nail. The prisoner gave it a mighty kick and the officers rushed into the bedroom.

As the door crashed through, the frail house resounded with a woman's shrieks. The woman was Mrs. Witherell, the young wife and mother, who had been missing for six days. A flashlight revealed her lying on a filthy bed in a corner.

[An officer] ran through the bedroom and into one of the front rooms. A rusty iron bed with dirty coverings was the only article of furniture in this room. [Another officer] looked under the bed, then he ran his hand between the quilts. They were still warm. He knew an enemy was not far away. In one hand the officer clutched a shotgun, in the other a flashlight. Instinctively, he looked for a closet and found it.

Jerking the closet door open, [he] thrust his light into the darkness. A savage-visaged man with gray hair and a gray mustache stood in the doorway of the closet with a 45-caliber Colt automatic leveled at the officer's heart. The officer stood firm, still covering the man with the shotgun.

"Throw up your hands," the officer yelled, "or I'll blow you through the wall!"

The man with the automatic slowly raised his arms above his head in surrender. He was then dragged from the closet and handcuffed. He said his name was Floyd Carr and that he was a cousin to Jack Carr. He objected to the handcuffs and in the fracas that followed he emerged a badly battered person.

"For God's sake—don't kill me," he pleaded. "I'm not at the bottom of this."

Neither of the Carr cousins were at the "bottom" of the Witherell kidnapping—or so they said. They were nothing more than dupes, paid snatchers and transporters of the victim. The real culprits were men in higher places, men they did not know.

It was an interesting story, but it was nonsense. Gladys related:

The day before the rescue, [Floyd and Jack] talked over the reward. They said that they might take the reward if they could not get the ransom.

Yesterday I had a feeling that something was going to happen. Floyd got ready to go to town. [He] left at 6:45. A few hours later [I] heard a car drive up. I became frightened and rushed into the corner of the room. It was only Floyd. He limped in and said he had an accident and wrenched his back. The car ran into something and Jack would have to go to town instead. He gave Jack all the instructions and Jack left.

Floyd sat on the edge of the bed and talked to me. He told me he thought I was a wonderful girl, had lots of nerve and all that. Then Floyd talked of his family and his life. We talked till late and then Floyd nailed me into the room and went to sleep.

In the middle of the night the stove went out. I called him and he said, "Never mind," and went back to sleep.

Jack was not due back till daylight. I was alone in that dark room. I thought I would go mad. Something in me kept on telling that there was trouble in the air. The night was terribly long. I called to Floyd again, and said I was frightened. He said, "Don't be afraid. There is nothing to harm you."

Then, after some more long, dark hours, I heard a whistle and a car stopped. I called Floyd three times. I thought the "gang" had come, and felt my mind going insane. There were voices, and then I heard Floyd loading the automatic. I heard Jack's voice, and then all was a mad jumble of sounds.

At that point, Gladys heard a familiar voice. "Oh, is it you? Is it really you? Can it be you?" she sobbed, looking into her husband's face.

"It was a scene such as none of the veteran officers, callused as they are to displays of human emotion under all kinds of stress, had ever witnessed before," wrote the *Times*. "Worn by the sleepless days and nights of search and overjoyed that they had been able to find Mrs. Witherell unharmed, the officers to a man bowed their heads in the presence of the young reunited couple."

"Did they harm you, sweetheart?" asked O. S. "Did they touch you?"

"No," she replied. "No. They treated me as nice as they could, but I want home—house and baby." Then she added, "They treated me good, only they wouldn't let me go. Look," she said, reaching under the bed. "They even bought me a new pair of shoes. You see, I lost one of my own shoes in the fight coming out here. And they bought me a new curling iron, too."

According to the *Times*:

The automobiles were all brought up to the house and their glaring lamps flooded the rooms with light. In the four dingy rooms there were no carpets. Rubbish littered the floors. In the kitchen was a small stove, a cheap table and an old cupboard. On the table was a small typewriter, used in the writing of the notes demanding ransom. In the cupboard was a cribbage board and several sets of false teeth.

Only beds were found in the separate rooms occupied by Mrs. Witherell and the Carr kidnappers. In the men's room were many old hats, which had been used as disguises during visits of the men to the city.

The police returned Gladys and her husband to their Hollywood bungalow and shuttled the Carr cousins off to jail. Scores of police officers, dozens of detectives, and a number of deputy sheriffs spent the afternoon guarding the pair. A howling mob packed the space between the courthouse and the county jail shouting, "Hang them. Lynch them. Let's string them up." But the officers kept the unruly crowd at bay.

With astonishing speed, justice was meted out. After discarding their tale of involvement by "higher ups," the kidnappers were arraigned in Justice Court at 2:30 in the afternoon. Both plead guilty. Two-and-a-half hours later both plead guilty a second time in a preliminary hearing in Superior Court. Bail was set at $50,000 each, with sentencing scheduled for 9:30 the following morning.

What usually required weeks, or even months, was completed in the space of a few hours. The morning after their capture, the court sentenced the Carr cousins to an indeterminate term of from ten years to life imprisonment. As the *Times* noted, the kidnappers had been "run through the greased chute of justice."

"Well," said Jack Carr, "we've danced to our music and I reckon we're payin' the fiddler."

"Yep," agreed Floyd, "we played our game and lost. We hold no malice toward any man, not even the officers who grabbed us. They treated us rough, but that's their business."

At six o'clock that evening, the heavily shackled and closely guarded prisoners boarded a train for San Quentin. "Boys," said Jack Carr to police officers and reporters, "before we leave, we want to let the world know that Mrs. Witherell is the pluckiest little girl in the world."

"You tell the world she is," added Floyd. "She's too good to wipe her feet on any man."

Moments later, the failed kidnappers were en route to the penitentiary.

Chapter 3: A Cowardly Fox

Christmas 1927 was but ten days away when twelve-year-old Marian Parker and her twin sister Marjorie left home on a Thursday morning to attend classes at Mt. Vernon School in Los Angeles. Following their routine, the girls boarded a streetcar at the corner of Wilton Place and Venice Boulevard. "We were sitting together on one of the car seats," recalled Marjorie, "when a man drove by the car at about Third Avenue and Venice Boulevard. He smiled at us several times and motioned to us to get off the car and go with him. We looked the other way, but finally saw him turn off at Fourth Avenue."

Figure 3.1 Twelve-year-old Marion Parker.
Los Angeles Public Library

Earlier that morning, Lorna Littlejohn, a schoolmate of the twins, saw the same man sitting in a small coupe parked at Sixteenth Street and Wilton Place, about a block from the Parker home located at 1631 South Wilton Place.

Just after the noon hour, the same man strode confidently into the office of Mt. Vernon School and approached Mary Holt, school registrar. He explained that Perry M. Parker, the twins' father, had been seriously injured in an automobile accident and was calling for his "youngest daughter," Marian.

Referring to twin Marian as Parker's youngest daughter should have alerted Holt that something was amiss. It did not. "Oh, I can think of many things I could have done now," she later lamented. "I never would have let Marian go but for the apparent sincerity and disarming manner of the man."

The well-groomed stranger gave Holt a name and address, which she failed to note. "I am an employee of the bank where Mr. Parker is chief clerk," he told her, "and if there is any doubt in your mind, here is the bank's telephone number. You may call there."

She did not make a call.

On Holt's instructions, Naomi Britton, an assistant, called Marian from her classroom about 12:13 P.M., just as classes were about to be dismissed.

"Marian was nervous and excited when I told her that her father had been injured," related Holt. "The news completely broke up a little Christmas party the children were having in their room and Marian had some of the refreshments in her hands when she came into the [office]. But at once she forgot about everything but her father."

The stranger patted Marian's arm reassuringly and explained in soothing tones that he had been dispatched by her father to pick her up and take her to him.

Outside, the man helped the girl into a Chrysler coupe, patted her arm again, and got into the car beside her. There was a clashing of gears, and Holt watched from her office window as the car sped down the street.

Marjorie, too, watched as her sister rode away. She did not recognize the stranger as the very man who had tried to lure the girls from the streetcar earlier that morning.

It was the last time anyone, except her abductor, saw Marian alive.

"I can't understand why anyone would wish to hurt us," said the anxious father. "We live quietly and I am sure I have no enemies. We are of moderate means, not the type of family, it seems to me, that would be marked by kidnappers. It is the most puzzling situation I have ever faced."

Law enforcement authorities circulated a detailed description of Marian's kidnapper throughout the state of California. It read, "An American, 25 to 30 years of age, 5 feet 8 inches in height, slender build, thin features, smooth-shaven, medium complexion, dark brown hair which is oily and wavy, apparently well-educated, speaks good English, wears a heavy brownish-gray herringbone overcoat, dark gray hat and dark suit. He is driving a dark-colored coupe or convertible roadster with a spare tire in the rear."

The description was close to the mark, with one notable discrepancy. Marian's abductor was considerably younger than witnesses estimated.

"All we want, of course, is to get her back safely," said the young girl's distraught mother. "Nothing else matters. And I feel that we shall. We haven't given up hope, by any means. I have an idea that when her abductor realizes the effort that is being made to find her he will be frightened and will release her. She isn't the type of child whom anyone would wish to harm."

Two hours after his daughter's kidnapping, Parker received a telegram wired from Pasadena instructing him to do nothing until receipt of a special delivery letter. A second telegram, sent from Alhambra at 6:20 P.M., read: "Marian safe; use good judgment. Interference with my plans dangerous."

The following morning, Parker received a special delivery letter demanding $1,500 for the return of his daughter, and a warning not to notify police of the kidnapping. The letter was printed by hand and the word "death" was written at the top in Modern Greek characters.

The paltry sum demanded as ransom mystified police investigators, whom Parker had of course contacted. Rarely did a kidnapper demand a sum less than five figures.

"Fulfilling these terms with the transfer of the currency will secure the return of the girl," the letter read in part. "Failure to comply with these requests means no one will ever see the girl again—except the angels in heaven. The affair must end one way or another within three days—seventy-two hours. You will receive further notice."

The letter was signed "George Fox."

Late Friday, the kidnapper called Parker at his home to say that he would call again the same night with instructions for delivery of the ransom money and arrangements for the return of his daughter. The second call came and a meeting was arranged at Tenth Street and Gramercy Place. It was thwarted by sloppy police work when the kidnapper spotted police vehicles trailing the Parker automobile.

Saturday, Parker received another special delivery letter. The kidnapper admonished him for notifying the police and outlined what he called the "final chance terms" for getting his daughter back alive. Enclosed was a heart rending letter in Marian's handwriting:

> Dear Daddy and Mother:
> I wish I could come home. I think I'll die if I have to be like this much longer. Won't someone tell me why all this had to happen to me? Daddy please do what the man tells you or he'll kill me if you don't.
> Your loving daughter,
> Marian Parker.
> P.S. Please Daddy, I want to come home tonight.

At 8:00 P.M. that evening, near Fifth Street and Manhattan Place, Parker went to meet the kidnapper for the second time. Shortly

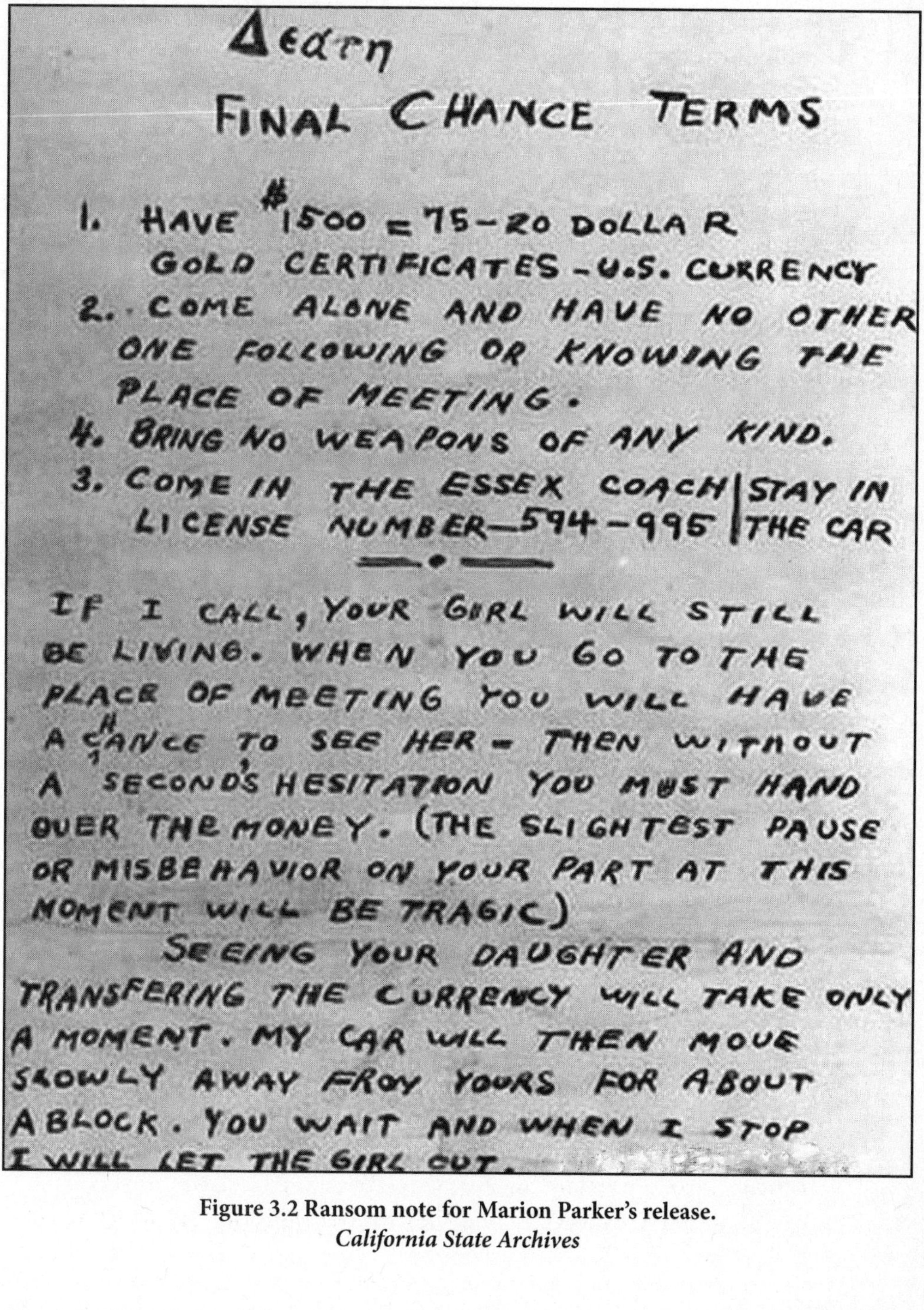

Δεατη

FINAL CHANCE TERMS

1. HAVE #1500 = 75-20 DOLLAR GOLD CERTIFICATES - U.S. CURRENCY
2. COME ALONE AND HAVE NO OTHER ONE FOLLOWING OR KNOWING THE PLACE OF MEETING.
4. BRING NO WEAPONS OF ANY KIND.
3. COME IN THE ESSEX COACH|STAY IN LICENSE NUMBER—594-995|THE CAR

IF I CALL, YOUR GIRL WILL STILL BE LIVING. WHEN YOU GO TO THE PLACE OF MEETING YOU WILL HAVE A CHANCE TO SEE HER — THEN WITHOUT A SECOND'S HESITATION YOU MUST HAND OVER THE MONEY. (THE SLIGHTEST PAUSE OR MISBEHAVIOR ON YOUR PART AT THIS MOMENT WILL BE TRAGIC)

SEEING YOUR DAUGHTER AND TRANSFERING THE CURRENCY WILL TAKE ONLY A MOMENT. MY CAR WILL THEN MOVE SLOWLY AWAY FROM YOURS FOR ABOUT A BLOCK. YOU WAIT AND WHEN I STOP I WILL LET THE GIRL OUT.

Figure 3.2 Ransom note for Marion Parker's release.
California State Archives

49

after he arrived, a Chrysler roadster drove alongside the Parker automobile and the banker saw what appeared to be his daughter seated beside the driver.

The kidnapper wore a handkerchief over the lower part of his face, and through the open car window he leveled a pistol at Parker. "Here's your child," the man said. "Give me the money and follow instructions. She is asleep now."

Parker handed the kidnapper $1,500 in seventy-five, new $20 gold certificates, the serial numbers recorded by authorities. The abductor, following their agreement, drove ahead of the Parker vehicle and deposited Marian on the front lawn of a home located at 428 South Manhattan Place.

As soon as the kidnapper drove away, Parker rushed frantically to his daughter's side. He took her in his arms and knew at once that his child was dead. Marian had been brutally murdered and horribly mutilated.

Parker, on the verge of collapse, telephoned Los Angeles chief of detectives Herman Cline. Within minutes, the greatest manhunt in the city's history was on.

The kidnapper's Chrysler roadster was found Sunday evening abandoned at a parking lot in the Westlake Park district. Fingerprints lifted from its windshield matched perfectly those found on one of the ransom notes. Stolen from a Kansas City physician in early November, the automobile was the first substantial lead in the case.

Meantime, five separate bundles containing missing parts of the slain child's body, all found in Elysian Park, made for a gruesome discovery. A man named Britton discovered packages containing the arms and legs of the victim, and less than an hour later two small boys recovered the remaining part of the body—the viscera.

"Swooping down from the sky, airplanes carrying Los Angeles detectives last night halted an east-bound bus at Las Vegas, Nevada, and arrested Lewis D. Wyatt ... as a suspect in the Marian Parker kidnapping and murder case," reported the Monday morning issue of the *Los Angeles Times*, in most dramatic fashion.

"Two airplanes carrying the Los Angeles officers headed off the bus just as it came to a stop in Las Vegas to take on gas. They removed Wyatt and escorted him at once to the police station where he was fingerprinted and photographed."

The story made compelling headlines, but the Los Angeles police department could have put the money paid for chartered airplanes to better use. Wyatt had no connection to the Parker case. His purchase of a ticket to Terre Haute, Indiana, using two $20 gold certificates, had triggered his arrest.

Although not as dramatic as Wyatt's arrest, the LAPD took seven additional suspects into custody. Before the day ended, however, each was exonerated and released.

The city and county each offered rewards of $5,000 for the capture of Marian's slayer. Warner Brothers' radio station, KFWB, announced pledges of more than $20,000 in listener contributions towards a reward fund. Station KMIC in Inglewood received promises of contributions totaling some $4,000. At Angelus Temple in Echo Park, famed evangelist Aimee Semple McPherson sent out a plea to followers for contributions. In time, the reward fund multiplied to nearly $100,000.

The odious task of putting Marian's body back together fell to an autopsy surgeon named Wagner. A next-door neighbor of the Parker family, he had known the young girl most of her life and was visibly shaken during the procedure.

Late in the afternoon, Parker asked the police to rope off the block surrounding his home. Some 25,000 morbid curiosity seekers had driven by the house during the day. The constant purring of motors and tooting of horns was wearing Parker's wife's nerves to a frazzle.

At six o'clock Monday evening, the police issued a murder warrant for 19-year-old William Edward Hickman. Fingerprints taken from the windshield of the Chrysler "death car" matched with those of a check forger arrested the previous June by the LAPD.

A towel stuffed in the torso of Marian's body revealed the name of the Bellevue Arms Apartments at 1170 Bellevue Avenue. Through photo identification, witnesses confirmed that Hickman lived there. The previous Saturday night, he was seen carrying a suitcase and several bundles to an automobile parked near the building's rear entrance. The engine was running and the car's lights were on.

From police photographs, K. D. Jackson, owner of Jackson Pharmacy at 1400 Sunset Boulevard, identified Hickman as the man who held him up on the night of November 27. Searching for chloroform and ether, the bandit forced Jackson to lie on the floor while he ransacked the store. Failing to find what he wanted, he took $80 in cash and some sleeping pills.

Two other druggists identified Hickman as a holdup man. He robbed both L. D. Welch, owner of a store at 2829 Glendale Boulevard, and Harry Packer, owner of a store at 1801 Glendale Boulevard, on the night of December 5. He took chloroform, ether, and $36 in cash from Welch's store, while Packer was relieved of $120. According to Packer, the bandit drove a Chrysler roadster.

At the time of his forgery arrest in June, Hickman was employed as a messenger in the bank where Perry Parker worked as personnel officer. The young man pleaded guilty to the forgery charge, but because he lied about his age, his case was heard in juvenile court. Hickman was placed on probation in his mother's custody. Mother and son soon moved to Kansas City from whence they came. Some months later, the Chrysler "death car" was stolen there.

"It's a terrible mistake," said Eva Hickman upon learning of her son's arrest warrant for murder. "This crime is the work of a fiend. My boy is a good clean boy. I'll never believe it until I hear it from his own lips."

Eva said her son left Kansas City a few months before to "make his way in the world alone." She last heard from him in October. He

was working
as an usher
in a Chicago
theater and
she thought
he was still
there. He was
a "good home
boy," she said.
He attended
church regu-
larly and was
a leader in
Sunday school
activities.

Figure 3.3 Hickman's apartment, on left.
Los Angeles Public Library

Officials at
Central High
School, Hickman's Kansas City alma mater, were shocked when told
of the charges lodged against him. Principal Otto F. Dubach said he
had been an exceptional student. Hickman was described as "mild
mannered" and "popular," and his scholastic resume was impressive. Elected to the student council three years in a row, he served
as vice president of his senior class in 1926. He was president of the
central chapter of the National Honor Society, president of the Central Webster Club, president of the Central Classics Club, a member
of the debate team, business manager of the school paper, literary
editor of the school year book, and was voted by his peers as the
school's "best boy orator."

William Edward Hickman was a dichotomy.

On Wednesday, December 21, another $20 gold certificate turned
up, used for purchases in a Seattle clothing store. Bearing the serial
number K-68016970, it was the sixty-ninth in the series of seventy-
five certificates Perry Parker paid Hickman as ransom for his murdered daughter.

"A blockade was immediately placed about the northern city to cut off every avenue of escape from the hunted man," wrote the Associated Press. "Its harbor is being watched for any and all suspects. Tense policemen were stationed on every important traffic artery."

Despite its careful preparations, Hickman's capture would not be at the hands of the Seattle police department.

Thursday morning found the fugitive in Arlington, Oregon, a small town on the Columbia River some 85 miles west of Pendleton. There he cashed another of his telltale $20 gold certificates before speeding away in a stolen green Hudson sedan. Just before noon, Edward Aldrich, editor of the *East Oregonian*, telephoned Tom Gurdane, Pendleton chief of police, to alert him that Hickman had been spotted. The wanted man was headed east on the Old Oregon Trail, a macadam state highway that paralleled the winding Umatilla River.

Gurdane and state traffic officer Buck Lieuallen jumped into Lieuallen's squad car and drove west along the same route, stopping near one of the roadway's numerous curves. Lieuallen was about to light his pipe when an automobile swung around the curve, some 300 yards distant.

"Here comes a Hudson," Gurdane remarked.

"That's not him," replied Lieuallen. "It has Washington license plates. His car has California plates."

The automobile drew nearer.

"To hell with the license," said Gurdane. "It's a Hudson and it's green."

As the Hudson sped by, the officers noticed that the driver wore dark glasses.

"I figured that there was something wrong when a young fellow was wearing dark glasses on a day when it was cloudy," said Gurdane later. "I knew that it was Hickman so we turned the car around."

By the time the officers completed a U-turn, Hickman had pulled a mile or more ahead of them, driving at about forty miles an hour. It was a high rate of speed given the primitive conditions of the roadway.

For a mile-and-a-half or more, the law officers chased the fleeing vehicle at speeds of forty-five and fifty miles an hour.

"I didn't have much time to see just how fast we were going," said Gurdane. "I was watching the Hudson."

As they drew close to the Hickman automobile, they pulled on the siren. The fugitive maintained his speed and showed no indication of stopping.

"Keep behind him," said Gurdane. They were certain Hickman was armed and the officers did not intend to be his targets.

They were four miles east of Echo, and twenty-two miles west of Pendleton when, unexpectedly, Hickman pulled his car over to the side of the road. Gurdane jumped out, covering the alleged slayer with his gun, as Lieuallen rushed to the other side of the Hudson.

"I covered him with my gun," said Gurdane, "and opened the door with my left hand and told him to get out. When he started to get out, a .45 automatic dropped to the running board. He pretended to make out that he was being arrested for speeding."

The officers scoffed.

"I knew you all the time," said Gurdane. "What are you doing with that gun?"

"It's customary to carry a gun when you are traveling," Hickman replied.

"You don't need to keep it between your knees," the lawman told him.

They ordered Hickman out of the car, telling him to keep his hands up high. Gurdane held Hickman's hands, keeping him covered, while Lieuallen searched him. "Here's one of the bills," said Lieuallen, as he rifled Hickman's pockets.

Lieuallen then searched the car, which rendered an additional $1,400 in bills. Hickman glanced at the twenty-dollar bills, and then looked at the officers. "Well," he said, "I guess it's all over."

Hickman's only response to the handcuffs placed about his wrists was a hysterical burst of laughter.

The Associated Press reported:

> William Edward Hickman late today positively denied that he knows where the body of Marian Parker was dismembered and declared that his part in the crime was to handle the messages to the father and collect the money. He said he turned the girl over to Andrew Cramer Thursday night after taking her to the Rialto Theatre in Alhambra and did not see her again until Cramer came to the apartment with her remains in a suitcase.
>
> "This is going to be interesting before it is all over," Hickman remarked to Buck Lieuallen … as he sat down to relate the details of the crime.
>
> "Do they only kill by hanging in California?" he queried. "Oh, this is not California, is it?" he asked before they could reply, answering his own question.
>
> When asked to pose for a photograph, he said, "What should I look like, a crook?"

Hickman agreed to make a confession, but for reasons obscured by time, he offered it up to Parker Branin, city editor of the *East Oregonian*, rather than to the Pendleton police officers.

In a rambling diatribe that often made little sense, Hickman persisted with the story that he had been in cahoots with one Andrew Cramer, an older man whom he had picked up hitchhiking from San Diego to Los Angeles. Together, they held up drug stores, and, for reasons unknown to Hickman, Cramer insisted that the loot include chloroform and ether as well as money.

When Cramer approached him with the notion that they orchestrate a kidnapping, Hickman agreed. He reasoned that it would be an easy way to raise money to enable him to return to Kansas

Figure 3.4 William Edward Hickman at the Pendleton, Oregon jail, January 1928. Left, Chief of Police Tom Gurdane; center, Hickman; right, State Traffic Police Sergeant Buck Lieuallen.
Los Angeles Public Library

City and enroll in college. He limited his participation, however, to writing ransom notes and collecting the money. It was his idea to target Marian Parker as the victim, but he had no idea that Cramer intended to kill her. He was shocked when Marian was murdered and her body mutilated.

After the deed was committed and authorities were hot on his trail, Hickman fled to San Francisco where he planned to rendezvous with Cramer. Cramer, however, was nowhere to be found. Frightened and desperate, Hickman began his journey to the Northwest.

Hickman was a creative liar.

"I was stopped by four different Los Angeles police officers in making my getaway," he boasted to fellow inmates at the Pendleton city jail.

The boast was more in character than was Hickman's "confession."

He told inmates of cashing the first $20 gold certificate at a Los Angeles restaurant on Sunday. The waitress asked if he was not afraid of flashing about new $20 bills—no trifling sum in the late 1920s. No, he boasted, he was not afraid. They chatted for a while and when the waitress asked him his name, he said, "You sure would be surprised if you knew."

Hickman clearly enjoyed his role as a much written-about fugitive on the lam.

Almost at once, Pendleton became the news capital of North America, and Hickman was the star attraction. Because he had signed the first ransom note under the name George Fox, clever reporters dubbed him "The Fox"—a *nom de plume* he relished with childish glee.

The Los Angeles legal community moved swiftly. On the afternoon of Hickman's capture in Oregon, a grand jury convened. In one hour and two minutes, jurors returned an indictment against the boastful youth. It contained two counts: murder and kidnapping, with intent to extort money.

As extradition papers were being prepared, Los Angeles district attorney Asa Keyes, chief of detectives Herman Cline, chief of police James E. Davis, and other officers boarded a train for Pendleton to take charge of the prisoner.

Before departing, Keyes said the worst danger now was the possibility of Oregon residents taking the law into their own hands and lynching Hickman. Then he added, "In my opinion, Hickman had no accomplice in this brutal murder. If he did, it will be amazing to me. Until I talk with him and learn more about what he has to say, I cannot give a definite opinion, but it seems to me if he had help, he certainly would have had to split the ransom money with his accomplice."

Meantime, Hickman's capture had created havoc in Kansas City. "Newsboys became centers of scrambling masses of humanity as persons tore at one another to buy papers," wrote the Associated Press. "Many employees in downtown buildings rushed from their tasks when the cry of 'Extra! Extra! Boy killer captured!' went up, and Christmas shopping was stopped temporarily."

Eva Hickman was not one of those in Kansas City grappling for a newspaper. When told of her son's capture and partial confession, she collapsed. "It can't be true," she sobbed. "If they've caught the slayer of the little girl it can't be my son."

In El Paso, reporters tracked William T. Hickman, Eva's former husband and the alleged slayer's father, to a Southern Pacific Railroad yard where he was employed as a crane operator. Denying that his son was abnormal in any way, the father wept as he told of his last meeting with the younger Hickman in Kansas City in October 1926:

"I would rather be dead and in hell a thousand times than to think a child of mine would commit such an atrocious crime," he lamented. "I cannot understand what could have happened to him to change him into such a fiend as the murder indicates he is, if he really did it."

Much of the bravado was knocked out of Hickman when on Friday, December 23, he was told that Andrew Cramer, his alleged accomplice, had been the occupant of a Los Angeles jail cell since August. It was impossible for Cramer to have been involved in the diabolical murder and mutilation that Hickman had ascribed to him.

"I know Hickman," Cramer told the press with much disgust. "I don't know why he picks on me."

On Christmas Eve, Oregon governor I. L. Patterson signed extradition papers authorizing the removal of Hickman from Pendleton to California. When district attorney Keyes told the prisoner of his impending return to Los Angeles, charged with a death penalty offense, Hickman flew into a maniacal frenzy and collapsed in his cell. Writhing on the floor, he moaned, "I did not kill her. I did not kill her."

His jail mates, many of them hardened felons, sneered at Hickman and turned their backs on him. "He'll get his," was the sentiment common among convicts unsympathetic toward the alleged child killer.

Disgusted by his antics, Chief Gurdane quipped, "The Fox has become a rat."

During the night, Hickman tied a handkerchief about his throat and attempted to hang himself from a beam in the jail cell. Hearing a guttural groan, guards rushed to his cell. He was hanging limp and several minutes were required to revive him.

Then he attempted to beat himself to death by banging his head against the cell bars. He failed again when guards intervened.

"Listen, Hickman," seethed Detective Cline, "are you going to be a yellow cur or are you going to brace up and come along on this trip like a man?"

Hickman's reply was a woeful moan.

"Take him out," Cline ordered his officers.

It was just past daylight Christmas Day, when Hickman was taken aboard a prison coach attached to a Union Pacific train bound for Portland. From there, he would transfer to another prison coach attached to a Los Angeles-bound Southern Pacific train. En route to Portland, however, district attorney Keyes received a wire from Portland chief of police Jenkins, informing him that a mob of some 2,000 angry citizens had formed at Union Station. Jenkins insisted that Keyes remove his prisoner at Montavilla, five miles east of Portland. Keyes complied and when the train rolled into Montavilla, a police car rushed Hickman to the Portland city jail to await the Southern Pacific connection.

Soon Hickman was en route to Los Angeles. As the train clickety-clacked across the tracks, the youthful "Fox" did an about face. "I'm ready to talk," he told the district attorney. "I want to tell the whole story."

And so he did. Almost.

He admitted that, acting alone, he kidnapped and murdered little Marian Parker. The killing and dismemberment occurred the afternoon of Saturday, December 17, at his Bellevue apartment. When the beastly task was completed, he went to a moving picture show at Loew's State Theater, returning to his flat at 5:30. There he gathered the body parts and took them to his car. He drove on Sunset Boulevard to Elysian Park, where he disposed of the limbs and viscera. He then propped the murdered girl's torso onto the seat beside him and proceeded to his ransom meeting with Parker. After collecting the money and dumping the torso on a nearby lawn, he went to dinner at Leighton's Cafe where he cashed the first of the $20 gold certificates. Afterward, he returned to his apartment and went to bed. He slept soundly until morning.

It was a confession of torture, death, and butchery so depraved that even hard-bitten law officers were sickened.

The following day, as Hickman's train sped south along the California coast, his mother announced from Kansas City that she had retained attorney Jerome Walsh to represent her son. Walsh, 25 years old and the youngest member of the Missouri State Legislature, was the son of Frank P. Walsh, one of the Midwest's most celebrated criminal lawyers. Apparently, the young attorney, who had accepted the Hickman case *pro bono*, was out to make a name for himself.

On December 27, the Southern Pacific *Padre* rumbled closer to its destination. Hickman, awakened at 3:00 A.M., dressed and ate a hearty breakfast, then listened as officers discussed the temper of the Los Angeles public and their plans to slip the prisoner safely into the city.

"Newspaper men sat up all night in readiness, should a sudden dash be made [by Hickman and his escorts] from the train," reported the *Times*. "Presumably the messages from Los Angeles were reassuring, for he was kept on the train until it reached the point nearest the jail.

"… Restrictions were tightened as the car neared Los Angeles. Doors were bolted and Southern Pacific agents guarded the coach. At Glendale, a crowd of 1,000 ran along the train [tracks], eagerly looking for the man who called himself a fox."

The train did not come to a complete stop, but paused at Jackson and Alameda streets. There, detectives guarding the heavily shackled prisoner leaped with him from the train and dashed across the vestibule to five waiting police cars. In seconds, the procession sped off for the county jail. It was 10:10 A.M.

Five minutes later, Hickman was behind bars. At 11:30, he faced superior court judge George Carlos Hardy, who informed the accused that his arraignment had been postponed until 2:00 P.M. the next afternoon, in order to await the arrival of Walsh.

As the *Times* reported:

> The courtroom scene attendant upon Hickman's session was one seldom matched in local court history. News that Hickman had been lodged in the jail and would be taken before Judge Hardy for arraignment spread through the building and out on to the street as if by magic, despite the precautions taken by the officers and the speed with which they worked.
>
> Deputy sheriffs and a small army of uniformed officers from the city, and [officers of] the county motorcycle squad were hurried up to the eighth floor of the Hall of Justice, where the courtroom is located. They filled the courtroom. They filled the corridors. They guarded elevators and they guarded all entrances and exits.

The attention did much to pump air into the prisoner's inflated notion of self-importance.

After his court appearance, guards allowed Hickman to speak with reporters. "I'll plead guilty and stand by my confession regardless of what this attorney advises me to do," he announced, in a tone reflecting more than a hint of swagger.

Asked if he stood ready to suffer the consequences of his actions, he answered, "Sure."

"Suppose your attorney advises you to plead not guilty and stand trial?" someone asked.

"I would plead guilty anyhow."

"You want a speedy trial?"

"Yes, I want a speedy trial." Then after a pause, he added. "But not too speedy."

Meantime, in El Paso, Hickman's father spoke out: "Since he has confessed this awful crime, I've disowned him as a son and am content to let the law have him. I was hopeful William was telling the truth when he said he had not murdered the child. Kidnapping was bad enough. Now I want to see him punished according to the crime."

When rumors began to circulate that attorney Walsh would plead his client not guilty by reason of insanity, the *Times* uncapped its editorial pen:

> Society does not have to give up restraining criminals merely because a psychologist or so thinks he has discovered they are machines instead of beings with wills, souls and consciences.
>
> A dog that becomes dangerous is either muzzled or shot, according to circumstances, and no inquiry is made as to whether or not he is "responsible."

On December 28, the court arraigned Hickman for the kidnapping and murder of Marian Parker. Walsh, citing his need to become intimately familiar with the details of "this gruesome affair," requested that a delay be granted until Tuesday, January 3, before entering a plea. Judge Hardy granted the delay.

A bombshell exploded the following day when 16-year-old Welby Hunt, late of Kansas City, and a "pal" of Hickman, admitted to authorities that he had been involved with the confessed slayer in a string of armed robberies. These included Rose Hill Pharmacy on Christmas Eve, 1926, in which Hickman allegedly shot the proprietor, C. Ivy Toms, to death.

The *Times* reported: "The Toms murder confession came as a startling climax to Hickman's revolting statement admitting the murder and mutilation of little Marian Parker, whom he kidnapped from school two weeks ago. Hunt's confession, in which he admitted being present at the time of the shooting but denied firing the shot that killed Toms, added another chapter to the amazing orgy of crime directed during the past year by the brutal slayer of the Parker girl."

The noose about Hickman's neck drew even tighter when Hunt admitted that the accused had spoken of "cutting up someone." Hickman told Hunt "he had always had a desire to cut up someone and throw them along the highway." Hunt dismissed it as idle talk, noting that Hickman was "occasionally moody and silly, but not sick or insane."

Hickman readily admitted the Toms killing, adding that a few days later he and Hunt went by train to San Francisco where they "robbed a number of places [and] stole five automobiles." The pair returned to Los Angeles on January 15, 1927, where they continued their holdup spree.

Hunt found himself charged with murder and Hickman faced a second murder charge.

"My goodness!" exclaimed the naïve Hunt from his cell in the county jail. "They can't charge me with murder. I never even fired a shot."

On January 3, 1928, Hickman, who with much bravado had insisted he would plead guilty to the kidnapping and murder of

Marian Parker, entered a plea of not guilty by reason of insanity. His trial date was set for January 25.

In essence, the proceeding was both a trial and a sanity hearing in which life or death figured in the balance. Should the jury find Hickman guilty and sane, the trap door of the gallows would be released. If, however, the jury ruled him guilty and insane, he would be committed to life in the State Hospital for the Criminally Insane. However, should the latter verdict be rendered there was yet another wrinkle. If at any time during his confinement in the state hospital, it could be determined that his sanity had returned fully, the gallows doors would again swing open.

The same evening, defense counsel Walsh and deputy district attorney Costello left on the Santa Fe Railroad for Kansas City and other Midwestern points, seeking a number of depositions and affidavits regarding Hickman's past.

The prisoner, meantime, embraced with enthusiasm his role of insanity. Whenever jail personnel or officials connected to his trial were present, the normally boastful, gregarious inmate would stare listlessly at the wall of his cell or indulge in babbling fits of incoherence.

Jail mates, appalled by his vicious crimes and disgusted by his antics, strung a large photograph of Hickman over a rafter. They punched a hole in either side, placed a rope about the neck, and hanged Hickman in effigy.

Welby Hunt appeared before Judge Hardy on January 10. He entered a plea of not guilty in the murder of druggist C. Ivy Toms. Hunt petitioned the court to be tried separately from Hickman— who would stand trial for the Toms killing upon completion of the Parker murder trial, scheduled to commence fifteen days hence.

The judge denied the petition, and the Toms murder trial was set for February 15.

The *Chicago Tribune* reported on January 13 that a young boy, influenced by news reports about Hickman, "wrote a ransom letter to his former employer, the neighborhood butcher, demanding $10,000, and threatening to kidnap the butcher's daughter. The youth made two mistakes, however. He failed to say where the money was to be delivered, and he signed his own name."

The impressionable youngster earned himself six months probation.

Five days before the scheduled trial date, Hickman's father, William Thomas—who claimed to have disowned his son—chugged into town to tell of an alleged strain of mental illness that ran through his ex-wife's family. "If placed on the witness stand, I will testify that Edward is suffering from hereditary insanity," he stated. "I do not think Edward should ever be permitted to walk the streets. He is a dangerous being, and if I felt entirely satisfied as to his mental condition, then I would expect him to pay the supreme penalty. There is no place in this country for such a beast as he has proven to be, except solitary confinement, if insane. If he is sane, then the gallows."

Three days later, Eva Hickman and another son, Alfred, arrived in Los Angeles. Eva met at length with the confessed slayer, but refused to pose for photographs with him and declined to speak with the press.

Most surprising was an affidavit filed by Walsh on the eve of the trial, seeking the removal of Judge Hardy. In it, he stated that Hardy's actions were improper in assigning the trial to himself, when, as presiding judge of the criminal division, he should have assigned the case to another court. Perhaps more to the point, he declared that Hardy had made disparaging remarks about Walsh's efforts to obtain depositions for the defense, and he had made prejudicial remarks about the defendant.

Hardy denied the allegations, but voluntarily removed himself from the bench. J. J. Trabucco, superior court judge of Mariposa County and considered one of California's leading jurists, was appointed in his stead.

Figure 3.5 Crowd outside courthouse during Hickman trial.
Los Angeles Public Library

On Wednesday, January 25, in Department 24 of Los Angeles County superior court, the trial of William Edward Hickman, the press-styled "Fox," commenced.

With blistering sarcasm, the *Times* wrote:

> The old stock company is back for another stand.
>
> Playing tragedy.
>
> Some new faces, props, a slight change in the plot, but in the main just the same old troupers, same old scenery, same old theme.
>
> Written in blood, staged by the State and featuring this time a wavy-haired, shifty-eyed, pasty-faced fiend, civilization's shameful tragedy, "a famous murder trial" is here again for an undetermined run.

By 5:07, Friday afternoon, twelve jurors were in place. When court reconvened on Monday, Walsh read into the record eighty-five pages of depositions. And that was just the beginning. The defense counsel insisted on the reading of some 600 pages before calling a single witness, each deposition an attempt to establish hereditary insanity in the defendant's maternal family.

A deposition from Benjamin Harrison Bailey, brother-in-law of Otto Buck, Eva Hickman's brother, stated that Buck was "insane."

Thomas Lewis, uncle of the defendant, said Otto Buck's mind was "feeble." He further stated that Becky Buck, the slayer's grandmother, had a "mind weak and was feeble like a little child."

Irvin Harris declared the grandmother was "insane" when she died, and Otto Buck was "crazy."

Dr. W. D. Hunt of Poteau, Oklahoma, testified in his deposition that he had treated Eva Hickman from 1912 to 1920. He said that she had once tried to commit suicide and later was confined to an institution for the insane. "In my opinion she was insane," he concluded.

Sarah Stankard, a former neighbor of the confessed killer's mother, characterized her as "a little bit queer," and attested to Eva's attempted suicide.

Artie Smith, Hickman's paternal aunt, told of Eva experiencing "dancing fits" that convinced her that the woman was "insane."

Mae Forrester testified that Hickman's father had a reputation of "running around with women," which contributed to Eva's "nervous" condition.

The readings went on and on.

At the conclusion of the day's testimony, prosecution alienists* who had interviewed the defendant declared that the depositions read were meaningless and that none had application to the young man on trial.

But never mind. The depositions continued.

---

*An archaic term then commonly used for doctors skilled in the treatment of mental disorders associated with medical jurisprudence.

Otto F. Dubach, Hickman's high school principal, told of girls who had been acquaintances of the young man, but stated that he knew of Hickman having no real girlfriends.

A classmate testified that the defendant had never accompanied a girl to a dance, but preferred to "take girls away" from other lads and escort them home.

Other instructors said that he was "a very bright boy," in the upper 10 percent of his class, with a 3.5 grade-point average.

In other depositions, schoolmates and friends testified that Hickman seemed to "go through a change" between his junior and senior years. Some thought he was "insane," others that he was "different."

One deposition stated that the "change" in Hickman had occurred after he had experienced defeat in several oratorical contests.

Another student testified that the killer had been a leader in a school YMCA club, but after a time, he had lost interest. The members asked him to resign. Hickman "flew into a passion" and wrote insulting letters to other members of the club, accusing them of not being Christians.

February 1 was Hickman's twentieth birthday. It also marked the conclusion of the tedious reading of depositions, and it was the day counselor Walsh introduced the young man's confession to kidnapping, murder, and mutilation as "evidence for the defense." The lawyer was certain that the jury would find Hickman's unconscionable brutality the act of an insane man.

The first witness to offer oral testimony was Los Angeles detective Lieutenant Richard Lucas, who was among the officers present when Hickman confessed in the Pendleton jail. In a deep, husky voice, his hands gripping the arms of the witness chair, Lucas recounted the ghastly story he heard from the defendant's lips.

The detective then testified that Hickman:

> ...told me that he would throw a fit for the judge and asked me what I thought of the fits he had thrown in the Pendleton

jail. I told him that he might be able to fool the officers in the north, but that he couldn't fool the [Los Angeles] officers with any of his fits.

Hickman went into great detail with me, relative to the selection of the judge and a jury, and then stated that he didn't want to be tried by a jury, but would plead guilty and take his chances before Judge Hardy [who removed himself before the trial began].

The prisoner told me that Judge Hardy had handled his case before [in the check forgery conviction], and that he was against capital punishment and that he would not hang him on account of his religious affiliations.

Evidently, Hickman had known that Hardy was a follower of Aimee Semple McPherson's Four Square Gospel, and a worker at her Angelus Temple.

The next day, Chief of Detectives Herman Cline took the stand and retold Hickman's confession in bloody detail.

Then, shocking spectators and throwing the jury into disarray, defense counsel Walsh introduced into evidence a series of graphic photographs showing the dismembered body of Marian Parker.

Standing abruptly as though she would flee the courtroom, a woman juror swayed back and forth and looked as if she might fall over the railing of the jury box. District attorney Keyes rushed to her aid and thrust a glass of water into her hands. The woman seated beside her, in scarcely better condition, held the glass as the dazed juror drank, and then she was administered smelling salts.

Male jurors were observed gritting their teeth and kneading their palms.

The gruesome photos were repulsive to all.

Welby Hunt, accused with Hickman in the Toms murder, testified that the defendant once said, "I want to get someone and chop them up and string them along the highway."

Dry-eyed and seemingly composed, Eva Hickman testified to her unhappy life. The *Times* took up the story:

She told of her detention in an insane asylum shortly after Edward's birth, and also corroborated her [ex]husband's charges that she had suffered from mental ailments that caused her from time to time to threaten both suicide and murder of her whole family. She told of an attempted suicide and stated her mental condition was always much worse just before the birth of her various children, and reached a climax a few months before Edward, her youngest son, was born.

"At times I hated my husband, and many times I told him that I would kill him," Mrs. Hickman testified. She also astonished the courtroom by announcing that the infant, who nineteen years later was to slay the little Parker girl, was himself born dead, but was revived after doctors had worked over him for hours.

"My mind at times was blank, and I cannot now recall all of the things that I did."

Later testimony was offered by a defense alienist named Fettes, who said he had made a complete examination of the defendant and found him to be suffering from cirrus meningitis, which he explained was an inflammation of the covering of the brain.

A doctor named Shelton then testified that Hickman suffered from dementia praecox and megalomania, and that he considered the defendant paranoid.

Shortly after 3:00 P.M., Friday, February 3, the prosecution opened its case. Almost immediately, Hickman's insanity defense was struck a telling blow. Introduced into evidence was an astonishing document written by the defendant and slipped to a fellow inmate in the county jail. It read:

> Listen Dale:
>
> I believe you and believe I can trust you. Give me your advice on which one of these plans would be better. All of these depositions aren't enough to prove me insane. I've got to throw a fit in court and I intend to throw a laughing, screaming, diving act before the prosecution finishes their case—maybe in front of old man Parker [the slain girl's father] himself.

Then to bewilder the jury, before the case is ended—I'll get up and ask the judge if I can say something without my attorney butting in. Then I'll get up and give all that shit about me wanting to do some good by living.

I intend to rap Mr. Keyes before the thing's over and pull some trick on him in the crazy line.

Shorty, think these things over and tell me whether it is best or not.

For God's sake tear this thing up because it would ruin me if it got out.

See you in the morning.

William Edward Hickman,

Alias "The Fox,"

Ha! Ha! Ha!

P.S. You know and I know that I am not insane, however.

As the note was read, Hickman's jaw dropped and he looked over at his attorney. Unable to restrain his anger, Walsh's face reddened and he glared with disgust at the defendant. Hickman's jailhouse note could be his undoing.

Dr. Reynolds, prosecution alienist, testified that "Hickman's dominant characteristic is callousness, and callousness has long been recognized as the hallmark of the criminal. But if he presents no signs of insanity from the medical standpoint, he presents even less from the medico-legal standpoint. It is abundantly clear … that he knew the nature and quality of his act at the time it was committed, that he knew it was wrong, and was in no sense disoriented. Moreover, his act was performed under circumstances that fulfilled all the requirements of a wrong act without mitigating circumstances."

Expert after expert testified to Hickman's sanity but, perhaps, no testimony was as damning as the note slipped by the defendant to "Dale" in the county jail.

On February 9, the prosecution rested its case. After deliberating thirty-six minutes, the jury of four women and eight men reached its verdict on the first ballot. The jury declared Hickman sane.

"The die is cast and the state wins by a neck," the killer flippantly remarked as the guards removed him from the courtroom. "Perhaps I should have my body cut into forty-eight pieces and send a piece to every state."

On February 14, Valentine's Day, Judge J. J. Trabucco sentenced Hickman to hang on the 27th day of April, 1928.

The next day, jury selection began in the joint trial of Hickman and Welby Hunt, accused of murdering druggist C. Ivy Toms. The trial dragged on until March 10, when the jury found the defendants guilty. Each was sentenced to life imprisonment.

In Hickman's case, however, the length of his life sentence depended on how quickly the appeals process expired, and the time it took a hangman to knot a noose to punish Hickman for the savage slaying of Marian Parker.

To the dismay of many, April 27 passed without incident.

Times columnist Harry Carr wrote, "The irony of it is that this wretched little butcher is resigned to death on the gallows. He knows that what he would get at the hands of the convicts at San Quentin would be worse than hanging.

"Yet, between him and the gallows, will be a poison gas screen of miserable legal technicalities thrown up to block the operations of the law."

Given today's standards—Carr's comments notwithstanding—justice moved expeditiously in the Hickman case.

Hickman's appointment with the grim reaper was reset for October 19. On the 10th, Jerome Walsh, still pleading the slayer's case, petitioned Governor C. C. Young for commutation of the death sentence.

"I will treat the Hickman case as any other that might come before me," said the governor. "I will not grant executive clemency unless there is some new and positive evidence proving the innocence of the prisoner."

There was none.

"I have made up my mind to take my medicine," Hickman wrote in a statement to the Associated Press from his San Quentin prison cell.

Apparently, convict 45041 had gotten a last-minute surge of religion: "I know very well that I have been a most guilty sinner. Nevertheless, I have confessed my sins and I am now trying to do what is right. I am sorry for having offended God and man. I desire punishment and ask no personal favors...."

Religion aside, when Hickman was not listening to jazz records on the phonograph in his cell, sent to him by admirers, he was preening his ego by writing replies to the hundreds of "fan" letters he received.

Not one to give up easily, Walsh went to the capitol at Sacramento where, on October 15, he met with Governor Young. It was all for naught. The governor pointed out that the state constitution provided that a twice-convicted felon could not seek commutation of sentence without the assent of a majority of the members of the state supreme court. And, such assent appeared to be impossible to obtain.

Walsh then asked Young to appoint three psychiatrists to examine Hickman and ascertain his sanity, or lack of it. The governor politely declined.

The condemned man then sent off an orgy of "Please forgive me" letters, writing to various police chiefs across the country, confessing to heretofore-unknown crimes he had committed.

Three days before his scheduled execution, Hickman told reporters that when he graduated from high school he planned to become a minister and carry on a life of crime under the "cloak of the holy cloth." He added that he wanted to become a fiend and a "demon incarnate" to test his philosophy of life and self-sufficiency.

Then, in a chilling confession, he said he slew Marian Parker to test his capacity to deliberately take a human life under the most revolting conditions.

On October 17, Hickman "mounted the seventy-five steps from the inner yard to the old shops building housing the death cell which opens only to the scaffold," reported the *Times*.

> As taps sounded [at 9:00 P.M.], Warden Holohan went to the cell occupied jointly by Hickman and Russell St. Clair Beitzel, another Los Angeles murderer, and rapped on the grating. Hickman immediately stepped forward, bidding Beitzel goodbye, and was taken out to the steel runway which flanks the cell house like a balcony.
>
> The death cell, in reality, is composed of two wooden-barred cages, fitted only with a mattress and two blankets in the center of a room forty-feet square on the third floor of the old shops building. The room is double-lined with steel mesh.
>
> Almost immediately after entering the death cell, Hickman began to pray. As he prayed he looked at the signs, symbols, and marks that his predecessors have left on the walls as their last words to a mundane world.
>
> By turning his eyes to the right … Hickman could see the door which opens on the short path to the gallows.
>
> "The door is scheduled, barring a last minute change of plans, to open for him a few seconds before 10 a.m. Friday. Immediately beyond the door is a short ramp which can be covered in about three average-size steps. Next come the thirteen steps which end at the gallows trap.

The next day, Hickman breakfasted on fruit, scrambled eggs, coffee and rolls. Then he wrote a letter to Beitzel, his former cellmate:

"I'm very comfortable up here, Russ. I'm not a bit frightened either. Tomorrow I'm going to walk up [to the gallows] like a man."

That letter was followed by one to his Oregon captors, Tom Gurdane and Buck Lieuallen:

"I am most sorry to have pretended insanity in your jail," he wrote.

It was Hickman's last letter.

Friday, October 19, 1928 arrived.

At 2:30 A.M., after fitful sleep, the condemned man awakened and asked guard Charles Alston to fetch his phonograph, which he had played almost constantly the day before. When the machine was brought in, Hickman put a recording of "In a Monastery Garden" on the turntable and, while reading his Bible, listened to the record repeatedly.

At last, he tired of the music and launched into a recital of his life, including every lurid detail of the Parker slaying. According to Alston, he talked incessantly until 7:00 A.M.

After a breakfast of grapefruit, which he merely picked at, and coffee, Warden Holohan entered the cell and read him the formal notice of execution. Hickman listened impatiently, and then cried out, "Now let me read you something."

He read the last letter he had received from his mother, then broke into tears.

The minutes ticked ceaselessly by, and then it was time.

"Hickman did not mount the thirteen scaffold steps with the unfaltering tread he had predicted he would," noted the *Times*:

> About halfway up the fatal flight … he slumped, and the guards, with a hand under each armpit, had to help him.
>
> As they did so, his spiritual zealousness seemed to return momentarily. He flung his head back with his eyes toward the whitewashed ceiling and rafters of the death chamber and began to pray. His lips moved and his face twitched. The words were audible, but not distinguishable.
>
> Not once did he drop his eyes or alter his passionate plea to the time when the black hood was dropped over his head….

And then—never mind his new found religious bent, or the blusterous bravado that was his trademark—the man who had savagely murdered a 12-year-old schoolgirl to "test his capacity to deliberately take a human life under the most revolting conditions" fainted.

Wrote the *Times*:

> His strapped body sagged and fell sidewise. He was unconscious. In that split second, the hangman raised his hand and three men with poised knives behind a screen on the gallows platform drew the blades simultaneously across three strings. One of the strings released the trap and the swaying form slipped through.
>
> The trap was sprung at 10:10 A.M., and it was 10:25 before the physician stepped back and nodded his head to signify the presence of death.

"Hickman is dead and the world is cleaner for his going," editorialized the *Times*. "His page is turned and the rest of the pages are brighter by contrast. The Hickman case is over. Now let's forget it."

Generations would pass, but Hickman's beastly brutality would not be lost to history.

Basking in the Limelight

In Los Angeles, word of Hickman's capture, three days prior to Christmas 1927, "swept the city." Radio broadcasts were interrupted with sensational "flashes" and newspapers rushed "Extras" onto the streets. "Men and women fought over them and a scene the like of which has not been equaled since the great Armistice Day [which signaled the end of World War I] followed," noted the *Los Angeles Times*. "Crowds collected around excited readers who called aloud from the papers they held with trembling hands."

In Pendleton, Oregon, arresting officers Cecil Leon "Buck" Lieuallen, State Traffic Division sergeant and Chief of Police Tom Gurdane were treated as heroes. Described as "two steel-nerved, straight-shooting peace officers"—never mind that no shots were fired—the men became instant celebrities and Pendleton was fixed, briefly at least, in the American consciousness.

The small Oregon city became a destination as well. The *Times* made much ado about dispatching two reporters and a photographer to the Northwest in a "sleek cabin monoplane." The newspaper was not alone. Oil flares burned at the Pendleton "aviation field" in anticipation of "aeroplanes" stuffed with newspaper and wire service reporters, newsreel cameramen, and California law enforcement officials carrying extradition papers. The man in charge of the airfield asked to be notified of incoming aircraft "so that markings on the field can be swept clear of light snow."

It was a wasted effort. Snow played havoc with visibility and not a single plane made it to Pendleton. Grounded at Yreka, the *Times* reporters experienced a memorable landing when their chartered aircraft "cracked" its landing gear: "The plane skidded around and buried a wing in the ground, but no one was hurt."

Getting there by any means possible, a horde of newspeople converged on Pendleton—and so did ordinary folks. Noted the

Times with great drama: "From the wheat lands of Washington, from the potato farms of Idaho and from the cattle country of Eastern Oregon, thousands of residents of this inland empire are here to welcome gravely officials of the land of oranges and olives who come to claim that strange human being charged with the most revolting crime the western world has known."

In fact, the thousands of people who converged on Pendleton were not there to greet California lawmen. They came specifically to admire the "steel-nerved, straight-shooting" officers who captured Hickman and, hopefully, to catch a glimpse of the criminal himself.

While Hickman languished in the Pendleton jail, Lieuallen and Gurdane "donned their sombreros, mounted the horses they ride annually in the Round-up [a local rodeo] parade, and accompanied by several prominent business and wheat men, rode up and down the street in front of City Hall for the benefit of the camera and motion-picture men."

Hickman was, however, the star attraction and, after much hesitation, Chief Gurdane gave in to public demand. "One of the strangest parades that ever filed through the picturesque streets of this western town shuffled down an alleyway beside the City Jail today to get a glimpse of William Edward Hickman," reported an Associated Press dispatch. "Gaudily-blanketed Indians stared impassively at the youth; pretty women stopped to peer into the grated room; grim cowmen, with their own ideas of justice, stalked past with audible comments, and businessmen made hurried trips to the scene and took their places in the line."

The town's moment of fame ran it course on December 25. "Half the populace of Pendleton deserted the Christmas festivities at their home firesides and came through the chill morning air to see Hickman taken from the police station. Hickman ran into a battery of motion-picture and press cameras. His face was waxen and carried no more expression than a death mask. When the police car pulled away from the jail for the [railroad] station the crowd broke and ran for vantage points near the prison car waiting on a siding."

Three days later, when the train steamed into Union Station, Tom Gurdane and Buck Lieuallen climbed down from the prison car. They were the toast of Los Angeles. Wearing ten-gallon hats and dressed in flashy Western dude outfits, the Oregon lawmen spoke to reporters from their suite in the Alexandria Hotel.

Surrounded by well wishers, fruit baskets, flowers, and telegrams, Lieuallen stretched back on a divan and said, "We haven't done so much."

"Shucks no," added Gurdane. "We are police officers and get paid for catching criminals."

"We are not used to talking to you newspaper chaps and we don't know what to say," interjected Lieuallen. "We are so tired, we are dumb."

"We have had offers from theatrical chaps," volunteered Gurdane. "Pantages, West Coast, and other agencies, but we don't know what we are going to do."

Added Lieuallen, "There is only one thing I can do, and that is ride horses and shoot fairly straight. I can't see what good we would be in a theater."

The following day, the *Times* announced that the "steel-nerved, straight-shooting" heroes would open on the stage of the Pantages Theater for a week's run, "afterward going to San Francisco for a short engagement."

The "Ah, shucks" officers had signed a contract for $5,000.

Chapter 4: In the Garden of Aphrodite

Aimee Semple McPherson was an American phenomenon. Savvy, sexy, silver-tongued, she was arguably the most celebrated evangelist of her time and, without question, the most renowned woman evangelist the world has known.

Aimee also was a dichotomy.

Called the only woman alive whose first name alone was sufficient to carry a headline on the front page of any newspaper in North America, she was born Aimee Elizabeth Kennedy in a chronically mortgaged farmhouse near Ingersoll, Ontario, Canada, on October 9, 1890. Her parents were James Morgan Kennedy and Minnie Pearce Kennedy—and from the moment of her birth, Aimee's life was seeped in controversy.

James Kennedy married Elizabeth Hoag in the early 1860s, and three children, Mary, William, and Charles were born from this union. In 1886, Elizabeth fell ill. Daughter Mary nursed her mother as best she could, but with her own children to care for, her time was limited. James placed a newspaper ad for a live-in housekeeper, and Minnie, a 14-year-old girl, orphaned to the Salvation Army, found herself employed. Within a few months, Elizabeth was dead.

Minnie stayed on.

Tongues wagged.

Before the year was over, James married his attractive young housekeeper. Never mind that he was 50 years old and Minnie had just turned 15.

Three years later, this curious couple celebrated the birth of a daughter, whom they named Aimee. Tongues wagged anew. It was most unseemly, after all, for a man to father an offspring who, in infancy, became an aunt to his older grandchildren—whose mother was twice the age of his wife.

A pillar of the Methodist Church, James kept to himself a nagging chagrin at Minnie's activities as a tambourine-thumping devotee of the Salvation Army. Aimee, however, whose formative years were anchored in New Testament exhortation, cared not a whit about hue or polish, and found felicity in each sect.

A crisis arose when, in her mid-teens, Aimee became enamored of things secular—dime novels, ragtime music, lipstick, and cheek-to-cheek dancing. Then came Robert Semple, a boilermaker by trade who fancied himself a preacher. Semple was tall, handsome, and ten years her senior. His sententious mark of righteousness enraptured Aimee. Into her soul, Semple breathed the fire of fundamentalist Protestantism—and she promptly became pregnant.

The starry-eyed couple joined in wedded bliss, and soon they were off to China to coax heathen souls to the bosom of Jesus.

Within a year, Semple dropped dead of dysentery.

Converting heathen souls lost its romance for Aimee, who set sail for New York. Broke, alone, and with a young daughter to care for, the resourceful 18-year-old widow married Harold McPherson, a 21-year-old accountant for a Fifth Avenue restaurant—a man who did not fancy himself a preacher.

Aimee had a son by McPherson and the family moved to Providence, Rhode Island. However, domesticity was not Aimee's strong suit; she loathed her new life. Later, she would claim that desperation and loneliness were the only reasons she married McPherson.

After enduring three years in Providence, she suffered a nervous breakdown, recovered, and promptly divorced her young husband.

Aimee returned to the sidewalks of New York. Meanwhile, Minnie, not yet 40, decided that James, now in his 70s, could do quite well without her. She packed her bags and moved to New York, where she worked as a missionary for the Salvation Army and operated a boarding house. Then, when Aimee abandoned Providence, Minnie joined forces with her daughter. Never was there a divorce, but never again would Minnie and James occupy the same dwelling.

Then a fortuitous event occurred, an event of such import that Aimee's life—and Minnie's as well—would forever be changed. The Holy Ghost appeared to the young Aimee and told her to go out among the people and preach the word of God.

And that is what she did.

Henceforth, and forever more, Aimee became Sister Aimee, and Minnie became Mother Kennedy. Together they would slay the mongers of perdition—or so the reasoning went.

The two set out—babes in tow—on the tent and sawdust circuit of the Atlantic seaboard, armed with Aimee's effusive oratorical skills, Minnie's keen eye for the bottom line, and a rattletrap automobile.

Success was not immediate. One-night stands followed one-night stands. Often as not, the nightly take from the offerings plate proved insufficient to cover their expenses. For the lack of a better way to explain their failure, they reasoned that God moved in mysterious ways.

Still, all was not in vain. A following of sorts had come to admire the young evangelist's work. Word got around, and now and again stories about her rousing revival meetings received mention in the local papers.

Then, for reasons inexplicable, Aimee's ministry exploded with success. She was in demand, and she made demands in return. No

Figure 4. 1 Aimee Semple McPherson on the road, 1914.
San Francisco History Center, San Francisco Public Library

longer must she fret about paying for gasoline, meals, or lodging—such incidentals were the province of the host churches who invited the comely evangelist to preach. She made headlines. She made money.

God spoke to her. He told her to go west. He told her that California was her destiny.

God had spoken, and west went Aimee.

The evangelist and her mother pooled their resources and purchased a spanking new seven-seat Oldsmobile touring car. With Aimee's children outfitted comfortably on the rear seat, they departed New York on October 23, 1918.

They did not travel unnoticed. On one side of the automobile was a sign that read, "Jesus Is Coming Soon—Get Ready." On the other side was a sign reading, "Where Will You Spend Eternity?"

Aimee was off to gloryland.

Californians began hearing the McPherson name. Aimee's press notices preceded her arrival. However, she did not meet with instant success. She preached for a time at Victoria Hall, a small upstairs mission on Spring Street in Los Angeles. Nevertheless, as word about this dynamic young woman spread, she began to attract such crowds that the hall was outgrown. Other halls were outgrown as well and, at last, Aimee moved her revival meetings to Philharmonic Auditorium, which boasted the largest seating capacity of any hall in the city.

Aimee had arrived.

By the mid-1920s, Aimee wanted not for fame or fortune. She had established the Four Square Gospel Church, with a membership of some 25,000 devoted followers, and had erected Angelus Temple, a 5,300-seat auditorium in the Echo Park suburb of Los Angeles. A powerful radio station, KFSG, carried her message far and wide, and within the temple was erected the Tower of Prayer, where devout volunteers prayed for the souls of sinners 24 hours a day.

Her evangelic endeavors enjoyed only short-lived support among local clergy, who came to resent their loss of congregates, as Aimee's following swelled. Humble preachers eking out a living from obscure pulpits scorned the millions of dollars that flowed into her coffer. The well-known Reverend Bob Shuler, jealous of the young upstart evangelist, preached sermons intended to debunk her teachings, and he even went so far as to publish a pamphlet attacking her.

It was all for naught. There was no stopping Aimee.

A McPherson church service was no ordinary revival meeting. Hell, fire, and brimstone were prominent, but these elements were cloaked in pageantry and orchestrated with theatrical precision. Salvation was the message, but the messenger—Aimee—was the central attraction.

And central to Aimee's attraction was sex appeal. While not beautiful in a conventional sense, the buxom young woman exuded sensuality—an asset finely honed and skillfully exploited.

Aimee was 36 years old and at the pinnacle of her success when on May 18, 1926, newspapers around the world carried the startling headline: "Aimee Semple McPherson Reported Dead."

Thus began one of the strangest incidents in American history.

In the company of Emma Schaeffer, her private secretary, Aimee had driven to the Ocean View Hotel at Rose Avenue and Ocean Front in Venice for an afternoon dip in the sea.

Schaeffer, a non-swimmer who did not join her employer in the surf, told police that Aimee went into the water for a few moments, came out for a while, and then went back into the water. While the evangelist was swimming the second time, Schaeffer went to the hotel just a few steps away to use the telephone. When last she saw Aimee, the evangelist was swimming only a short distance out into the water.

"She smiled, waved her hand to me, and called out something," related the secretary. "I thought it was 'The water's fine—I'm all right, honey.'"

Schaeffer completed her call and returned to the beach, but Aimee was gone. She was not in the water, she was not on the beach, and she was not in the small tent the couple had erected as protection from the sun. Aimee had vanished.

The evangelist was considered a proficient and powerful swimmer. That fact led lifeguards and beach police to believe that Aimee had suffered a fainting spell or had been seized with cramps while in the water.

The water was unusually quiet. There were no heavy swells, no rip tide. Of the handful of persons on the beach, no one heard an outcry.

It was a most unusual disappearance.

Santa Monica police summoned an aviator, who flew his plane back and forth over the beach. He saw nothing out of the ordinary.

Later, a telephone call came to the manager of the Ocean View Hotel stating that Aimee had been spotted near the Santa Monica pier. A search ensued, but nothing came of it.

At Angelus Temple, some 5,000 people gathered to hear what would have been the last in a series of illustrated talks about Aimee's recent tour of the Holy Land. Mother Kennedy broke the news to the congregation, telling Aimee's supplicants that their spiritual mentor was dead. "We know she is with Jesus," said Minnie. "Pray for her."

A moan of grief, as if uttered by a single person, arose from the congregation and echoed about the temple. The notion that the shepherd would not return to her flock was incomprehensible.

"Followers flocked to the beach and tonight were frantically pacing the shore," reported the Associated Press. "Some of the more devout worshipers threatened to throw themselves into the water, police reported. All available police have been dispatched to the beach to keep the crowd under control."

The next day, May 19, Mother Kennedy announced a $500 reward for the recovery of her daughter's body. She also revealed that Aimee had left a will disposing of her personal effects, but she claimed not to know its general provisions. The last of Mother Kennedy's pronouncements made clear that she would take command of Angelus Temple. She would carry on Aimee's ministry, "along the lines laid down by her."

"To the hundreds of men and women who wait in a huddled and silent mass beneath the open sky on the beach between Venice and Ocean park, Aimee Semple McPherson, their beloved leader, still lives," commented the May 20 *Los Angeles Times*:

> A faith as strong and deep as the ocean they watch hour after hour with aching eyes, holds them there.
> "She can't be dead. She can't be dead."
> It is almost a refrain, repeated time and time again, an expression of faith which flings defiance into the teeth of death itself.

"God wouldn't let her die. She was too noble. Her work was too great. Her mission was not ended. She can't be dead."

The crowd remains hushed and tense. The words are alike. They come only in answer to direct questions. The speakers say them as if quoting. Then their eyes turn back to the sea.

The elements of tragedy and hysteria are there. They flare occasionally as some woman breaks under the vigil and sobs. Otherwise the crowd remains fixed and motionless. Few words are exchanged.

Through the fog-bound, chilling night and then through the weary, scorching hours of the day, the followers of the evangelist have kept their places on the sand in the hope of seeing their leader again.

Mother Kennedy's words to Aimee's followers were equally dramatic:

It is for us to carry on, feeling that as Christ spoke through her, so must we tell others.

How often I have heard her say that she didn't want to live to be old and stricken with disease. She did not want to live to old age, and I feel as I believe you do, too, who loved her so well, that she has passed on as she chose.

The same day, a Culver City police captain insisted that he had seen Aimee in an automobile driving toward Los Angeles. "I looked up and saw Mrs. McPherson and I'm sure I couldn't be mistaken," he said. "If it wasn't Mrs. McPherson that I saw, then it certainly was her double."

It was a curious sighting.

Day and night, the search for Aimee continued. Hundreds of Angelus Temple congregates scoured the beach, their eyes fixed on the near horizon, watching each breaking wave that splashed onto the shore. Airplanes flew above and a Coast Guard cutter, dispatched from San Pedro, trolled the sea with grappling hooks.

Aimee had been missing two days when follower Doris Leland reported to authorities that for several days prior to the disappearance, a strange man had stood across the street from Angelus Temple watching those who came and went. He stood in the same position each day, and his facial expression was a "half-sneer."

The inference was, of course, that Aimee may have been a victim of things sinister.

William Walberg, a Temple employee whose duty it was to keep worshipers from rushing the platform during healing services, announced that the evangelist had appeared to him in a vision. She told him she was in Buenos Aires and that "everything is alright. There is no need for excitement."

"If her body is found the third day," said Walberg, "and if it is brought to the platform and all her followers pray, she well be revived."

Mother Kennedy was not enamored by the notion of public resurrection. "Her spirit is with God and cannot return," she said emphatically. "Nor have we any wish that it should even if it were possible. We know Aimee is in heaven; we would not bring her back if we could."

More dramatic than Walberg's vision, however, was Minnie's contention that her daughter had been the victim of foul play. "A blow on the head must have caused her death," she asserted. "She was such a strong swimmer that I cannot believe she was drowned by an ordinary current or tide. The more I think of it, the more I believe she took her life in her hands when she stood on the plat-form at Angelus Temple and said she would rather see her daughter dead than in a Venice dance hall."

Mother Kennedy's reference was to a recent election in which voters had passed a measure to allow Sunday dancing in Venice. Aimee had been vociferous in her opposition, and had come under criticism in many quarters.

During Saturday evening services at Angelus Temple, a Pasadena man rose from his seat and rushed down the aisle, hands waving, declaring that he had been ordained to take Sister Aimee's place in the pulpit. Church workers led him away as he shouted, "Hallelu-jah!" and turned him over to temple security officers. They released him after his promise to go home.

He did not. About fifteen minutes later, he interrupted the service a second time by rushing down the aisle toward the rostrum, again proclaiming his call to succeed Aimee. Police were about to take him off to jail when temple workers prevailed, insisting they would escort him home.

After this most unusual service concluded, hundreds of ad-ditional supplicants signed up to patrol the beach in search of the evangelist's body, augmenting those already there. A written protocol was given each volunteer, admonishing them to remain at their respective stations at all times; to refuse to enter into "controversy" or "argument" about "the matter most sacred to our hearts"; to make no outcry if the body were found, and then to shield the body from curious onlookers.

"The temple patrol," reported the *Times*, "extended … from El Segundo to Malibu Ranch, covering from fifteen to twenty miles. Hundreds, if not thousands, of Mrs. McPherson's followers, includ-ing women, took part in the work."

Aimee's disappearance was five days old when, on Sunday morn-ing, her fifteen-year-old daughter, Roberta Semple, took to the pul-pit of Angelus Temple. Dressed in white, with a Bible beneath her arm, the comely teenager walked dramatically to the altar, closed her eyes, and lifted her right hand.

"Praise the Lord," she said solemnly. "The Lord has given and the Lord has taken away. Blessed be the name of the Lord.

"Mother isn't here to give the altar call, but I believe she would want me to bring you to Jesus. Everyone bow your heads and close your eyes. Raise your right hands and tell Jesus how much you need him. Help us carry on, as I am sure Mother, looking down from heaven, sees this sight. So put up your hands, as Mother would want you [to do] and Jesus would have you do. You must be saved to go to heaven, too."

After the service, Mother Kennedy announced that Roberta would succeed her mother in the pulpit "when she hears the call." In the meantime, Minnie would run the show.

The notion of foul play was bandied about again when, on the following Wednesday, the Associated Press reported, "a new and thorough investigation of the disappearance … will be undertaken by authorities of Santa Monica and Los Angeles if the body … is not found within 48 hours." This investigation, authorities indicated, would be along lines contrary to the accepted theory of her thousands of followers and others that the Angelus Temple pastor was accidentally drowned …."

The following day, Los Angeles district attorney Asa Keyes announced that he intended to question "Mrs. Minnie Kennedy, mother of the evangelist, Miss Emma Schaeffer, Mrs. McPherson's secretary, who reported the disappearance, and Kenneth G. Ormiston, formerly radio operator at Angelus Temple, now reported missing."

It was the first mention of Ormiston's name. It would not be the last.

"The circumstances," said Keyes, "are such as [to] warrant an investigation on my part to determine if any other elements entered into the disappearance than the fact that Mrs. McPherson was last seen in the surf."

Keyes failed to mention why Ormiston, said to be a close friend of Aimee's, had become a subject of inquiry. The *Times* filled in the gap with a curious piece of information:

"… Ormiston is thought to have registered some time before the evangelist disappeared at a beach hotel close to the spot where Mrs. McPherson was last seen."

Recently separated from his wife, Ormiston had installed KFSG, Aimee's radio station, in 1923, and had operated it until a few

Figure 4. 2 McPherson on air with engineer Kenneth Ormiston at radio station KFSG.
Corbis

months prior. Keyes said he could not overlook the fact that Ormiston had been a close friend of the evangelist, and that he felt their close association might provide a valuable lead in tracing the missing woman.

In San Francisco, the former radio operator heard a radio report stating that the district attorney wanted a word with him. Of his own volition, he traveled to Los Angeles and, the next day, met with Keyes. The detective determined that Ormiston "could not aid ... in solving the mystery."

Much to her chagrin, word leaked out that the radio engineer had met privately on the beach at Santa Monica with Mother Kennedy. Responding to insinuations that there might be more to the relationship between Aimee and Ormiston than met the eye, Minnie scoffed: "Aimee led a spotless and blameless life. As for Mr. Ormiston, he is a nice boy...."

However, even more intriguing were comments from Ormiston's mother stating that Aimee was the cause of her son's failed marriage. He and his wife had separated three months earlier, "following a quarrel over Mrs. McPherson," she stated bluntly.

"Ruth was always jealous of Mrs. McPherson," she added, "but I don't believe there was any foundation for her jealousy. My son had the deepest respect for Mrs. McPherson, but he and his wife quarreled over her a number of times. The disagreements finally broke up the family."

From her family home in Australia, Ruth Ormiston inadvertently contradicted her mother-in-law when she announced that she intended to return to Los Angeles and instigate divorce proceedings. Aimee, she said, would be named as the correspondent.

The public's collective tongue wagged.

Aimee's disappearance was ten days old when Minnie made the startling announcement that she would offer a $25,000 reward for the return—alive—of her missing daughter. At the same time, however, she reiterated her belief that the evangelist had met with foul play and was dead.

Then, in direct contradiction of Emma Schaeffer's story, a Venice police captain swore in an affidavit that he was at the beach at the point and time that Aimee was said to have disappeared in the water, and that "no person, man or woman, was swimming there."

Contradictions were mounting.

Meantime, kooks were crawling out the woodwork. "Send $50,000 and she is yours," wrote a would-be extortionist to Mother Kennedy. "Put the money in a west-bound streetcar …. Wear a bright red suit. Don't bring police or she'll die within ten minutes. We'll deliver her within half-an-hour after pay. Mum's the words. Keep police away."

Police officers were certain the letter was either a hoax or the work of a crackpot.

Ormiston's name surfaced again on May 29, when he was seen in San Luis Obispo driving a blue coupe. With him was a woman said to be Aimee's age, who wore driving goggles and kept her coat collar up about her face.

For reasons not made specific, authorities sought to question Ormiston again, but regardless of occasional sightings here and there, the man could not be located.

"While an airplane strewed white and crimson roses over the gentle swells of Santa Monica Bay," reported the Associated Press the following day:

> "...thousands of [Aimee's] followers crowded ... into Angelus Temple ... to conduct a memorial service for the beautiful and magnetic woman whom they firmly believe is 'with her God' after death in the Pacific surf:
>
> In contrast to the attitude of mourning for the missing church leader were the preparations going forward ... in official circles for a thorough investigation of the unsolved mystery of Mrs. McPherson's disappearance.
>
> Twelve days have passed and the sea has not given up its dead. Police and investigators of the sheriff's and district attorney's office, while reiterating that ... drowning is the most plausible solution, nevertheless are preparing to launch this week a definite hunt on the theory that the missing evangelist may be alive, a voluntary absentee for private reasons, a captive of kidnappers, or a victim of amnesia, or [the] least tenable theory of all, a murderer's victim.

Aimee sightings were becoming commonplace. On June 3, she was seen having breakfast at a cafe in Biggs, a small town north of Sacramento. The following day, a woman in San Francisco reported that a friend had met with Aimee and was told that the evangelist would return to Angelus Temple within two weeks. The next day, a private detective in Alberta, Canada, telegraphed the LAPD that he had seen Aimee in Edmonton.

The $25,000 reward for Aimee's safe return was to have expired at midnight, June 5. For reasons known only to her, however, Minnie extended the offer until midnight, June 12.

Aimee had been missing more than a month when thousands of followers flocked to Angelus Temple, where three memorial services—morning, afternoon, and evening—were conducted to mourn the death of their leader.

Mother Kennedy petitioned county coroner Frank Nance to issue a death certificate, but Nance declined, declaring, "there was no evidence that the woman was dead and expressing his personal belief that she is still alive."

The coroner was correct. Aimee was alive. The evangelist was very much alive and holding court in a Douglas, Arizona, hospital room.

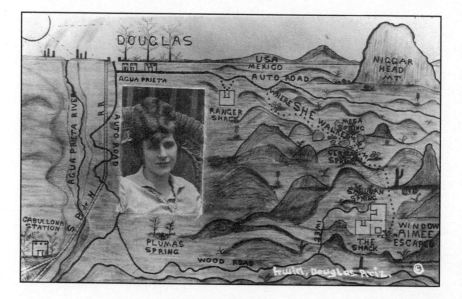

Figure 4.3 Postcard from Douglas, Arizona, detailing
Aimee's alleged escape route.
W. Lane Rogers

"Resurrected From Dead; Aimee Safe," read the bold splash of a headline on the front page of the June 24 issue of the *Arizona Daily Star*. In startling prose, other headlines proclaimed, "Kidnapped from Beach"; "Evangelist Held for Ransom"; "Staggers to Border"; "Relates Lurid Story of Adventure and Cruelty."

Then, in prose most billowy, reporter Gilbert Cosulich wrote:

> Despite her weakened condition after her harrowing experiences on the Mexican desert, Mrs. McPherson received [this] correspondent ... with the graciousness of manner that has won her multitudes of followers.
>
> From time to time, as she spoke, she would raise a well rounded white arm to smooth her luxurious brown hair .... Clad in a becoming pink *crepe de chine robe de chambre*, Mrs. McPherson sat propped up in bed in the west wing of the hospital. During the recital of her experiences, she would occasionally stop to take a deep breath, close her eyes a few moments, as if to gather strength, and then she would proceed with her narrative.
>
> Her room was filled with gladioli and other flowers sent by the chamber of commerce, several of the churches, and others.
>
> Outside of the hospital hundreds gathered on the street to catch a glimpse of the famous evangelist, and occasionally a favored few would be admitted to her room for a few words and a handshake.

The tale told by Aimee was, indeed, an unusual one:

> ... Tuesday afternoon [May 18], I went to the beach to take a dip with my secretary, Miss Emma Schaeffer .... I wore a dress over my bathing suit on the way to the beach for being an evangelist I knew that I had to be rather careful about these things.
>
> When we arrived at the beach, I thought of some details concerning our meetings and I asked Miss Schaeffer to attend to them ....
>
> While she was away I decided to take a dip, and walked into the water, waist deep.

Suddenly I heard my name called by someone on the beach. I was annoyed at being disturbed.

I saw a woman and a man standing on the beach. They began crying and told me that their baby was dying and they wanted me to pray for it. The woman ran on ahead, after having given me a long coat to wear, which she had conveniently at hand.

"Hurry," the woman said, "or my baby will die."

The woman had been holding what seemed to be a baby but it turned out to be a bundle of clothing, which she clapped over me and made me smell something which I later found to be chloroform.

This happened at two o'clock in the afternoon, as nearly as I could judge. It was dawn of the next day when I awoke in bed. The room was in a house that I believe was in Mexicali or some where near San Diego, from what I could catch of the conversation by the people around me.

I felt very sick at the stomach. Three persons were in the same house. One was a woman they called Rose, who had black hair, dark brown eyes, full lips and weighed about 185 or 190 pounds, and who seemed to have been a nurse.

One of the men was called Steve. He was rather heavy set, but not fat, smooth shaven, with brown hair, and he wore a brown suit.

The other man's name I did not hear. He was tall and dark, was flat chested, had sparse hair and a gold tooth.

They told me that they wanted $500,000 ransom for me. When I told them that I did not have that much, they answered, "Pshaw, you have got millions."

I was in that room all the time, up to about four days ago. Then they moved me in the same auto, to another place during the night, and we reached our destination the next morning.

This time I was placed in a room that was very meagerly furnished. There were two cots, one for Rose and the other for me. The men slept in another part of the house, and their conduct towards me was respectful, except that one of them

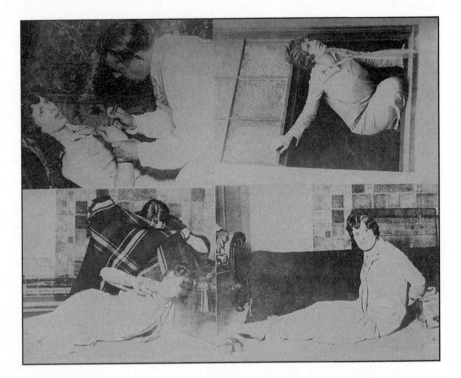

Figure 4.4 Aimee demonstrates how (1) her fingers were burned by a cigar wielded by one of her abductors; (2) the kidnappers swathed her in blankets; (3) she was tied up; and (4) she managed to escape before struggling across the desert to safety. *Corbis*

burned one of my fingers with a cigar while trying to get some information.

About four days ago Rose told me she had to go away to get supplies and said she would have to bind and gag me. "You don't mind dearie." She always called me dearie. "For after Friday everything will be all right if your mother does the right thing."

I had noticed a can in one corner of the room. It looked like a varnish can. I knew that if I could get to it I could cut off the flat bands with which Rose had tied me by using the sharp edge of the can's lid.

I rolled off the cot, and cut off the strands that bound me. I was nearly wild with joy when I found that I was succeeding, and I gave thanks to God for giving me strength to do it.

I ran out into the desert. I suppose I wandered about for 20 miles during that afternoon and evening. It was terribly hot and I had no water. I ran gasping and feverish among the cactus and got considerably scratched up.

Finally I struck a road, and ran along the highway for about eight miles. At about 9:30 that night I came to the outskirts of a town and heard dogs barking and a man swearing at his dog. He seemed to be clad in his underwear. I asked him to telephone to the police, and he asked me what I had done. I answered that I had done nothing, but that I had something done to me and I needed help. He invited me to spend the night in the house, but when I found that there were no women there, I moved on.

Finally I was picked up by someone else and brought to this hospital. I have been a rather brave girl, don't you think?

The tale would be told, retold, embellished, and altered here and there to suit the situation, but this, essentially, is what Aimee expected the world to believe.

"Through the halo of joy that surrounded the temple," wrote the Associated Press, "there penetrated today the cold eye of official investigation."

"How was a woman like Mrs. McPherson, known almost all over the civilized world, kidnapped in broad daylight on a crowded beach?" District Attorney Keyes asked rhetorically. He continued in the same vein:

Why was a $25,000 reward offered for her safe return withdrawn, then re-offered, and withdrawn again on June 12?

Will the approximately $15,000 collected at Angelus Temple during the special memorial services last Sunday for the purpose of creating a lasting memorial to Mrs. McPherson's memory be returned to the donors?

> The circumstances of this case, in the opinion of the district
> attorney's office, call for an investigation both in justice to
> Mrs. McPherson and to the public, and I intend to see that it is
> made.

That said, Keyes and chief of detectives Herman Cline boarded a train for Douglas, Arizona.

When reporters attempted to interview Emma Schaeffer, Mother Kennedy balked: "No, you must not see her. She is so nervous and she can't talk very well. She just isn't that sort, you know. She doesn't know [anything]."

With that, Minnie and Aimee's children, Roberta and Rolf, boarded the same train for Douglas.

A posse headed by Douglas police sergeant Alonzo B. Murchison, and accompanied by two expert trailers as well as Mexican officers, searched the desert southeast of Douglas all day long in pursuit of the alleged abductors. "There were few clues as to the place where the evangelist was held prisoner," Murchison told the Associated Press, "but [he] expressed belief that he could find it, possibly to-morrow ...."

However, the "place"—a "shack," as Aimee called it—where she claimed she was held captive eluded them the next day. And the next. Its location would remain a daunting mystery.

Meantime, the Bisbee, Arizona, *Daily Review* joined the fray by reporting that the shoes worn by Aimee during her "twenty miles" of wandering in the desert showed no scuffing or damage in any way. In examining the area below the Mexican border described by Aimee, Cochise County sheriff James F. McDonald and his men returned with "their boots scratched and their clothing covered with dust. No such evidence of the desert wastes appeared on the clothing or shoes of the evangelist."

As Aimee's story unfolded, Conrad Schansel, proprietor of a slaughterhouse just south of Agua Prieta, Sonora, Mexico, came forward to say that it was at his house where the evangelist heard barking dogs, and he was the man she saw in the yard in his underwear. When he invited her in, she became frightened and fled toward the lights of Auga Prieta.

Aimee next appeared at the home of Ramon and Theresa Gonzales. Ramon heard a woman call out and when he answered her call, she asked if he had a telephone. He did not. She asked if there was a woman in the house. There was. When Ramon and Theresa came out of the house, they found the woman slumped at their gate. Ramon thought she was dead and rushed across the street to the home of Ernesto Boubion, Presidente (mayor) of Auga Prieta. Boubion was not at home and when Ramon returned, the woman had stirred. He carried her to the porch, placed a pillow beneath her head, and covered her with a quilt. Theresa noticed the woman's hair tucked neatly into a silk hairnet.

The strange woman regained consciousness and was speaking rapidly in English, which the Gonzales couple did not understand. Just then, Boubion arrived at his home. He listened for a moment, then left to fetch Police Chief Sylvana Villa and Johnny Anderson, an American who operated a taxi service between Douglas and Auga Prieta.

It was quickly determined that the woman was an American, and Anderson agreed to transport her over the border to the Calumet and Arizona Hospital at Douglas. After admission to a private room, nurse Margaret Attaway undressed the patient. She saw red marks on her wrists and two small blisters on her toes. Otherwise, the woman's condition was remarkable for one who claimed to have wandered twenty miles in the desert. She was not sunburned or emaciated, and she showed no signs of dehydration. Her lips were not cracked or swollen, and her vital signs were normal.

It was most unusual.

At 8:00 A.M. the following morning, the Golden State Limited steamed into Douglas. Los Angeles law enforcement officials disembarked, and so did Minnie and her entourage.

"After Mother Kennedy … had held Aimee in a embrace lasting three or four minutes, had posed for a half dozen flashlight pictures, and had given her first interview in Douglas … she sallied in and held informal religious services off the porch of the west wing of the hospital," wrote the *Star*. "Plump, genial and ingratiating, the little woman's improvised services were an undeniable success …."

A circus atmosphere prevailed in the little city of Douglas. The *Star* described the scene: "Motion picture artists taking pictures of the Mexican constabulary just across the international line at Agua Prieta. A still camera taking pictures of the motion picture cameramen. And then another motion picture camera taking a picture of the still cameras taking a picture of the other motion picture camera and the Mexican constabulary."

The *Star* reported:

> [Airplanes arrived] every hour or so bringing more photographers and taking back more film ….
>
> "Never been mugged so much in my life," said one border agent. "I have posed for still cameras by day and by flashlight and for movie cameras in every conceivable position except standing on my head. I would say off hand I have been photographed every five minutes for the last 24 hours."
>
> … Within an hour of the time [Aimee's] presence in the city was announced, one soda fountain displayed a sign bearing the notation that "Aimee sundaes" can be purchased for 25 cents. In another soft drink emporium an "Aimee," presumably a drink, can be had for 5 cents.

Johnny Anderson, the taxi driver who delivered the evangelist to the hospital, accosted potential customers on the street with the question, "Do you care to ride in the seat that Aimee Semple McPherson rode in?"

A young woman employed at a local drug store took a more cynical view of events unfolding: "The stuff that the newspapers are printing about Aimee is all bunk. Why, I've walked all around these mountains, and I know what they'll do to a woman's shoes. You know, I believe that this whole thing is ... [expletive deleted by the newspaper]."

The drug store clerk was not, however, the only person skeptical of Aimee's tale. Douglas chief of police Percy Bowden was one of the first to see the evangelist after her alleged Mexican drama:

"... I had been looking her over ... [and] I told her that I could not believe her—that this whole thing was a hoax. At this, I thought she was going to faint. She put on quite a show for a few moments. Then she straightened up and asked me why I doubted her word and on what grounds. I told her first that, if she had been kept in an old adobe shack for a month, that her clothes as well as she [herself] would be filthy dirty ... that her hair would be in knots, and if she had walked so far through the desert on a hot day like this one, that her clothes and shoes would be in shreds. I also told her that she had planned her story very poorly; that she should have gotten hold of one of the old desert rats if she wanted to know what it is to walk several miles through rocks and brush such as ones encountered in this country. At this, she pulled a fainting spell and requested to be sent to a hospital where she could see a doctor. This request we granted."

Learning that the police chief doubted her daughter's story, Mother Kennedy stormed into Bowden's office, telling him that "I had [no] right to doubt a minister of the gospel. She wanted to know what kind of police department we were running. She said that she would call in her own investigators if I kept giving out false reports on Sister. At this point, I had my say, telling her that I had made a complete check in Agua Prieta and had proof that the whole affair was a hoax."

Hospital officials, alarmed by their inability to keep hordes of curiosity seekers away from the grounds, and concerned about the truly ill in their care, insisted on Aimee's removal to a suite at the Gadsden Hotel.

It was at the Gadsden that a curious incident occurred. William Critchley, a bellboy, was asked to examine a man's photograph. Had this fellow been seen at the hotel? Indeed, he had been. He had checked into room 242 two nights before. The face in the photograph belonged to Kenneth G. Ormiston, Aimee's elusive radio operator.

"Newsmen gathered around me like flies," said Critchley, but Ormiston—if the man was Ormiston—had disappeared.

Asked about the shack in the desert, Pedro Demandivo, chief of the Mexican border patrol—which had searched for three days—said, "[My] men know every foot of ground within fifty miles and none of them know of such a cabin. If one did exist, we would know about it within two days after it was built."

Nonplussed, Aimee offered a five hundred dollar reward to anyone who located the shack. A skeptical *Los Angeles Examiner* added one thousand dollars and offered an additional ten thousand dollars for information about the kidnappers.

When Aimee and her entourage prepared to leave Douglas, the Southern Pacific put eight railroad detectives at her disposal, and they even furnished the evangelist with a special car.

A late afternoon "community service," billed as the largest gathering ever staged in Douglas, drew mixed results. An army band from Camp Harry A. Jones regaled a crowd of some five thousand to military marches, followed by music from a choir representing every church in the city. When Aimee, known for long-winded oratory, spoke to the gathering, her sermon was disappointingly brief. Then, in what many believed was an affront, the evangelist refused to shake hands with members of the crowd, and was whisked away by detectives to her hotel suite to await her departure time.

The train left Douglas at 9:13 P.M. and arrived in Tucson at 1:10 in the morning, where about a hundred people waited at the depot hoping to catch a glimpse of the famous evangelist. Aimee did not disappoint them: "… [She] arose from her berth … [and] from the vestibule of her sleeper she delivered a brief talk to those who had stayed up to wish her Godspeed."

Moments later, the train steamed into the darkness, but long before it reached its destination, the *Los Angeles Examiner* reported that two Tucson men in an automobile had given a lift three or four nights before to a woman closely resembling Aimee: "They were driving east from Tucson, which is in the direction of Douglas and Auga Prieta, when they overtook a woman walking in the same direction. They offered her a ride and she got into the car. Noticing a resemblance to the missing pastor, they asked her if she was Mrs. McPherson. She neither confirmed [nor] denied it. When they said they would take her to the police station, she begged them not to, and got out of the car."

Late Saturday afternoon, June 26, after an absence of thirty-four days, Aimee arrived in Los Angeles. "'Praise the Lord,' was the first exclamation of the famed pastor of Angelus Temple," reported the International News Service.

> Many in the great throng tried to kiss her, others pressed her hands and others pelted her with a deluge of beautiful flowers.
>
> Mrs. McPherson briefly thanked her welcomers, and then declared that no doubt many had accepted the account of her kidnapping with some skepticism.
>
> "How many of you dear people believe in me?" asked the evangelist. "I do," was the loud affirmative chorus from a hundred throats.

The following afternoon, before a congregation of some 7,500 people, packed belly to back in cavernous Angelus Temple, Aimee took to the pulpit and laid her problems at the "door of the devil":

> ... And so [the devil] finally said, "if I could just get hold of Sister McPherson—if I could just get her away, [the Four Square Gospel] would crumble." Some months ago, the newspapers of our city came out saying that there was a plot—that two people were to be kidnapped. One was a motion picture actress, very well known—I need not mention her name;* the other was Aimee McPherson. I laughed at it at the time and threw down the newspapers, saying, "They would have a hard time getting me."

---

*McPherson's reference was to film star Mary Pickford.

Now I realize that even then the devil was laying his plans.

The devil notwithstanding, Los Angeles law enforcement authorities pressed their investigation of Aimee's alleged kidnapping.

Lashing out at skeptics, Aimee declared, "The sword which should be turned against the criminals has been turned against me …." She insisted it was ridiculous that she would "stage a disappearance" in order to rest, or to gain publicity, or that she "should wander off in an attack of amnesia."

The evangelist was most annoyed, however, with those who intimated a love tryst. "In love?" she demanded. "With whom? Isn't it remarkable that, with all the investigation and hullabaloo that has been made, the name of the man, if there was one, has never entered the case."

Aimee was, of course, mistaken. Kenneth Ormiston's name had been mentioned prominently—and would be mentioned time and time again.

On June 30, the Associated Press reported:

> The joint investigation by police and the district attorney's office [has] failed to produce a single clue to substantiate the evangelist's version of her strange disappearance.
>
> Mrs. McPherson, however, contends that the burden of proof falls upon those who doubt her … [and] the woman pastor announced she was preparing to strike back legally at those who have cast "blackening insinuations" upon her story. The evangelist said two libel suits were being drawn up by her attorneys, each suit seeking $200,000 damages. She would not divulge who she would name in the suits.

Her threat was mere bluster. Aimee sued no one.

Meantime, law enforcement officials in Douglas, still searching for the alleged kidnappers and the elusive shack, reported that "not a new clue worthy of any consideration has been found."

An interesting twist developed when Aimee reported that she had received a letter purportedly written by "Rose," the female member of the kidnapping team. Rose told her she harbored no hard feelings about Aimee's escape, and sought her forgiveness: "Pray for me even if I did make you suffer."

The LAPD was not impressed.

Then, with much ballyhoo, Aimee announced that she and her mother would return to Douglas to accompany searchers in their quest for the much-sought shack.

While Aimee was en route to Arizona, the *Tombstone Epitaph* took a potshot at the evangelist. In a July 1 editorial titled "Thanks, Aimee, Call Again," the newspaper noted the notoriety given Cochise County by her visit to Douglas, but concluded the piece with skepticism:

> Hard boiled officers of the law are noncommittal, to say the least. Their attitude seems to be that no gentleman would dispute the word of a lady, but up to [this] date we have had no word of a posse, either Mexican or American, scouring northern Sonora for a trace of the kidnappers of Aimee Semple McPherson; neither has a cabin or shack been found within a radius of twenty-five miles of Agua Prieta that corresponds to a description of the place where the evangelist claims she was detained as a captive three or four days prior to her thrilling escape.

After spending one day and visiting eight shacks in the Sonoran desert, and declaring the excursion fruitless, Aimee and Minnie returned to Los Angeles. "There is a deep plot behind this," intoned Mother Kennedy. "It is not over, and Aimee is still in danger."

When footprints were found outside a shack near Agua Prieta—it was not the shack Aimee described—Ernesto Boubion, the mayor, remarked:

> The tracks were made by a woman's shoes and went both to and from the road and the shack. We compared the tracks with one of the shoes that had been worn by Mrs. McPherson on that occasion and they matched absolutely.

The same tracks reappeared at a point by the side of the road about two miles nearer town. They lead to the slaughterhouse, which is about one mile east of Agua Prieta. At the slaughterhouse, they were lost again.

My belief is that Mrs. McPherson was taken by automobile to a place 200 yards from the shack and deposited there and that she walked from the automobile to the shack and back again to the automobile several times. Tracks made by shoes were found all around the shack, but not beyond, though a search was made as far as Gallardo, nine miles away.

I further believe from the investigations made by me and by those under my supervision that she was picked up by the same automobile, say, within an hour from the time she was taken out and brought back to a place on the road where the tracks start toward the slaughter house.

My opinion is that the entire transaction was consummated during the afternoon or evening of June 22, the day before Mrs. McPherson appeared in Agua Prieta.

Boubion, in essence, had called Aimee a liar.

The embattled evangelist declined comment about Boubion's statement, but Mother Kennedy shot back, "That's Mexico, Mexico," implying that the mayor's ethnicity precluded him from making sensible judgments.

With Boubion's report just released, the district attorney convened a grand jury to investigate the case. Minnie brushed the news aside with a wave of her hand: "We are glad to welcome a grand jury investigation, or in any other way assist in clearing up this matter."

Then on July 5, it was announced that officials had obtained new and "startling information" from law enforcement officers in Douglas, germane to the McPherson case. At the same time, the LAPD revealed that they wanted very much to question Kenneth Ormiston about Aimee's alleged kidnapping.

The next day, District Attorney Keyes formally laid the entire case before the grand jury, issuing subpoenas for Aimee, daughter Roberta, Minnie, and assorted Angelus Temple workers.

Meantime, the grand jury requested that officials at Douglas and Agua Prieta travel to Los Angeles and relate details of their independent investigations conducted along the border.

On Thursday, July 8, the Associated Press reported that Aimee "today addressed the Los Angeles county grand jury—the smallest, perhaps the least responsive, but the most analytical audience to which the Angelus Temple pastor has ever talked."

The AP also noted that, in pure Aimee fashion, "two lines of Angelus Temple workers robed in white and blue and each carrying a hymn book, formed a pathway into the justice hall."

New evidence developed on Friday, when Keyes let it be known that Ernesto Boubion had telegraphed from Agua Prieta stating that "a large blue automobile had been parked near Niggerhead Mountain, a well-known landmark," on June 22, the day before the evangelist appeared in the Mexican border town. Several persons asserted that they had seen a similar automobile at different points near the border areas, carrying, among others, a woman who closely resembled Aimee.

The next day, the grand jury subpoenaed the much-sought Ormiston to appear before them, and investigators drove to Riverside, his suspected locale.

They returned empty-handed.

When testimony before the grand jury resumed Tuesday, July 13, Mother Kennedy—"unheralded, unguarded, and unattended"—took the stand for approximately an hour. What she said was, of course, unrecorded, but it did not escape the notice of reporters that her entrance was far less grand than her daughter's had been.

Had a rift developed between her and Aimee? Certainly not, she said flatly.

The following day, the grand jury learned that Mother Kennedy received a telegram sent from Oakland at Angelus Temple three days after Aimee's disappearance. "Your daughter is O.K.," it read. A Western Union employee identified Kenneth G. Ormiston as the man who ordered it sent, and handwriting experts expressed their belief that Ormiston wrote it.

Minnie was having none of it. It was the "work of a nut," she insisted.

As the grand jury heard a bevy of witnesses who claimed to have seen Aimee and Ormiston together, or one or the other separately, during the evangelist's 34-day absence, Mother Kennedy declared, "The fires of hell are burning and they must burn themselves out, but we are not afraid."

Meantime, the search for Ormiston switched to Norfolk, Virginia, but that proved to be another dead end.

The grand jury turned over its report on July 20, ruling that the evidence presented was insufficient to warrant an indictment.

"The official investigation not only bears out her story and proves it true," read a statement from Aimee's attorneys, "but reveals her to the world as a truthful, upright woman, who has withstood the attacks in a religious, God-fearing manner."

Samuel W. McNabb, United States attorney for Los Angeles, announced the next day that it was most improbable that a federal grand jury would be called to investigate the case.

For all practical purposes, it appeared that Aimee's troubles were over.

They were not.

Six days after the grand jury concluded its investigation, startling new evidence was uncovered by deputy district attorney Joe Ryan. Sleuthing south of Los Angeles, Ryan revealed that Aimee, in the company of Kenneth G. Ormiston, may have spent several days in a secluded cottage at Carmel-by-the-Sea, immediately following her May 18 disappearance.

"I'm positive that Ormiston was the man at the cottage," Ryan told district attorney Keyes. "I have samples of handwriting [from the cottage] which I believe to be that of Mrs. McPherson."

Figure 4.5 The back of the Carmel love nest as seen from the beach. It is located on the west side of Scenic Road exactly half-way between Ocean and 8th. The current home now sports a wrap-around addition to the original structure. *Henry Golas, Frasher's Fotos*

Ernest Reinert, driver of a coal truck; Ralph Swanson, a grocery boy; Mrs. Percy Parkes, who lived near the cottage; and William Michael, who was repairing the roof on the house next door, each identified photographs of Aimee and Ormiston as the couple who occupied the cottage for ten days.

Ormiston, the witnesses claimed, traveled freely about the town. Aimee rarely ventured from the cabin. When she did, she wore driving goggles and a close-fitting hat.

When asked by chief of detectives Herman Cline to go to Carmel and face the witnesses, Aimee refused. She also refused to have her fingerprints taken, and she refused to provide police with handwriting samples.

For a woman who claimed her innocence of any wayward activities, the evangelist's refusals were, indeed, curious.

"I have been chosen," said Aimee, "the lamb for every kind of slaughter, but I won't be slaughtered, either financially or morally."

Cline and Ryan, father-in-law and son-in-law respectively, were, according to Aimee, "both Catholics persecuting a Protestant minister." Now if that convoluted bit of logic was not outlandish enough, she claimed the two were determined "to dig up dirt and filth wherever they could and hurl it at me."

Aimee was in trouble and she knew it.

The grand jury was recalled and a new investigation was opened. Like it or not, Aimee was subpoenaed to appear before the Carmel witnesses.

On July 30, Minnie gave police a telegram she claimed she received from Chicago and that had been sent by Ormiston. It read, "Sworn statement concerning Carmel incident. Clearing you [Aimee]. En route. Deeply regret Ryan's terrible error."

It was a timely device, but Ormiston was not en route.

Ten days elapsed before investigators discovered that key evidence taken from the Carmel cottage had disappeared. Whether by accident or design, a member of the grand jury had tossed alleged samples of Aimee's handwriting down a courthouse drainpipe.

A flush of water had weakened the case against the evangelist.

A woman calling herself Lorraine Wisemann appeared at the office of Aimee's attorney on August 23, claiming that her sister, not Aimee, had shared the Carmel cottage with Ormiston. This she knew because she had spent several days there with them.

"I have been unable to sleep since this thing happened," said the woman. "Although I know it means that I will lose the position I have had for three years and also may ruin my name, I can't stand by and see another woman suffer for an indiscretion in which she was not connected in any way."

Then on September 11, Wiseman—who was not Lorraine Wiseman at all, but Lorraine McDonald Wiseman Sielaff—was jailed for passing a number of worthless checks. She claimed, however, that not she but her twin sister was the guilty party.

Sielaff did not have a twin sister. Nor did she have a sister who had spent ten days at the Carmel cottage with Ormiston. Sielaff was a liar.

Two days later, she admitted that her story had been a fabrication for which Aimee had paid her $5,000. "It was a pure premeditated hoax, born in Angelus Temple and launched from that source on glib and golden promises. Mrs. McPherson and her mother at various times gave me money to use for expenses in framing the hoax. They were always free with cash."

"The whole thing is a pack of lies," declared the angered evangelist. "Anything Mrs. Wiseman has said at the county jail, she had found in her own imagination and there is no truth in it as far as I am concerned. I am convinced that she has been prompted by enemies of me and my work to make such dastardly statements and I am positive they will fall of their own weight."

Sielaff was a liar. So was Aimee.

The next day, the evangelist admitted that she had given Sielaff money. The funds, she claimed, were to enable the woman to carry on an independent investigation of the Carmel cottage accusation. "We did just as we did with detectives and others who believed they could obtain evidence in clearing up my case. We gave her considerable money with the understanding that it would be returned to us providing she did not obtain the facts as she represented."

"She fooled us completely," Mother Kennedy said of Sielaff, "and we would have advanced her a great deal more money if she had requested it, so complete was our confidence in her apparent integrity."

At afternoon services, Aimee told her congregation that she expected "to be arrested any moment and I may be in jail tonight. Saint Paul and Saint Peter were arrested. When I get to heaven, I shall say, 'Saint Peter, I have been in jail, too, so I know how you felt.'"

The evangelist's premonition proved only partially correct. On September 16, district attorney Keyes announced that he had ordered the arrest of Aimee, Minnie, Kenneth G. Ormiston, Lorraine Sielaff, and John Doe on charges of criminal conspiracy to defeat justice.

As if on cue, Aimee collapsed at Angelus Temple. "Mrs. McPherson," reported her doctor "is suffering from one of the most dangerous infections I know of, which is abscess of the nose close to her brain. There is very, very great danger that it may go to her brain. Death, I fear, would follow."

Whether or not her "brain-threatening" illness was a ruse, it worked. Aimee posted $2,500 bail, pending arraignment. However, she was not formally arrested and taken into custody.

Minnie was arrested, but after spending forty minutes in the district attorney's office, where she plead not guilty and waived reading of the complaint, she posted bail in a like amount and was released. "It's the martyrdom of John Bunyan," said the long-suffering woman.

Ormiston's mother surfaced again when she told an Associated Press reporter in San Francisco that she was "tired of all the deception," and she called on her son to come forward and tell the truth. "We tried to bring him up as a God-fearing, righteous man," said Mrs. Ormiston, "and until he met Mrs. McPherson there was nothing to mar our joy and pride in him. Since then there has been nothing but trouble."

Four days after the announcement of Aimee's "life-threatening" illness, the redoubtable evangelist was back in the pulpit of Angelus Temple looking none the worse for the wear and spewing hellfire and brimstone to her adoring congregation. Hers was a miraculous recovery.

On Monday, September 27, Aimee's hearing got underway in municipal court. Before the day was over, six witnesses took the stand and testified that they had seen Ormiston and the evangelist together at the Carmel cottage.

"They talked as if they were hypnotized," said Aimee in summation of the witnesses' testimony. "Such ridiculous stories they told."

Following one of the longest preliminary hearings on record, the judge finally issued his ruling on November 3. "After a full examination of the entire evidence there is sufficient cause to believe the defendants guilty," said Judge Samuel R. Blake. He bound Aimee over to superior court to stand trial on charges of criminal conspiracy.

"As God is my judge," said Aimee on her way out of the courtroom, "I am innocent of these charges."

On December 9, as the evangelist awaited her day in court, newspapers announced Kenneth G. Ormiston's capture. Living under an assumed name at the Penn-Harris Hotel in Harrisburg, Pennsylvania, Ormiston "expressed astonishment" that he had not been apprehended sooner.

Returned to Los Angeles on December 17, the wily radio operator was released from jail two days later on $2,500 bail. In his only comment to the press, Ormiston said, "Intrigue and hokum are as thick as a fog." He did not elaborate.

On December 29, district attorney Keyes startled the public when he told the Associated Press, "The McPherson case is now in such a muddled state that a conviction is almost impossible and the charges probably will be withdrawn."

Calling Lorraine Sielaff a "perjurer" and "turncoat," Keyes said she had told a "different story every day," and cited the "collapse" of her testimony as the reason he would drop the charges.

If the McPherson case was "muddled," Keyes was doing little to unmuddle it, for the next day he told reporters, "Emphatically, I will not drop this case. While Mrs. [Sielaff] has changed her original story in part, it is not diametrically opposite to that she told on the witness stand …. Instead, it is more of an elaboration of the vague parts of her previous testimony."

The prosecutor's intentions had, indeed, become confusing.

Eleven days later, on January 10, 1927, Keyes stunned the nation when charges against Aimee, Minnie, Lorraine Sielaff, and Ormiston were dismissed. "In asking the dismissal," wrote the Associated Press, "Keyes did not vindicate the Four Square Gospel leader of charges that she left here last May 18, not in the hands of kidnappers, but in the automobile of Ormiston bound for a cottage at Carmel, California. He reiterated the state's contention that Mrs. McPherson had perpetrated a hoax but declared that he could no longer proceed on the often-changed stories told by Mrs. Sielaff, the evangelist's chief accuser."

Thus it was that the case against Aimee transferred from a court of law to the court of public opinion.

"While Aimee's followers had roamed the beach at Venice searching for her body, several of whom caught visions of her rising from the waves and ascending to Heaven," wrote a magazine called the *Haldeman-Julius Monthly*, "The Rev. 'Sister,' alive and pulsating, had been a dweller in the Garden of Aphrodite; that when airplanes were scattering flowers over her watery 'grave,' the lady was devoting herself to the shrine of Venus."

In a blistering editorial, the *San Diego Herald* wrote:

> The failure—or perhaps the innate inability—of some women to keep their legs crossed has been the cause of more wars, murders and general crimes than all the other reasons in the catalog.
>
> … As a modern lesson to a modern world it has made Aimee Semple McPherson out to be the most chuckleheaded liar that ever dallied with her Lothario in a bungalow by the sea or tasted the delights of forbidden love in a cottage just big enough for a folding bed that never folded, and a stove that at its best was a good deal cooler than the flaming desires of those who giggled beside it in the dark.

Figure 4. 6 Led by Aimee, delegates to the 1942 19th Annual Four Square Gospel Church Convention wept, sang, prayed, and fainted in the ecstasy of prayer during their Holy Ghost Rally.
Bancroft Library, University of California, Berkeley

Her followers will still follow, the merry jingle of the collection plate will rise as sweet music to her ears, the blue cape will still flaunt itself in the breezes of Los Angeles. Aimee will ride the crest, and when the time comes for her again to uncross her legs, Aimee will attend to the uncrossing with the same thoroughness she has done in this case, but we doubt not that she will prepare a better alibi.

"How she will resume the pulpit of the Temple; what she will do next; how her amazing career will end; these are questions only a bold prognosticator will venture," wrote *Vanity Fair* magazine. "Aimee is not a guessable quantity. The average life of an actress is somewhere between five and ten years. But Aimee is to be classed only with the Duses and Bernhardts; it is quite possible that she may give farewell performances the rest of her life."

As the years rolled on, so did the McPherson bandwagon. Aimee's Four Square Gospel established more than 400 branches worldwide and the money poured in. Still, all was not well in gloryland. There was much dissension in the ranks of temple workers, and Aimee became the brunt of a plethora of lawsuits.

In a violent disagreement about monetary policy, Aimee doubled her fist and broke Minnie's nose. An estrangement followed.

Roberta, Aimee's daughter and heir apparent, joined in a lawsuit against her mother. Another estrangement followed.

Aimee married again, but it was not much of a match and a nasty divorce followed.

On September 27, 1944, Aimee and her son—now the Reverend Rolf McPherson, who replaced Roberta as heir apparent—traveled to Oakland where they dedicated a new Four Square Gospel church and conducted a revival meeting. After services, Aimee retired to her suite at the Leamington Hotel. She did not awaken the following morning, but purportedly died from an overdose of prescription barbiturates.

"Aimee Semple McPherson died unexpectedly today after thirty-four years of spectacular evangelism frequently punctuated by sensational episodes in her personal life," wrote the *New York Times*, with studied understatement.

At 53, the mistress of hallelujah revivalism had preached her last sermon.

Figure 4.7 Angelus Temple, 1924.
California State Library

AIMEE'S TEMPLE

On a day in 1919, Aimee and Mother Kennedy drove out Glendale Boulevard scouting for land. The evangelist was approaching 30. Her children were young and needed permanence. So did Aimee. For nearly half a lifetime, the exuberant evangelist had traveled the tent and sawdust circuit, preaching here and preaching there, and moving on to the next meeting in the next town. It was time to put down roots, to have a church of her own where folks would come to her instead of her to them.

Aimee found the land she wanted adjacent Echo Park, where Glendale and Sunset boulevards intersected. Lush greenery fringed a tranquil lake and the site was distant enough from downtown Los Angeles to have a country feel.

Sufficient funds—$5,000—were available to buy the land, but Aimee had no money for construction. Unfazed, she quickly devised a master plan that would produce a whirlwind of activity and mounds of ready cash. In the two years following, Aimee crisscrossed the nation. She preached before myriad congregations and conducted thirty major revivals—a brief revival lasted a week, a long revival extended a month or more.

Wherever she went, she made her purpose clear to local clergy, adoring crowds, and fawning reporters. Aimee was on a mission to save souls and raise money. If the stress seemed more on money than on souls, no matter. The edifice she wanted to build would be a reflection of her larger-than-life personality, and that kind of building did not rise on the cheap.

Aimee, whose instinct for promotion was nearly flawless, shamelessly mimicked tactics employed by the government to peddle Liberty Bonds during the late war. She reasoned that if Woodrow Wilson could inveigle the public to dole out money for bombs and bullets, surely she could inspire a similar dole for the Lord. "How could she fight the devil without funds for ammunition?" she asked repeatedly.

Another stroke of brilliance was Aimee's play on America's love affair with the stock market. She did not ask congregants to become shareholders, but to become "chair-holders"—that $25 would put a seat in her church and in that seat would sit a sinner Aimee would save.

In less than a year, the enterprising evangelist raised enough money to break ground and begin construction. The project was under Aimee's watchful eye, and costs were carefully controlled. The contractor was forbidden to use credit—his or hers. It was a pay-as-Aimee-went proposition. Until cash was in hand to buy materials and pay labor costs, neither the contractor nor his crew was to drive a nail or saw a board.

In mid-1922, Aimee concluded an immensely successful road tour and returned to Los Angeles to witness completion of her most ambitious project. By the end of December, her 5,300-seat auditorium was ready for occupancy. Remarkably, the enormous structure was debt-free, its $1.2-million price tag met in advance by thousands of donors.

Never mind that the finished product looked more like a baseball stadium than a house of worship, Angelus Temple was an impressive monument to Aimee's perspicacity.

On New Year's Day, 1923, "a crowd of several thousand people assembled before the doors of the great building," noted the *Los Angeles Times*. Traffic was tangled for blocks and people arrived from far and wide, some in automobiles "gaily decorated with colorful ribbons and lace."

"Today is the happiest day of my entire life," gushed Aimee. "I can hardly believe that this great temple has been built for me."

Disbelief aside, Angelus Temple was built for no one other than Aimee. No one but Aimee could pack to capacity its cavernous hall. Three times a day, every day of the week, thousands of zealous devotees flocked to Aimee's temple to bask in the presence of this dynamic woman.

Time passed and so did Aimee. Angelus Temple weathered the decades. In April 1992, as it approached it seventieth birthday, the building was listed on the National Register of Historic Places.

Chapter 5: Baby Bandits

B aby Bandits—it must have been humiliating for youngsters
in their late teens to read that term. Nevertheless, a clever
reporter gave the name to a collection of misfits and it followed
them through a brief and bloody career in banditry.

Thanksgiving, 1936 segued to a fretful weekend for residents of
the San Francisco Bay Area. Apparently, a gang of hooligans—bold,
brash, and armed with deadly weapons—was on the loose. No
one knew how many—eight, twelve, twenty—were in the gang. It
moved quickly, struck at random, and covered a wide swath of ter-
ritory. Descriptions ran the gamut—tall, short, fat, lean. Agreement
converged on a single point: The outlaws were young.

The police traced nearly a dozen armed robberies to the hoodlums, all with similar *modus operandi*. Nevertheless, uncanny luck,
coupled with misinformation and incorrect assumptions made by
law enforcement agencies, kept the bandits a step ahead of the law.

That the gang numbered eight, twelve, or twenty was a fundamental miscalculation. Even the term "gang" was overblown.
Indeed, the Baby Bandits claimed exclusive membership of three
malevolent teenagers—Ernest Pla, Frank Sena, and William Daly.
Sena was nineteen, Daly eighteen, Pla seventeen. Each was a recent
alumnus of Preston Industrial School, a lockup for incorrigible boys
at Ione.

trio's reign of terror approached its apex on Sunday afternoon. With Pla behind the wheel of a stolen automobile, the boys stopped at a San Francisco tavern to replenish dwindling cash reserves. Pla kept the engine running while Sena and Daly went inside.

"Hands up," said the boys. Waving pistols and a shotgun, Sena and Daly ordered patrons to line up with their faces pressed against the wall. Daniel O'Connell, a 47-year-old off-duty watchman, was slow to react. His sluggishness cost him his life. Sena lifted the shotgun, pulled the trigger and put a gaping hole in the man's belly.

While O'Connell lay in a pool of blood, the tavern was relieved of its cash register receipts and the trio made a clean getaway.

Unnerved, perhaps, by the sheer brutality of a senseless killing, Pla left his partners to their own devices and headed for a rendezvous with friends at Merced. At the Southern Pacific depot in San Jose, temptation got the best of him when ticket clerk J. A. Montague leaned into the safe and manipulated its tumbler.

The moment the safe door opened, the 70-year-old clerk felt the barrel of a pistol jabbed into his back. "Get your hands up," Pla told the old man. Instead of complying, Montague whirled around and attacked the gunman. During the skirmish, the pistol fell to the floor. Pla fought his way loose, grabbed the gun, and fled the depot.

Later, sifting through mug shots at the San Jose police station, Montague was able to identify his assailant.

Meantime, Sena and Daly crossed the bay to Oakland.

Daylight was fading to dusk when twenty-one-year-old Harold Nickle reached the corner of 36th Avenue and East Eighth Street. His fiancée, nineteen-year-old Irene Bird, was about to leave the car and walk the few steps to her East Oakland home when two youths approached the automobile. The young couple thought the boys wanted directions, and Nickle rolled down the window.

Sena opened the door, pressed his gun against Nickle's ribs and said, "Move over." Without another word, he climbed into the driver's seat while Daly opened a rear door and settled against the backseat. Sena put the car in gear and drove away.

Moments later, Nickle's mother and sister watched from the front porch of the family home as the car drove by.

"That's not Harold driving," said Hanna Nickle to her daughter Helen. "I wonder who it is."

"But Harold and Irene are in the front seat with him," observed Helen.

Mother and daughter found it curious that Harold and Irene passed the house without waving, but thought no more about it.

"Do you know the way to Sacramento?" Sena asked Nickle.

The young man said he did and pointed the driver toward Dublin.

Sena leaned back and handed his gun to Daly. Gripping a pistol in each hand, Daly kept the captives covered. "If you do as we say, you won't get hurt," said Sena.

In an odd way, the bandits were considerate and courteous, and not for a moment did it occur to Harold or Irene that they were in the company of killers. Irene thought they were "just a couple of smart kids who wanted to get to Sacramento and [they] stole Harold's car to get there."

Certainly, Irene was apprehensive, but she was not afraid. "This is a poor way for you fellows to start out life," she told them. "Why don't you forget about it and go straight? This will never get you anywhere."

"It's too late," Sena replied. "This is a kidnapping. We're public enemies now."

Whether the comment was boastful or regretful was incidental. Sena's assessment was correct.

Irene recalled, "Once when Harold and I said something to each other, the fellow in the front seat remarked, 'Don't you two go planning anything because it won't do you any good.'"

Nearing Stockton, Sena decided to make the remainder of the trip on back roads. It was a bad decision. He lost his way and wandered aimlessly for more than an hour. Finally, he asked for directions and Nickle got him back on the right road.

On a patch of darkened roadway, Sena pulled over to relieve himself. He took Nickle along and left Irene under the cover of Daly's pistol. The only conversation was a warning from Daly that the gun was loaded and his finger was on the trigger.

Later, they stopped to accommodate Irene. "You be back in three minutes," ordered Sena.

"I could have yelled to several cars which passed," the young woman acknowledged, "but I was afraid they might shoot Harold."

With the lights of Sacramento in the distance, Sena pulled up to a roadside stand. He left the captives in Daly's care and went inside to buy a newspaper. None was available. Beer, however, was available in quantity and he purchased four bottles.

He returned to the automobile, passed out chilled bottles of beer and gave Irene a bag of cookies. "Here's something to eat," he said. "I thought you might be hungry."

Parked by the side of the road, kidnappers and victims sat in the car and drank beer, watching automobiles speed by. Harold and Irene wondered if unaware policemen were among the passing motorists.

After a while, Sena pulled onto the road and proceeded to the outskirts of Sacramento.

At about eleven o'clock, he stopped curbside near 56th Street and Folsom. On Sena's instructions, all four got out of the car. Daly asked Nickle if he had a driver's license and the young man handed his wallet to the gunman. He took the license and returned the wallet. "Here," said Daly. "We don't want your money."

Irene's eye fell on the boys' inappropriate clothing. They were lightly dressed, without hats and appeared cold. "Where are your overcoats?" she asked with motherly concern.

"We didn't have time to go home and get them," Sena replied with a hint of defensiveness in his voice.

"We have some good clothes but we had to leave them behind," added Daly, slightly embarrassed by his shabby appearance.

Sena redirected the conversation to matters at hand. "I know you got to report this," he said, "but we have to meet a fellow in Sacramento and we need forty minutes. If you wait forty minutes before notifying police, we'll leave your car in front of the Bank of America."

Harold and Irene agreed—naively.

The kidnappers returned to the automobile. As Sena opened the driver's door, he looked back. "If you need any money just say so."

Both shook their heads.

As he climbed behind the wheel, Sena said, "You're two swell kids."

The young couple kept their part of the agreement. They walked to a small coffee shop and ate dinner. After the passage of forty minutes, they took the shop's owner into their confidence and he drove them to the Sacramento police station.

In no time at all, Harold and Irene identified Sena and Daly from mug shots. Consequently, they inadvertently revealed the three Baby Bandits' identity, and police grudgingly acknowledged that this fearful gang was tiny in number and short on age.

After considerable questioning, they drove the couple in a police cruiser to the Bank of America. The kidnappers did not keep their part of the bargain—Harold's automobile was nowhere in sight.

The group drove about the city for several hours hoping to spot the car or the bandits. It was hopeless.

Later that morning, anxious family members greeted Harold and Irene at the Oakland bus terminal. While the weary kidnap victims were none the worse for the wear, they had come to realize how lucky they were to return home unharmed.

Descriptions of the wanted teenagers circulated to every police agency in California. Duped for days by a trio of kids, the law enforcement community was in a sour mood. Subsequently, they issued an astonishing "shoot to kill" order.

While the kidnapping played to its conclusion, yet another drama was set to open at Merced.

When Olga Pla learned that her errant son Ernest was wanted in connection with the San Francisco tavern slaying, she sought to find him. Determined to "rescue" him from his "evil companions," she reasoned that he had holed up with friends in Merced, the former family home.

Traveling more than a hundred miles to the small agricultural community in the San Joaquin Valley, the resolute mother set about her task. Her effort succeeded when she found her son in the company of friends. As only a mother could, she pleaded with the boy to surrender. At last, he agreed.

Spending money she could ill afford, Olga contacted San Francisco attorney Alexander Mooslin by long distance telephone. The lawyer listened to her story. Then he made his intentions known to San Francisco police detectives, and set out for Merced to connect with Olga's son. That afternoon, Mooslin accompanied Pla to the Merced police station where the boy surrendered to authorities.

It was Mooslin's call that placed San Francisco chief of detectives Charles Dullea in Merced when the most dramatic chapter in the Baby Bandit saga unfolded. Dullea had gone to the police lockup to claim Pla when "all hell" broke loose.

"We didn't know what was happening when we heard the sirens and saw all the excitement in the streets," he told a reporter for the *Modesto Bee & News Herald*. "We thought at first it was an accident."

In another moment, Dullea heard gunfire and knew it was no accident.

Unbeknownst even to Pla, Sena and Daly were in Merced.

Acting on a tip, Merced chief of police Fred Zunker and officer James Turner went across town to the Square Deal Café. Sena and Daly were at the bar were drinking beer. Zunker sat down beside Sena. Turner stood behind Daly.

"What is your name?" Zunker asked Sena. The young man handed him a stolen union card.

"And what is your name?" Turner asked Daly.

Daly was not inclined to answer. Instead, he reached into a shoulder holster for a pistol while Sena burst into action with flailing fists to keep the officers at bay.

The *Fresno Bee Republican* takes up the story: "In the melee Daly backed toward the front door. Zunker leveled his gun at him but the officer's arm was struck by Sena. Daly gained the sidewalk just as Officer Turner opened fire. The first shot was placed at his feet, the second knee high. As the bandit ran, Turner fired two more shots but thought he had missed since Daly did not stagger."

Daly ran around the corner of the café building, across an open lot and through a garage. Rather than give chase, Turner rushed back into the Square Deal where a fierce fight raged. Zunker and the bartender struggled mightily to subdue Sena.

"Sap him!" hollered the chief.

Turner's nightstick came down over the bandit's head—to no avail. With remarkable endurance, Sena continued to fight. Not until Turner had struck half a dozen blows did he immobilize the young man.

After Sena was cuffed and in custody, all available Merced County sheriff's deputies and highway patrolmen were called into town to help track down Daly. Deputy Sheriff Rex McBride and highway patrol captain William A. Burch went to the garage into which Daly had disappeared. From there they followed a trail of blood across two streets, through a lumberyard, and then through the backyards of several homes. Finally, at the Second Baptist Church, the blood trail ended.

Figure 5.1 Mrs. Charlotte Daly, William Daly's mother.
San Francisco History Center, San Francisco Public Library

Moving through an opening in the side of the building, the two officers entered a crawl space beneath the church. McBride lit a match. What appeared to be a body lay at the opposite end of the structure, partially obscured by a low cement retainer.

The officers crawled on all fours until they reached the site. There they found Daly—dead. A bullet hole fringed by powder burns was visible in his head, and a pistol lay across his chest.

Refusing capture, Daly had shot himself to death.

Sometime later, Charlotte Daly, the suicide victim's mother, said, "He won't get into anymore trouble now. After his release from the Preston School a short time ago, he told me he would never go back to a reformatory. He would kill himself first. It seems best that it is all over."

The police transported Sena and Pla to San Francisco to await charges of first-degree murder. They held them on the heftiest bail ever fixed in the bay city—one million dollars on multiple charges of armed robbery. Nevertheless, the staggering sum was a mere formality. There was no bail for a capital murder charge.

The teenagers confessed to ten armed robberies and admitted their participation in the killing of Daniel O'Connell. Not

Figure 5.2 Ernest Pla and Frank Sena at their arraignment.
San Francisco History Center, San Francisco Public Library

surprisingly, however, they named the dead Daly as the trig-german in the slaying.

When the brash Sena was led to his cell, he asked officers, "When are you going to put a rope around my neck?"

No rope was necessary. The next morning they found his body dangling by the neck from a pair of suspenders attached to the ceiling of his cell. Sena was dead.

Just a few yards away, Pla slept soundly through the night.

"All my life and all my money have gone to keep my boy out of trouble," said Emma Crone, Sena's mother. "Now it is all over and I don't care. Yes, I do care, I guess. But it has never been any use."

As prosecutors eyed the gallows, Ernest Pla, sole survivor of the Baby Bandit triumvirate, turned contrite. Noting the suicides of his two companions, he told authorities he had no intention of "taking

Figure 5.3 Ernest Pla, with his lawyer and mother.
San Francisco History Center, San Francisco Public Library

the easy way out." Then he begged for mercy. He would, he said, provide authorities with "all the information they asked for" to clear up robberies and other crimes.

Still, the saga of the Baby Bandits was not over. A few days prior to Christmas, a seventeen-year-old usurper named Leonard Cruz crawled out of the woodwork. An escapee from Preston Industrial School who had been on the loose since late October, sheriff's officers found the disagreeable boy at his parent's San Jose home.

"In thick, guttural tones, the lad reeled off to the deputies a tale of beatings, robberies, car stealings, and local crime that marched steadily forward since he escaped," wrote the *Bee*.

The brazen youth claimed to be the fourth member of the now-defunct Baby Bandits, and he even appropriated a role in the O'Connell murder. Still, he would never be brought to trial, he told

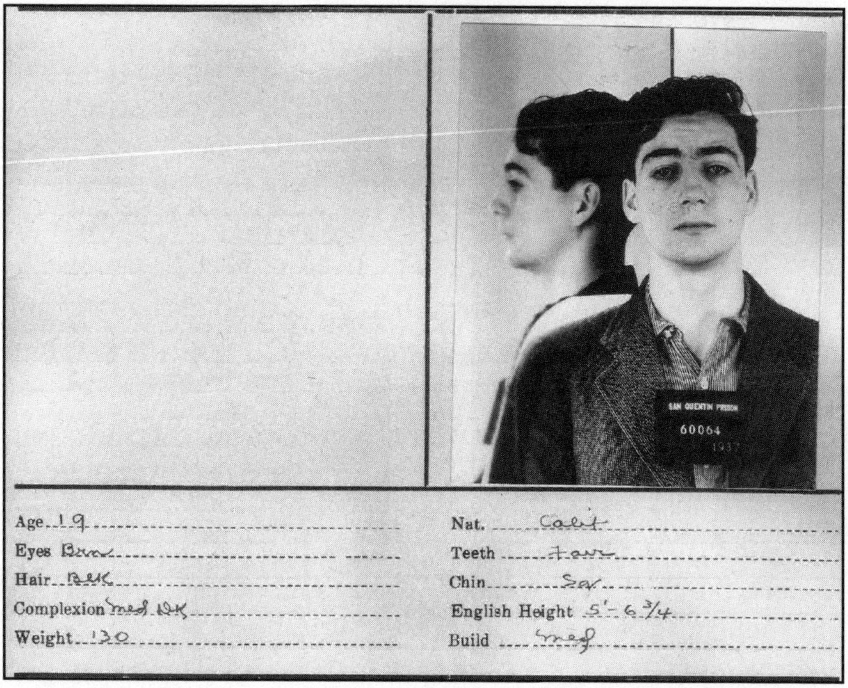

Figure 5.4 California State Prison Record Card, San Quentin, Ernest Pla.
California State Archives

his captors. The "suicide pact" he entered into with Daly, Sena, and Pla precluded him from ever seeing the interior of a prison.

As officers led him away, he turned to his parents and said, "The next time you see me, I will be in my coffin. I'm going to finish myself the first opportunity I get."

The sigh uttered by the teenager's father may have indicated relief. "We've just about given Leonard up," he said.

Authorities were skeptical of the boy's story. Ernest Pla shook his head in wonderment.

A few days later, Cruz recanted the entire confession. "I was lying," he said. "I just wanted to meet Pla."

Remarkably, Ernest Pla was the boy's hero.

Indicted on a charge of first-degree murder, Pla's trial was set for February 23, and then delayed until March 2, 1937. Defense attorney Mooslin stated that his client would plead not guilty and not guilty by reason of insanity—never mind that a panel of psychiatrists ruled Pla perfectly sane.

On March 1, Harold Nickle and Irene Bird, the Baby Bandit kidnap victims, sent their parents telegrams announcing their elopement to Reno. The California press was uniform in its congratulations.

Nothing was uniform about press reaction when newspapers learned that the prosecutors and Ernest Pla cut a deal, with superior court judge Sylvain J. Lazarus nodding his approval. In return for a guilty plea, they removed the potential for hanging Pla. There would be no trial. There would be no story for hungry reporters. The young man was sentenced to life in prison.

"I am opposed to capital punishment," Lazarus told the press. "My own investigation of this case disclosed that the defendant was a victim of poor health, poverty in his family, and a weakness that caused him to succumb to the temptations of other young criminals."

The kindly judge named Folsom Prison as the place of confinement. Pla bridled. He argued that San Quentin possessed better educational facilities. Impressed by the lad's apparent ambition to become a scholar of sorts, Lazarus dispatched the young man to the penitentiary of his choice—to live out his life.

Chapter 6: The Basket Case

Virginia Lee Cookson was a most unusual person. Variously described as a "farmerette" and "rancherette," she was—not of her own admission—between 45 and 48 years old. A "comely" woman, she was mistress of a ranch in the Forest of Arden at the head of Santiago Canyon near Santa Ana, California.

Walter M. Cookson, Virginia's sixth husband, had abandoned a position as post office inspector to become a handsomely paid executive of Bennet Financial Service in Los Angeles. Walter chose to live in his city of employment, visiting the ranch—and his most unusual wife—on occasion.

DID KIDNAPPERS SEIZE HER?

Virginia Lee Cookson, novelist and wealthy ranch owner of Santa Ana, Calif., startled the country when she returned after a mysterious disappearance with the claim that she had been kidnapped by Mexican white slavers, who kept girl victims chained to posts. California officials, however, scouted her story, Sheriff Jernigan declaring it a figment of her imagination.

Figure 6.1 Virginia Lee Cookson July 23, 1925. *Danville Bee*

Said to be the daughter of a Texas rancher, Virginia had resided with other husbands in Chicago and New York and, under the pseudonym Lee Chambers, she had enjoyed minor success writing fiction for various publications. Most assuredly, Virginia possessed a fertile imagination.

She came to California in 1909, and became Mrs. Benjamin Lemmon, wife of a Los Angeles newspaperman. Like her other unions, it was not a marriage marked by bliss and the couple divorced. In 1916, the much-married woman chose Cookson as her new mate.

The "rancherette's" name made a splash in the press when, in 1923, a feud developed between Virginia and the Modjeska Ranch Company, an outfit which ran a large spread adjacent to hers.

Virginia made a land purchase from Modjeska. It was her intention to subdivide the acreage into housing lots and sell the properties at a tidy profit. A waterline ran from a dam on the Modjeska Ranch to her land and, after her purchase, the ranch company decided to shut the water off.

Virginia was having none of it and for several hours sat guard over the waterline with a shotgun resting on her knees. This led to her arrest for trespassing and to the filing of suits and counter-suits for damages and injunctions. She won the first round of suits when an injunction was issued against Modjeska. The legal battle raged on and on until, at last, an out-of-court settlement was reached.

"The wind-up of Mrs. Cookson's water feud came in March [1925] when Judge Williams of Santa Ana awarded her $200 damages for false arrest ...." reported the *Los Angeles Times*. It was a paltry sum given the fact that Virginia had originally sued for $50,000.

The *Times* article continued: "Judge Williams ruled that the publicity attending Mrs. Cookson's arrest had not hurt her, as it set her out as a courageous and resourceful woman. But for five hours spent in the Santa Ana Jail, he held that she should be compensated."

Four months later, this "courageous and resourceful" woman disappeared. The *Times* reported to its readers on Wednesday, July 15, 1925: "The hills and canyons in and around Orange County Park were being searched tonight following an unsuccessful dragging of Orange County Park Lake for the body of Mrs. Virginia

Lee Cookson …. That [Virginia] had premonitions of evil for some time was confessed by her in a letter to her sister, written, but not sent, Monday."

The letter, addressed to Mary McKeever of Los Angeles, reflected Virginia's concerns. More accurately identified as Virginia's "foster sister and lifelong friend," Mary had left the Cookson ranch that very morning after a week's stay.

> Hello, my Mary darling,
>
> Are you not...[surprised]...that I am writing to you so soon? Oh, Mary, won't you come back and stay with me for a little while, just until this feeling of terror goes away? I know it sounds unreasonable, but for once I cannot help it. Something terrible seems pursuing me and I can't shake the odd feeling. It seems to me I'm going to meet it—it is as if invisible hands hold me forward and back, like voices almost that say "Don't! Don't! Don't!" And I don't know what to don't. I wish I knew. It is a dreadful thing to recognize fear—I never felt it before in my life and it swamps me completely. I am a nervous wreck today with what I feel and can't see.
>
> Of course, it's silly, I know, but my God, Mary, something is wrong, so you see you've almost got to come. Get Lulu to drive you down or telephone and I'll come and get you. But, Mary, please come. I'm an old fraidy-cat, but so help me Moses, there is some kind of warning sounding in my soul.

For reasons known only to Virginia, after completing the letter she tore it into scraps and tossed them into the waste can.

She spent Monday evening at the home of Mrs. W. E. Clement on South Grand Avenue in Orange. She told her friend of being "followed by a mystery automobile, which tried to crowd her off the road on three occasions."

Virginia left the Clement home shortly after midnight Tuesday morning. No one saw her after that.

"The route through Orange County Park is the most direct one from the Clement home to Mrs. Cookson's ranch," noted the *Times*, adding that Virginia "...expressed no fear of traveling it alone in the early hours of the morning, though it is a lonely road and there are few dwellings in the vicinity."

At daylight, a park caretaker and a deputy sheriff discovered Virginia's coupe in Orange County Park. The *Times* reported: "There were some indications about the car that a struggle had taken place; one of Mrs. Cookson's [slippers] was found wedged between the brake pedal and the handbrake, the other beneath the car. A few feet away lay Mrs. Cookson's hat, crumpled, a handful of hair clinging to it. And from the car to the...lake led a faint but clearly defined trail of footsteps—made by the shoes of a man. [At the lake] the trail ended."

Appearances lent credence to Virginia's premonition of evil, and foul play was suspected. "Sheriff [Sam] Jernigan of Orange County and Deputy Sheriff McClellan expressed the opinion that she had been murdered or kidnapped...." wrote the *Times*, but then added, "... [they] are not overlooking the possibility that she might have run away or killed herself."

They twice dragged Orange Park Lake with grappling hooks. The lake covered about a quarter of an acre, having a maximum depth of two feet. Nothing of significance was retrieved.

According to the *Times*: "Mrs. Cookson's car was found with two wheels off the highway. The ignition key was missing, evidently having been taken out of the switch. While officials pointed out that the [pavement] was hard at that point and would not show signs of a struggle unless [it was] an extraordinarily severe one, they also pointed out that there was no blood in or about the car or blood marks on Mrs. Cookson's...hat. The position of the second shoe indicated...that she might have been dragged out head first."

As investigators studied clues at the scene, C. S. Kelley, a Santa Ana druggist, came forward to report a "mysterious man hovering about the Cookson ranch Monday at 10 P.M." Authorities determined, however, that over several days folks had sighted the man hunting in the vicinity.

Meantime, Walter Cookson left his Los Angeles abode and rushed to the ranch. He was able to offer authorities little information but told investigators that he, too, had been privy to Virginia's premonitions of danger.

J. F. Lewis, Jr., of Orange, was another who had heard Virginia speak of a "mysterious pursuer." On Saturday, he said, she told him of her encounter with a car she described as "a large sedan which had forced her from the road."

Mary McKeever, the "foster sister and lifelong friend," held court with lawmen in her Los Angeles apartment. "My sister was a fearless woman," she said, curiously, speaking of Virginia in the past tense:

> She was afraid of no one until this strange man began to molest her.
>
> Three times this man—whose identity is a mystery—attempted to crash into my sister's car and force her from the road. Each meeting occurred at the same spot, the lonely spot where my sister's abandoned automobile was found...about 200 feet from the lake. These three meetings on the road all occurred during the latter days of last week.
>
> "I am afraid of that man," she told me last Saturday. "I always get panicky when I see that mysterious car tearing down the road toward me."
>
> She was so afraid of him that she went into town Saturday and insured her automobile, feeling certain that the stranger would wreck it in a collision with her.

"She seldom wrote to me," added Mary, making reference to the letter written and destroyed by Virginia. "And I can't understand why she should write a letter to me on the same day that I departed from the ranch, unless it was because she feared to remain there alone and wanted me to hurry back to the ranch. I feel that something terrible has happened to her."

Calling the case an "enigma," the *Times* reported the following day that there was little progress—no progress would have been more accurate—in the case.

Under close supervision, fifteen county jail prisoners joined hands in a human dragnet, sweeping Orange County Park Lake. The *Times* noted: "The...prisoners waded through every foot of the shallow lake, feeling their way at each step in the hope of finding some clew on the floor of the lake. But they found nothing.

"Forest rangers and deputy sheriffs scoured almost every foot of the rugged country about the park. They also reported that they found no trace of the missing woman."

Law enforcement officials feared the worst: "Only three possible explanations of the disappearance, each of a sinister nature, are seen by Sheriff Jernigan. He believes that she was either murdered, kidnapped, or wandered away and became lost in the rugged country while suffering from a temporary mental derangement."

Unbeknownst to dedicated lawmen searching relentlessly for the missing woman, Virginia was very much alive. She was alive and well down near the Mexican border, pouring out a tale of woe to local authorities. And the tale she told was bizarre.

Unharmed, but hysterical at times, Virginia turned up in Calexico and, according to the *Times*, "told police as weird and fantastical a tale as they have ever heard in their police experience."

Virginia, so went the story, left the Clement home in Orange shortly after midnight Tuesday morning. While driving through Orange County Park, a large sedan bore down on her coupe. Moments later, it forced the terrified woman to the side of the road. From the sedan sprang three men—a Mexican and two Americans—who attempted to drag her from her car. Not intending to become the docile victim of kidnappers, she tore off one of her slippers and struck wildly at her attackers. It was all for naught. One of the men doubled his fist and struck her in the chin. The blow rendered her unconscious.

When Virginia's senses returned, she found herself captive in the trio's large sedan, unable to move. A quick glance revealed a strap binding her arms and midsection, and another binding her legs.

Curtains drawn over the windows shrouded the interior in eerie darkness. The Mexican instructed her to remain quiet and she would not be gagged. She did as told, sitting silently for what seemed a journey of interminable length.

When they reached their destination at last, the men carried Virginia from the automobile into an underground room. It was pitch dark. A Chinese boy, himself a captive, brought her food and attended her needs.

After a while, an elderly Mexican man looked in on her. The Chinese boy referred to the man as Old Don.

Apparently, Old Don wanted a wife and he chose Virginia to satisfy that need. He told his prisoner that her marriage to Walter Cookson was not legal, that she was living in sin. Prepared to rectify the situation, he had summoned a priest. Old Don and Virginia would become man and wife.

Later, the Chinese boy told her that she was an "S.O." Upon inquiry, he explained that an "S.O." was a "Special Order" bride. Never mind the thousands of women Old Don could have chosen from, he wanted Virginia.

While the kidnap victim ruminated on her plight, a beautiful young American girl was brought into the room and chained to the posts of an iron bed. The girl was hysterical and, after awhile, she was taken away.

Virginia failed to explain how—given that the underground room was pitch black in darkness—she noted the girl's beauty. Regardless, the Chinese boy told her that the other unfortunate captive was a "T.B." A "T.B.," Virginia soon learned, was a girl meant for "Trade and Barter."

Uncanny instinct led Virginia to praise lavishly the Chinese boy's culinary skill, and to make a great display of eating with chopsticks—

an art she had mastered in New York's Chinese restaurants. The ploy worked. The young man became so enamored of the older woman that he agreed to aid in her escape.

Old Don, she learned, was a "hophead." When he next appeared in the underground room, Virginia and the boy conspired to fill him full of dope.

When at last the old man was in an opium-induced stupor, the Chinese boy fetched a basket large enough to accommodate Virginia. With little hesitation, she climbed inside. The lid was closed and the basket was loaded onto a waiting truck. Off it sped with Virginia jostling about. But no matter, she was en route to freedom.

The truck crossed into the United States. At Calexico, it stopped near the edge of the city and a Chinese man—a stranger—opened the lid. He helped Virginia out of the basket and told her to hasten to the police station. With that, the truck sped away.

Disoriented, Virginia sought the nearest house. Wrote the *Times*, "Attired in an old dress, stockingless, and with an old pair of slippers on her feet, her eyes swollen from weeping and her hair in fairly good condition, the woman appeared...at the home of Roy Rose, a Calexico garage man...."

Rose drove her to the police station.

At least, that is the story Virginia offered the world.

Almost.

"On the way up from Calexico," reported the *Times* the following day, "Mrs. Cookson retold her story to the sheriff and changed it in some particulars."

"Some particulars," indeed.

As a large automobile—related Virginia in the second telling—forced her from the road, she was strapped onto a cot and placed in an ambulance "in which she made the journey to [the] white slave den she described so graphically."

She said a "woman of culture" received her there. The woman told her that resistance would be useless, that her only hope was to take things as they came.

The addition of a "woman of culture" might easily be explained by a lapse of memory during the first telling. The "cot" and the "ambulance" were problematic. She had told in detail of her kidnapping across the border on the back seat of a large sedan with its curtains drawn. A cot had little in common with a back seat; a sedan had little in common with an ambulance.

The *Times*, now a bit skeptical of Virginia, noted that, "If there is such a [white slave] den it is not on the Mexican side of the international line." The newspaper added, "Immigration officials declared no ambulance had crossed into Baja, California in more than six months, and no truck bearing a clothes hamper crossed to the American side yesterday."

Declining an immediate interview with Sheriff Jernigan, the "fiction writer and rancher" claimed to be in seclusion in order "to recover from her nerve-wrecking experiences...."

On July 21, newspapers stated that the self-alleged kidnapping victim would appear the following day before district attorney A. P. Nelson and sheriff Jernigan: "Her story...is to be thoroughly probed by the officials."

After the latest telling of Virginia's story, Jernigan set out for Mexico to conduct his own investigation. Upon his return on July 25, he told reporters that he "...found nothing that would lead to any arrests, but said that he learned two things: first, that it would be impossible for Mrs. Cookson, or anyone else, to be taken across the international boundary line in an ambulance....Second, that it would be equally impossible for a Chinese boy to bring her back across the border in a truck, while she was hidden in a laundry basket."

Basket or not, the notion of a Chinese boy driving Cookson across the international border into the United States was a flight of fancy. The 1882 Chinese Exclusion Act, and subsequent immigration restriction acts which barred Asian immigration altogether, were not rescinded until 1943. Cunning as he may have been, the boy and his truck would never have gotten across the border.

Jernigan declared that "he was continuing his investigation in a quiet way and that the probe was not ended by any means."

In fact, the sheriff's "quiet" investigation soon became a silent one. Virginia's moment of fame was over.

A few headline-filled days had given the public much to chatter about. Perhaps, they had also given the oft-married "rancherette" fresh plots to write. The local prosecutor must have believed her or taken pity on her. She was never charged with staging her own kidnapping, although she disappeared again later that year only to turn up in El Paso, Texas. No tale of a kidnapping followed this second disappearance.

Virginia Lee Cookson died ten years later on April 20, 1935, from injuries she sustained in an automobile accident near Del Rio, Texas. Her husband, Walter Cookson, claimed she had been en route to Houston from California. Her disappearances remain a mystery.

Chapter 7: Tapping Midas

I thought the whole affair was just another prank of Bill's," said James P. Wolf, wealthy furniture manufacturer and close friend of millionaire William F. Gettle:

> Bill and I were at the bar, he on the serving side. We were chatting and joking. Suddenly I felt a poke in the back and saw a second man with a handkerchief over his face stick a revolver at Bill. In a voice barely a whisper they ordered, "Stick 'em up, gentlemen." Bill and I raised our arms above our heads. Then they motioned us to leave the recreation room and walk beyond the swimming pool.
>
> The fellow prodding me along—Bill and his captor were out in front—whispered as we walked alongside the pool, "This is no stick-up; this is a kidnapping." I still thought it a joke, but then something made me think it was a robbery. I reached in my hip pocket and dropped my purse containing some $200 in the pool.
>
> We walked very, very quietly, and outside of the whisper to me, I don't believe there was another word said, unless Bill's man was talking to him.

The gunmen said nothing until they reached the estate's seven-foot stone wall, surmounted by barbed wire. A ladder, used by gardeners for pruning, was conveniently in place. Wolf's account continued:

As we neared the wall—it was pitch dark—we halted for a moment. Then our hands were bound with our [neck] ties. Mine were tied behind my back. I heard Bill moving up the ladder and I'm sure one of the men was behind him. I was still on the ground. I heard Bill apparently stumble, then [I heard] a thud as he dropped to the other side.

Just as Bill hit, I heard him groan. I think he was badly hurt in the fall. As I glanced up, I think I saw the top of an auto just over the wall. I can't be sure, it was so dark.

Then my captor bound my mouth and nose with adhesive tape. He did a good job of it, too. Only my eyes were left open. Then he bound my feet and sat me down on the ground. He leaned over me and whispered, "Stay where you are for an hour or we'll kill you. This is no stick-up. It's a snatch."

With this warning the man climbed the ladder and then I heard the car drive away. It moved almost without sound.

What Wolf initially interpreted as a practical joke was no joke at all. Indeed, his good friend Gettle, host of an informal party to celebrate completion of a new swimming pool, had been snatched from his walled estate in what appeared to be a carefully orchestrated kidnapping plot. It was the night of May 9, 1934.

Wolf reported: "My tennis shoes were not tied and I wiggled my feet out of them. Soon I worked the binding from my ankles— they weren't very tightly bound, as it was done in a hurry—then I worked myself over to a small tree. Working against this tree for a few minutes, I was able to stand on my feet. I then hurried to the recreation room."

Not more than twenty minutes passed from the time of the abduction to the moment of Wolf's return. Consequently, their absence stirred no alarm from their spouses or from the third couple at the residence, Albert Hitchen and his wife. All that changed when Wolf, his hands tied behind his back and his mouth taped shut, burst into the recreation room.

The party at Gettle's country estate began in the afternoon, extended into the evening, and continued well into the night. At about 10:00 P.M., the Gettles and those remaining as overnight guests—the Wolfs and the Hitchens—christened the new pool. Then, after their late night swim, the wives decided to turn in. Gettle and Wolf retired to the bar and Hitchen escorted the women to their sleeping quarters.

"When I returned to the recreation room both the boys were gone," said Hitchen. "I waited a few moments, thinking they were outside, when suddenly Wolf came into the room. With his face and wrists taped and tied, he was a frightful-looking creature. I jerked the adhesive from his mouth and he mumbled the story of the abduction."

Moments later, Hitchen called the police. A search began immediately. Coordinated by Los Angeles County sheriff Eugene Biscailuz, it became a massive effort that included state and local law enforcement agencies, as well as "secret operatives" of the federal government. Authorities in Nevada and Arizona began tracking leads as well.

"Prostrated" and placed under a physician's care, Fleta Gettle, the kidnap victim's wife, told authorities that the family was never threatened and that "my husband has no enemies." Given a police guard, they moved her from the country estate, taking her to the couple's palatial home in Beverly Hills where an agonizing vigil commenced.

Born in Oklahoma in 1887 of modest circumstances, William F. Gettle amassed a fortune of several million dollars and retired at 42—missing the mark he set for himself by two years. In the five years since, he established offices in the Bank of America building in Beverly Hills where, at his leisure, he managed an impressive portfolio of oil and mining interests and brokered occasional deals.

His business career began in 1913 when, as a young man of 26, he took a position in Kemmerer, Wyoming, as manager of a J. C. Penney store. In 1918, he came to California's San Joaquin Valley, where he opened a store in Bakersfield. Within a few years, he controlled twenty-two Penney's outlets, and became a major stockholder in the corporation and one of its key executives. Meantime, he invested heavily and profitably in oil, mining, and real estate.

During the spring of 1929, Gettle watched as the nation's business climate began to chill. Nevertheless, the public gorging in stocks continued apace until fall. With every rumor of a merger or a split—and they were legion—stock prices soared and a buying frenzy followed. Much of the public bought on margin, inflating prices even more and adulterating an already fragile market.

Gettle was among the more enlightened investors who recognized that all was not well on Wall Street. Consequently, he cashed out his holdings in the department store chain, sold large chunks of prime real estate, and liquidated questionable investments from an otherwise fat portfolio of healthy oil and mining stocks.

When the market went belly-up in October, Gettle was ensconced in a newly acquired Beverly Hills mansion counting his profits. Economic sages estimated his net worth at $3,500,000—a fabulous sum of money in those days. As panic swept the land and the Great Depression gripped the nation, Gettle settled into a life of leisure and little worry. There was, however, one exception.

Despite his uncommon wealth, Gettle did not consider himself a candidate for the snatch racket. Nevertheless, he was exceedingly concerned about his four young children. Swift on the heels of the tragic Lindbergh kidnapping—the Lindberghs' twenty-month-old son was snatched from his crib in 1932 and murdered—armed guards were hired and the Gettle children remained under ever-watchful eyes.

The vigilance continued unabated when Gettle purchased a country getaway—a sprawling estate on five acres of land in Arcadia, situated at the base of the San Gabriel Mountains some twenty miles from downtown Los Angeles. It was there that the unthinkable occurred. As he and his friends celebrated completion of a swimming pool on that May evening in 1934, the perpetrators kidnapped at gunpoint, not one of his carefully guarded children, but Gettle himself.

Following a long and sleepless night in the Gettle household, Ernest E. Noon, the victim's friend and lawyer, emerged as the family spokesman. "We want Mr. Gettle back at once," he told reporters, confident that through the California press his words would reach the kidnappers. He emphasized the seriousness of Fleta Gettle's condition and asked the kidnappers to communicate quickly. "We are willing to follow instructions given by those who are holding Mr. Gettle. We are prepared to deal fairly, honestly, and confidentially with the kidnappers and will meet any reasonable demand. The money will be forthcoming as soon as the ransom demand is made, provided we have sufficient money to meet it."

Noon coupled his statement with a missive dictated to the kidnappers by Mrs. Gettle:

"I urge and beg you to communicate with our personal attorney. Mr. Noon is authorized by me to meet your ransom demands. You can be assured by me that any contact you make with Mr. Noon will be treated confidentially by him. He is working independently and exclusively in our interests."

The confidentiality guaranteed in both statements was, of course, poppycock. Beth Noon and Mrs. Gettle were working closely with law enforcement officials. Their fondest hopes were to secure Gettle's immediate release, and to see the responsible parties apprehended and brought to justice.

Lawmen were in general accord that the "job was pulled by bigtime kidnappers" from somewhere in the Midwest. The abduction was too effortless, too slick—or so the reasoning went—to have been orchestrated by inexperienced local thugs. Professional gangsters must be the culprits.

The assertion was not without a semblance of logic. John Dillinger, recently accorded the title Public Enemy Number One—he was the first criminal so named—conducted his reign of terror in unexpected places. Newspaper headlines exploited the bloody deeds of killers with catchy names—Pretty Boy Floyd, Baby Face Nelson—as they roamed the landscape tallying their victims. Misfits Bonnie Parker and Clyde Barrow, who shot innocent people in their quest for immortality, were unpredictable and very much at large. While none were known to frequent the California coast, a man of Gettle's wealth might inspire a trip west.

The press bought into the notion with such gusto that the *Los Angeles Times* was compelled to editorialize. By connecting Gettle's kidnapping to the abduction of a young girl in Tucson, it seemed "to point to an invasion of the Southwest by expert professional kidnappers from the East," asserted the *Times*. "Both crimes follow closely the lines of recent Eastern snatches and both show careful advance planning and practiced technique."

Then, having made a bold assertion, the newspaper lost its nerve and back-pedaled: "There is no certainty, of course, that the [Tucson] and Gettle kidnapping gangs are connected in any way, and a certain surface similarity between the cases should not lead to false conclusions. Investigating officers are keeping their minds open and the public should do likewise."

The editorial was more to the point when it admonished its readers that "the police need every bit of real information they can get and every man with eyes and ears in his head should use them in collecting it. The police also need to have fools, cranks, and publicity hunters kept out of the picture; in other words, amateur cooperative detective work needs an admixture of common sense. The community needs to keep its head and not get hysterical; such a public attitude could only impede the investigation."

Notwithstanding the newspaper's admonition, fools and cranks providing fatuous leads were in no short supply. A young lady, characterized by officers as "a great talker," talked herself into a three-hour police interrogation when she made light of the kidnapping and suggested to her landlady that she knew more than she could tell. She boasted of having underworld connections, predicted that the Gettle family would post a large reward, and babbled about what she would do with the reward money.

By the time she left the police station, a burst of profound reality tempered her overwrought imagination.

Officers from J. Edgar Hoover's Division of Investigation (DOI agents were the predecessors of FBI agents, and were loosely called G-men) were involved in a losing argument with the Mexican government over a mysterious flight. Apparently, a private airplane flew across the US-Mexican border about an hour after the Gettle kidnapping. Agents theorized that Gettle might have been flown across the border and lodged in an obscure hiding place. They insisted, to no avail, that Mexican federal police—the *Federales*—investigate. The Mexican government insisted that the *Federales* had more important things to do.

A curious shopper alarmed a UCLA student employed as a drug-store clerk. Crawford's Drug Store was located in the University Professional Building in Westwood Village, a property owned by Gettle.

"Who is the fat guy that has an office upstairs? He's the owner of the building, isn't he?" inquired the shopper, making an indelicate reference to the 230 pounds carried on Gettle's 5'8" frame.

"Why, that's Mr. Gettle," the student replied.

"He's pretty wealthy, isn't he? He owns quite a bit of property, doesn't he?"

The clerk replied that Gettle owned other property in Westwood Village, as well as property in Beverly Hills.

"Isn't Gettle the fellow who spends so much time in here playing the claw game?" asked the customer.

Apparently, Gettle spent spare change hoping to win trinkets. For a few cents, and a few seconds, players manipulated a claw-like device in an effort to retrieve cheap baubles scattered about the bottom of a glass enclosure. Those able to pluck up an item and drop it into a small tray-like opening won the game and pocketed the worthless gimcrack.

The student replied in the affirmative and the customer, his curiosity apparently satisfied, left the store. Then, after the kidnapping, the young clerk got to thinking about the odd conversation. It might be important, he reasoned, so he notified lawmen.

An automobile fell under suspicion when it was repeatedly seen by witnesses driving slowly about the vicinity of the Arcadia home. It was a black, Ford sedan bearing Illinois license plates. Four of the plates' six digits were recorded and departmental brass told their officers to be on the lookout. Should an officer spot the automobile, his orders were to apprehend the driver and hold him for questioning.

In Glendale, A. E. Kendall, a longtime business associate of Gettle's, suffered an acute case of jitters when unusual telephone calls were received commenting about his wealth and his connection to the J. C. Penney Company. At the same time, an automobile was seen driving back and forth in front of his home, and Kendall was certain the driver was "looking the place over." He notified the police but they found nothing out of the ordinary.

Meantime, Gettle's Beverly Hills neighbors—many of them motion picture stars and studio executives—took every possible precaution to protect themselves and their families. As the *Times* noted, their visibility and wealth made them "ready prey for gangsters and racketeers." Even before the Gettle kidnapping, Hollywood notables barricaded themselves behind fortress-like walls that were patrolled night and day by armed guards. Now, however, they tightened security measures even further, and Gettle's kidnapping was the talk of the day.

Some years prior, the ever-youthful Mary Pickford—billed as America's Sweetheart—was the object of a kidnapping plot unraveled by police. The culprits went to prison. Pickford and her dashing husband, Douglas Fairbanks, turned their lavish estate, Pickfair, into an armed camp.

Actress Marlene Dietrich, the recent recipient of a threat to kidnap her baby daughter, abandoned her Beverly Hills home for a secluded and heavily barred home in Santa Monica. Armed guards protected her child, each man being approved by sheriff Biscailuz before he was hired.

Crooner Bing Crosby, whose young son was threatened, not only employed guards but also finagled a deputy sheriff's badge, enabling him to carry a gun. Recently, his home was equipped with a costly and sophisticated burglar alarm system that was the envy of the neighborhood.

Film star Mae West, a personal friend of sheriff Biscailuz, lived behind triple-bolted doors. A bodyguard who carried a sawed-off shotgun protected her.

So fearful of kidnapping was actress Gloria Swanson that she sent her children to boarding school in Switzerland.

To protect his young son against kidnappers, Edward G. Robinson, famous for his tough-guy gangster roles, added a special wing to his home. Considered burglar-, bandit-, and kidnap-proof, the wing provided his son with a bedroom and playroom outfitted with a variety of security devices and armed guards were posted around the house night and day.

Some eighteen hours following Gettle's abduction, the San Bernardino post office cancelled a letter sealed in a plain white envelope, mailed to Mrs. Gettle by way of the Arcadia estate. Written on a half sheet of ordinary paper, the note said, "Get $40,000 in used bills, in $10s and $20s. Keep ready. Don't tell law. Will get in touch with you later." It was unsigned and the writer made several ink smudges when wiping the paper clean of fingerprints.

For reasons that were unclear, investigators determined that the letter was the work of a hopeful opportunist.

A more promising development occurred when Noon took a midday call at his office from a man claiming to be an emissary of Gettle's kidnappers. The victim's freedom could be bought for

$75,000, said the caller, who gave Noon explicit instructions for delivery of the ransom money.

Fortuitously, the caller was overheard and his location reported to authorities. The telephone receiver was still in the man's hand when lawmen converged on his apartment building. They took him and four others into custody. Much to their disappointment, police quickly determined that the caller was yet another opportunist who had nothing to do with the kidnapping. After intensive grilling, they released the three people arrested with him and jailed the man on charges of attempted extortion.

It was one among several calls made to Noon. Callers were either crackpots or calculating folks seeking to rake hay while the sun shined. One disingenuous stewbum offered a bargain basement rate of $500 for Gettle's return if Noon would deliver the money forthwith.

The kidnapping was two days old when, on Friday, May 11, the postman delivered a letter to Noon's office. Inside the envelope was a short note bearing Gettle's signature: "Have $60,000 ready. You may be able to get the money from the Gettle trading account at Hutton's [brokerage firm in Beverly Hills]. If not, try the Bank of America."

With due haste, a meeting of key law enforcement authorities was called. It included sheriff Biscailuz, Los Angeles chief of police James E. Davis, district attorney Buron Fitts, special agent Reed E. Vetterli of the justice department, and others. At the conclusion of the conference, Fitts told reporters that lawmen had agreed to curb their pursuit of the kidnappers until midnight Sunday to enable Noon to establish unfettered communications. "The [ransom] money," said Fitts, "was waiting in a Beverly Hills bank vault," and "no traps or tricks would be attempted that might frustrate ransom plans engineered by Noon."

The "limited truce" was, however, just that. Should the kidnappers not act with alacrity, a "sizzling ultimatum" contained "a threat to loose more than five thousand peace officers throughout Southern

California in one of the most intensive house-to-house man hunts ever devised."

Fitts concluded with a chilling rejoinder to the culprits that "the law specifically provides that the death penalty may be instituted when kidnappers harm or maim their victim."

Later in the day, Noon's office received a second note. It read:

> Have $60,000 ready. $40,000 in $10 bills, $20,000 in $5 bills. All to be old bills and not consecutively numbered. Do not mark any bills. If you do we'll burn them and collect another bunch in their place. Don't show this letter to any officers. Ask officers to stop all investigation until victim is returned.
>
> If you take officers into your confidence we are going to double the ante. If you shoot square with us, we'll do the same. If not, we might get hot. So think it over.

The balance of the note was devoted to instructions preparatory to delivery, and included a cryptic demand that Noon "get a Ford V8 coupe. Take right hand door off. Also take turtle back off."

Again, the missive bore Gettle's signature.

As lawmen digested the ransom note's contents, they found a third note on the steps of the Beverly Hills Community Church. It, too, was addressed to Noon and was signed by Gettle:

"If I do not get out of here pretty quick I may not be alive. Please complete this job today without delay. Please call off cops until I am returned home. Also see that no bills are marked."

Silence followed the flurry of notes. The Sunday deadline came and went. "While Noon remained in his office apparently expecting word that would send him on a journey to deliver the money," noted the *Times*, "no information was vouchsafed that any instructions had been received."

As frustration mounted, Fleta Gettle made what a reporter called "a pathetic appeal" to law enforcement authorities to extend the deadline. After much hesitation, Fitts announced, "We are giving an additional twelve hours to the kidnappers to make good their promise to deliver Gettle." He added, "There is an end to patience and we are near our limit."

Meantime, as friends and family members lent their support, Betty Weinberg, Fleta's niece, said, "She is bearing up bravely and is hopeful for an early and safe return of Mr. Gettle. The children have not been advised of their father's plight, and their only concern is 'how soon will daddy be home.'"

Yet another letter arrived at Noon's office. It contained detailed instructions for delivery of the ransom money, and stated that a follow-up telephone call would set a time for the payoff.

The long awaited call came Monday morning. Noon was told to find an emissary, because of the kidnappers' concern that the lawyer's visibility might cause him to be followed by thrill seekers or hijackers who would interfere with the delivery.

Carrying a black satchel containing $60,000, the emissary drove a modified Ford coupe to Laurel Canyon as instructed. There he found a stake to which a note was attached. It directed him on a roundabout route to another stake and another note, and further instructions. "Be sure not to drive over twenty miles per hour," admonished the kidnappers.

A third stake bore a note in Gettle's handwriting: "Go straight ahead until you find another stake and rag on the same side of the road. Stop and put suitcase about three to six feet from the post. Get in car and drive straight up Firestone and circle to left for Los Angeles."

The emissary did as instructed, but was unable to locate the final stake. Driving ever so slowly, he searched and searched, but to no avail. He followed Firestone Boulevard to the Los Angeles River, when all at once gunshots rang out from the opposite bank. Fearing that ransom hijackers had followed him, or that law officers had swooped down on the kidnappers, he put his foot to the throttle and sped away. He did not stop until he arrived at a sheriff's substation in Maywood, where he demanded protection.

Figure 7.1 James Kirk.
San Francisco History Center, San Francisco Public Library

His report of gunshots sent a score of police cars blazing into the area. It was a wild dash for no good reason. A quick investigation revealed that a local constable had shot at a fleeing burglary suspect.

Then, heavily guarded by a squad of Los Angeles police cars, the nervous emissary carried the $60,000 satchel back to Noon's office. The carefully orchestrated delivery effort was all for naught—but it made no difference.

Some four weeks prior to Gettle's kidnapping, two keen-eyed detectives attached to the robbery detail of the Los Angeles Police Department, lieutenants W. C. Burris and H. P. Gearhard, secreted a microphone attached to a dictograph machine into an apartment at 600 North Harvard Boulevard. Two men, James Kirk and Larry Kerrigan, both suspects in a string of bank robberies, lived in the building with women thought to be their wives. They resided in separate units on the same floor and met frequently in the apartment wired for sound.

Coincidentally, as the failed emissary headed toward Noon's office to return the ransom money, the attorney received another call from the kidnappers' contact man. Alert officers traced the call to a telephone booth on Western Avenue. Police cars rushed to the scene.

They arrived too late, but fortunately a witness watched a man dash from the phone booth to his car and drive away at high speed. The curious bystander jotted down the license number. A quick probe of vehicle records revealed that the automobile was registered to a man who lived at 600 North Harvard Boulevard.

Meantime, Burris and Gearhard, their ears tuned to the dictograph machine, heard a man say, "This is a nice cool spot that the cops don't know about."

Another voice said, "From the newspapers, it appears that the police are laying off."

The clincher came when one of the men said, "I'm going to write another note and give some instructions."

Like a bolt of thunder, it dawned on the two detectives that their bank robbery suspects might very well be Gettle's kidnappers. They reported their suspicion to Captain Harry Seager, head of the robbery squad, who, in turn, notified authorities in charge of the kidnapping investigation.

The morning was still young when Seager, Burris, and Gearhard, backed up by a hefty force of Los Angeles police officers, burst into the North Harvard Boulevard apartment building. Minutes later, James Kirk, Loretta Woody, and Mona Galleghen were led handcuffed and at gunpoint to waiting squad cars.

Officers took the trio to police headquarters, separated them, and subjected each to intensive questioning. Police found the business card of N. W. Zimmer, a La Crescenta real estate man, in Kirk's billfold. Written on its reverse side was Zimmer's home address—and the name Gettle.

Detectives rushed to La Crescenta. In quick time, they tracked down Zimmer and learned that, just a week prior, he had rented a house at 4256 Rosemont Avenue to several men. The detectives notified the sheriff's office and, within minutes, heavily armed sheriff's deputies surrounded the house.

They captured Roy Williams immediately. His companion, Larry Kerrigan, the other North Harvard Boulevard bank robbery suspect, escaped through the back door. However, he was arrested a few hours later in a Los Angeles drugstore.

On a raggedy bed in a small, dimly lit room, his hands and feet bound and his eyes covered by strips of soiled adhesive tape, lay William F. Gettle. He was dirty, disheveled, and dressed in the same suit he wore when kidnapped. When officers removed the tape, he blinked and rubbed his eyes, and complained about diminished eyesight. To relieve his discomfort, a deputy offered him a pair of "smoked" glasses. Otherwise, given the ordeal he experienced, the victim appeared in remarkably good condition.

Officers helped Gettle into the back seat of a squad car and rushed him to the sheriff's office at the Hall of Justice. Word of his rescue spread quickly. By the time the automobile carrying him arrived at the building entrance, a throng of some 500 people had gathered. A cordon of police cut a path through the excited crowd and whisked Gettle inside.

There, he told officers that he was "completely unaware that his absence had attracted more than passing attention. It all seems like a bad dream," he said, "and I've missed track of the time. My greatest worry … was for the anxiety my absence would cause my wife and family. I didn't suppose anyone else would be interested."

He was mistaken. Questioned but briefly, he was soon the principal occupant in a sirens-blaring, lights-flashing motorcade en route to his Beverly Hills estate. As word of Gettle's impending arrival spread, some 5,000 people lined the street leading to his home. John Barrymore, Joan Crawford, Leslie Howard, Winnie Lightner, and other Hollywood luminaries were among the enthusiastic revelers. Beverly Hills police had difficulty making way for the motorcade. As a black sedan carrying the rescued kidnapping victim maneuvered slowly through the crowd, a bedlam of cheers, shouts, and whistles erupted.

Gettle left the automobile and mounted the doorstep. Someone heard a child holler, "Daddy's home!"

The next morning, much refreshed by a hearty meal and a good night's sleep, Gettle returned to the Hall of Justice to reply to endless questions asked by representatives of various law enforcement agencies involved in the investigation. In a curious exchange, an officer asked, "Did you go voluntarily [with the kidnappers] or were you forced to go with them?"

"Well, they forced me to go, naturally," answered Gettle, wondering if the questioner had his wits about him. "What could a fellow do? They had their guns on me."

The snatchers had not mistreated him, he told investigators:

> They brought me sandwiches and drinks, and they told me they did not want to hurt me because, in fact, they said that I was the nicest fellow that they had ever had, because I was so agreeable. But, hell, there was nothing else that I could do. They had me.
>
> I had no idea where I was. I was surprised to find I was so close to home. When they kidnapped me, they blindfolded me and drove for several hours. I was under the impression they had taken me out somewhere near Riverside.

Later in the day, actress Winnie Lightner sent flowers to the Gettle home. "An orchid for you, Mrs. Gettle, for your courage and bravery," read the accompanying note. "An orchid for you, Mr. Gettle, for your safe return home."

The perpetrators received no orchids. Six days after the kidnapping, and one day after the victim's rescue, Roy Williams, James Kirk, and Larry Kerrigan, odd characters each, stood before superior court judge Charles W. Fricke. Despite press assumptions to the contrary, none of the trio was a "professional kidnapper." Nor were any of the three associated with big-time Midwestern gangsters. Kirk was an unemployed welder and boilermaker, and a one-time, small-time bootlegger. Williams was a failed poultry farmer and an

Figure 7.2 Roy Williams signs confession.
San Francisco History Center, San Francisco Public Library

unemployed mechanic and truck driver. Kerrigan, who possessed the longest rap sheet of all, was an unemployed, unskilled laborer.

Defiant at first, the trio wilted under the threat of district attorney Fitts to seek the death penalty should they plead not guilty and opt for a jury trial. Each thought better of the idea and, one by one, they pleaded guilty to kidnapping.

Just fourteen minutes passed from the time the Los Angeles County grand jury returned its indictment, to the time the culprits pleaded guilty, to the time Judge Fricke passed sentence—life imprisonment for each of the kidnappers. As the *Times* put it, "Justice moved with meteoric rapidity."

The convicted men appeared stunned. Given an opportunity to say anything they wished after the passing of sentence, they stood agape before the bench and said nothing.

Said Fricke, "Court is adjourned."

Meantime, a sign went up in front of the La Crescenta house: "See the room where Gettle was held. Ten cents admission." Ghoulish and exploitative as the venture was, it was not without pecuniary logic. Prior to its brief rental as a kidnapper's lair, the house stood vacant for the better part of four years.

A week to the day after Gettle's kidnapping, the convicted felons who orchestrated the crime were aboard a Southern Pacific train speeding toward the walls of San Quentin.

"I'd better have stuck to chicken ranching," commented Williams. "It didn't pay, but neither does snatching."

Kirk lamented the end of Prohibition. Bootlegging, he said, was a racket he "knew something about." He knew little about the snatch racket.

Kerrigan, who knew a lot about prison, "was the gloomiest of the three."

A month following their incarceration, the trio was returned to Los Angeles to stand trial in federal court. Each stood accused of using the United States mail for attempted extortion. Each was found guilty and sentenced to thirty-seven years in prison. If they were ever paroled by the state of California, the men would be placed immediately in a federal prison.

In the same courtroom, Mona Galleghen and Loretta Woody— each insisted she learned about the kidnapping from the newspapers—were found guilty on the same charge. The judge sentenced Galleghen to two years in prison and ten years probation; Woody to eighteen months in prison and ten years probation.

Had a reward been posted, officers Burris and Gearhard surely would have been the recipients. Neither had anything to do with the kidnapping investigation, but their dictograph surveillance of the North Harvard Boulevard apartment building was instrumental in solving the case. But no reward was offered. Perhaps to compensate in some small measure, Gettle presented the men with spanking new .38 caliber police specials—weapons that were "guaranteed to be poison to the underworld," quipped the *Times*.

Chapter 8: Sour Notes Played by Amateurs

The organ was Dr. Skeele's passion. It was the focus of his study at Oberlin College and figured prominently at Amherst, where he completed graduate and postgraduate work. However, necessity placed the organ in a modest role. He had assumed the role as dean of the school of music at the University of Southern California in 1895. It was Skeele's mandate to provide students with an education that encompassed the broad spectrum of serious music.

Quite naturally, the professor sought an outlet for his passion. Hence, since 1925, he spent Sunday evenings at a Los Angeles church where Dr. Skeele commanded what some musicians called the lion of instruments.

It follows, then, that Mary Bosworth Skeele, long the educator's devoted wife, spent Sunday evenings attending to her own interests. They were relaxing times dedicated to reading, chatting on the telephone with friends and family, or catching up on correspondence.

Shortly after 8:00, on the evening of February 5, 1933, Mary answered the telephone hoping it might be her son Franklin. Instead, an unknown man with urgency in his voice told her that Dr. Skeele, the victim of an automobile accident, was at North Side Emergency Hospital. A car was moments away, the man told her, and would pick her up and take her to the hospital.

Figure 8.1 Walter Skeele instructing a student.
Doheny Memorial Library, University of Southern California

Mary drew in her breath, braced herself, and placed a call to her son. Speaking as calmly as possible, she related details of the stranger's message. Franklin told her he would leave immediately and meet her at the hospital.

Just then, a car stopped in front of the house and she told Franklin she was leaving. A moment later, the bell rang and Mary opened the door to encounter a strange man wearing a concerned expression. She donned a wrap and followed him to a coupe parked curbside. He opened the passenger door and she entered the automobile.

Franklin sped to the hospital, arriving before his mother. With certain knowledge that she would do the same, he went directly to the desk and asked the clerk to direct him to Professor Walter F. Skeele's room. The young woman checked the register and looked at him askance. She told him she had no record of a patient by that name. With mild annoyance, he asked her to check again. Rechecking, she found no one named Skeele listed in her register.

Myriad thoughts coursed through Franklin's mind. Perhaps his father, forgetting his wallet, was lying on a gurney unconscious and unidentified. Quickly, he described Dr. Skeele—tall, bespectacled, dignified in demeanor, a habitual bow tie about his neck, 68 years old. The clerk shook her head. The hospital knew the identity of every patient, she told him.

Franklin was mystified. Perhaps he misunderstood his mother and had come to the wrong hospital. That Mary had not yet arrived lent credence to

Figure 8.2 Mrs. Mary Skeele. *San Francisco History Center, San Francisco Public Library*

the notion. Yet, still, he felt certain she told him North Side Emergency Hospital.

He crossed the lobby, entered a telephone booth, and asked the operator to connect him to his father's church. Perhaps someone there had information. While spilling out his story to an anonymous voice, the listener cut him short and asked him to hold. A moment later, Dr. Skeele came on the line.

Accident? What accident? His astonishment paralleled Franklin's own.

Father and son recognized immediately that something was seriously amiss. It was not in Mary's character to make up stories. They agreed to meet forthwith at the family home. Then, after his father signed off the line, Franklin clicked the receiver and told the operator to connect him to the Los Angeles Police Department.

Maneuvering city streets at a breakneck pace, the Skeele men arrived at the house—136 South Avenue 55—almost simultaneously, but mere seconds before detectives from the LAPD converged on the scene.

Wedged into the front door jam was a slip of paper. Pasted on the outside were the music dean's name, title, university affiliation, and home address. The inside text was formed by letters snipped from magazines and newspapers, inserted at intervals between typewritten letters. Mary Skeele, stated the note, was in the hands of kidnappers. Should Dr. Skeele meet a $10,000 ransom demand by 5:30 the following afternoon, they would spare her life, releasing her unharmed. Should he fail, Mrs. Skeele was a dead woman. Contained within the note were detailed instructions about delivery of the ransom money. It was decided immediately to assemble a dummy package. Under police surveillance, Dr. Skeele would satisfy the kidnapper's demands.

Following the note's instructions, they waited until the following morning. Then, lawmen escorted Skeele to a designated spot on Montecito Drive, a winding boulevard that began at Griffin Avenue, climbed a hilltop, and emerged on the other side at North Broadway. There, beside a culvert, they found a pasteboard carton. Beneath it was a hollow tile containing yet another note fashioned from letters scissored from publications and sandwiched between typescript:

"Walk to your left across the street to the [road] bank. Here will be a box in a hole in the bank with final instructions. We like tricks," concluded the cryptic missive, "but prefer to keep them out of business."

In the road bank some seventy-five feet distant, they found a cracker box containing additional instructions. The message was weighted by a stone, around which was tied a length of string. It read: "Tie package thoroughly to this end of string and go on your way."

The officers did as instructed—almost. Rather than leave the package of phony money and go on their way, they followed the length of string. It led them over an embankment to the lower level of a winding road, some 700 feet from its starting point. There, covered by dirt, the string ended.

It occurred to the officers that the deep ravine they were in was observable from any one of a number of higher points. It was a mistake to have followed the string. Mrs. Skeele's kidnappers might be watching them at that very moment.

Yet another thought occurred to them. The very complexity of the kidnappers' instructions, coupled with their demand to tie a $10,000 bundle of bills to a 700-foot length of string, was a strong indication that they were dealing with rank amateurs. It was a chilling notion. Amateurs were prone to panic, and panic often induced rash behavior. It was altogether possible that the LAPD had inadvertently put Mary Skeele at greater risk.

The officers did not make Professor Skeele privy to their uneasiness. Indeed, he found a modicum of comfort in the fact that they had met the kidnappers' ransom demand—ostensibly, at least.

Throughout the day, scores of detectives concealed themselves at strategic points within the immediate vicinity, hoping the kidnappers would make an appearance. They did not. Near the Montecito hilltop, however, police took a half dozen suspects into custody. They later released them all. Then, as the 5:30 P.M. deadline approached, a roadster carrying three suspicious-looking men stopped their vehicle near the money drop. In seconds, armed detectives surrounded the startled trio. They were not the kidnappers.

Meantime, detectives interviewed Skeele neighbors and relatives. They spoke with the professor's colleagues on the university music faculty, as well as members of the church where Dr. Skeele plied his passion. Not a single person knew of any reason why he would be the target of an extortion plot. It simply made no sense. The college dean was, by the very nature of his profession, a man of modest means. By any standard of reason, $10,000 in cash during the height of the Great Depression was an unapproachable sum.

Even had Skeele possessed $10,000, the kidnappers' timing could not have been worse. At that very moment, the nation's banking system teetered on the verge of collapse as depositors across the country queued up at tellers' windows to liquidate their accounts. The money supply was in a dismal state and few banks were in a position to accommodate such a large withdrawal.

The only substantial clue yet revealed was found on the outside of the ransom note. The kidnappers had cut Skeele's name and address from a page in the USC College of Music yearbook. Investigators learned that a limited number of subscribers had received the yearbook less than a week prior to the kidnapping. Nonetheless, the clue's implications were vague.

The 5:30 deadline passed with no attempt made by the kidnappers to claim the bogus ransom. Disheartening as it was, there was nothing police could do but push ahead vigorously with the investigation and hope against hope that Mrs. Skeele's abductors would contact her husband. They knew from experience, however, that with each passing hour the likelihood of finding the victim alive diminished.

They kept a vigil at the Skeele residence where, throughout the evening, the professor and his son Franklin stayed close to the telephone. The only calls came from concerned friends and relatives, each dropping off the phone quickly in an effort to keep the line open.

It was just past 8:00 P.M. when the doorbell rang. Yet another detective had arrived, thought Franklin, who crossed the room and opened the door. In an instant, Dr. Skeele heard his son cry, "Mother!"

Mary Skeele stood at the front door.

For reasons known only to them, the kidnappers released their victim. As a matter of fact, they drove her home and dropped her off just a block away from the Skeele residence.

Mary was unharmed save for a scratch or two, and, despite a traumatic ordeal pressed on a 65-year-old woman, her story was told with the kind of calm dispassion that marked her disposition.

As Mary's incredible tale unfolded, detectives followed promising leads. Two blocks from the ransom pickup point, neighbors told of odd behavior by a couple at 1195 Montecito Drive. The house, they knew, was owned by a woman, and rumor had it that the property was in foreclosure. It did not appear that the owner was living there—she owned another home in Pasadena—but occasionally she appeared at odd hours in the company of a strange man. They always parked down the block at a considerable distance from the house, and they always entered through a side door. A prying neighbor told the detectives that the man was her new husband. His name was Parsons, she said, and he worked at a Los Angeles rescue mission.

They considered the clue sufficiently important to rush a squad of detectives to 623 Buckeye Street in Pasadena. There, neighbors told stories about the "mystery woman of the neighborhood." Until perhaps six months prior, the woman lived there alone. Then the man materialized, but there seemed to be no consistency about his movements. For the last two weeks, the blinds were drawn night and day, and the only light was seen at the rear of the house.

No one in the area really knew the woman, but neighbors thought her to be in her mid-thirties. She drove a tan Chevrolet coupe. The neighborhood buzz claimed she was a graduate of USC, where she had earned a degree from the college of music about five years prior.

Immediately, the house was placed under surveillance and so was the dwelling on Montecito Drive. Hours later, following Mrs. Skeele's dramatic reappearance, a Chevrolet coupe stopped at the curb a few doors down from the Montecito house. A man and

Figure 8.3 Luella Pearl Hammer.
San Francisco History Center,
San Francisco Public Library

woman emerged from the automobile, walked swiftly up the block, and proceeded to the side door of 1195. A regiment of no-nonsense police officers met them there.

Arrested as suspects in the Skeele kidnapping were Luella Pearl Hammer and her companion, a man who gave his name as W. D. Howard. The police handcuffed the pair and whisked them off in a squad car to the Highland Park police station. During the booking process, officers discovered a slip of paper tucked away in the woman's purse. The paper had the names Mary B. Skeele, Walter F. Skeele, and Franklin Skeele written on it.

Hammer sought to diminish its importance by telling officers that for no particular reason she jotted down the names after reading in the newspapers about the kidnapping.

Although they had arrested the suspects solely on circumstantial evidence, police were confident that Hammer and Howard were the culprits they sought. They separated the two, with Howard kept at Highland and Hammer taken to the Lincoln Heights station. Hour upon hour of intensive questioning commenced.

It was learned that Hammer was a 35-year-old divorcée, born at Mountain Lake, Minnesota, in September 1897. She was a classically trained musician, who earned a degree in 1929 from the USC College of Music, where Dr. Skeele was her dean. An on-again, off-again music teacher, her principal source of income was buying, selling, and renting houses. Lately, however, erratic behavior, poor money management, and the vagary of the Great Depression were taking a toll on her finances. Hammer was chronically in debt and on the verge of losing two houses to foreclosure.

Fingerprints revealed that Howard was not Howard at all, but a 39-year-old career criminal named Earl H. Van Dorn, who sported a list of aliases the length of his forearm. He first came to the attention of California authorities during the fall of 1929, when he forged a stolen payroll check and bought a used Ford automobile from Standard Motors in San Francisco. He pilfered a set of license plates from another vehicle and got as far as La Mar, Colorado, where he was arrested by the keen-eyed chief of police and extradited to California. The court tried, convicted, and sentenced Van Dorn to San Quentin for a term of one to fourteen years. He gained parole in May 1931. Apparently, he met Hammer about six months prior to the kidnapping. Both claimed that he was her handyman.

As the interrogation continued, Dr. and Mrs. Skeele made themselves scarce. Their daughter, identified only as Mrs. Walter Humphreys, told a reporter for the *Los Angeles Times* that her mother was taking a needed rest: "She has always been a quiet little woman—and so sweet—and this has disturbed her. But she will be all right again soon. She just wishes to get away from it for a while."

Apparently, Mrs. Humphreys tended toward understatement.

Meantime, a thorough search of both Hammer residences unearthed a Royal typewriter, old and battered and hidden beneath clothing in an antique trunk found in an upstairs bedroom. In quick time, a police expert examined the keys and determined that the machine had produced portions of the ransom notes left at the drop. The giveaway was the pattern left by a chipped "t."

Detectives made a curious discovery in the garage of the Montecito house. There officers found five sets of 1932 automobile license plates. They found a sixth set in Hammer's Chevrolet coupe.

At the same time, a neighborhood postman came forward and told authorities he saw men in Hammer's backyard the afternoon of the kidnapping, busying themselves with what appeared to be a tangled skein of cord. When shown the string officers followed into a gorge near Hammer's Montecito residence, the man was unable to provide positive identification, but said it was similar in appearance.

It was a telltale sign of either financial distress or odd eccentricity that the interior of the Montecito house revealed definite signs of recent and continued habitation, yet the electricity was not in service, there was no running water and the telephone was disconnected. An oil lamp was the only source of light, and the dwelling was in a state of squalor.

During a second day of intense grilling, Chief of Detectives Joe Taylor repeatedly shouted at Van Dorn, telling him what a despicable thing it was to snatch a 65-year-old woman from her home and treat her roughly. At last, the suspect snapped. "We didn't treat her roughly at all," he blurted out, unthinkingly.

That cinched it. Hours later, a twenty-six page confession was in the hands of the LAPD. Immediately, the Los Angeles County grand jury, then in session, was asked to indict Van Dorn and Hammer on kidnapping charges. The court fixed bail at $100,000 apiece—ten times more than the imponderable ransom demand made by the kidnappers.

Hammer, who was no stranger to self-serving verbiage, had a long chat with a reporter from the Associated Press. "There is nothing I can say to excuse myself, and if I'm convicted, I'll just have to take my medicine," she told him, contritely. Then, feeling sorry for herself, she said, "I guess I am a victim of circumstances. But I'm not the first woman who has found herself in this sort of situation because she believed in a man whom she loved and allowed herself to be led by his judgment. And to think, here I sit in jail, faced, perhaps, with a life term in prison—I, who started out to be a great concert musician."

If police would bring Mrs. Skeele by, Hammer told the reporter, she would like to tell her how sorry she was.

Her statement revealed for the first time that a romantic link existed between the suspects. It revealed little else about Hammer's real disposition.

Later, she displayed a less engaging side of an inconsistent persona. When police came to the jail to take her before the grand jury, she burst into a fit of hysterics. She refused to leave her cell, and she refused to testify. "I didn't kidnap anybody," she screamed between sobs. "I didn't make a confession."

When reminded that she had confessed, she said she would deny everything. "I'm crazy," she shrieked. "I don't know what I said. Whatever it was, it wasn't true. I won't talk! I won't talk!"

Van Dorn, apparently roused by affection—or pity—for his beleaguered colleague, took full responsibility for the kidnapping: "I alone was instigator of the plot and by force and through fear used Miss Hammer against her wishes, by gaining her confidence and using her knowledge of facts."

He said he intended to "plead guilty at once" and "take it on the chin."

Not withstanding his magnanimous gesture, Van Dorn was loath to play it straight. He named two men, Billy Stillwell and E. R. Lindstrom, as accomplices and sent the LAPD on an extended fool's errand. Then to cover himself, he told authorities, "That may not even be their right names. They probably gave me a couple of bum ones."

In a matter of days, authorities concluded that the couple in custody acted alone.

In addition to phantom accomplices, there were glaring inconsistencies between his and Hammer's stories. Van Dorn said he inserted the ransom note in the Skeele door jam. Hammer said she did it. He claimed to have been alone when he fetched Mrs. Skeele from her home. She claimed she drove the car. Van Dorn insisted two other men were involved in the kidnapping. Hammer insisted that they acted alone.

Revealing titillating information heretofore untold, both parties agreed on one point: They needed money to save Hammer's properties from foreclosure. After all, they would need a place to live after they were blissfully wed.

The couple's marriage plan was not received with universal accord. Having followed the case closely, the *Fresno Bee-Republican* penned an acidic editorial: "It is likely to be some time now before they can be married, and that is not something to cry about. Married, they might produce more of their kind, and the world has far too many of their kind as it is."

Sifting through every scrap of paper found in both Hammer residences, police discovered an intriguing document written in the accused woman's hand. It was a list of motion pictures stars and included their addresses and telephone numbers. Among the actors listed were notable names: Mary Pickford, Constance Talmage, Harold Lloyd, Buster Keaton, Adolphe Menjou, and Mary Philibin.

When asked by police if they compiled the document as a list of possible kidnap victims, Hammer replied, "No, that's foolish."

Van Dorn appeared genuinely puzzled by the list. "I know nothing about it," he told lawmen, staring intently at it. Then he just shrugged it off by saying, "It looks to me like some of her monkey business."

An intriguing exchange occurred when a man whom police failed to identify walked into the Highland Park station and told officers he was an old friend of Hammer's mother and two sisters. The mother, he said, resided in Massachusetts, but the sisters lived in the Los Angeles area. The siblings requested that he act as intermediary between them and their incarcerated sister.

A decade prior, he asserted, Miss Hammer "got crazy notions." She left home, and a permanent estrangement followed. The sisters had no desire to see her, but they were anxious that she receive the basic necessities. They were anxious as well, he added, that the errant woman's predicament remain a secret from their mother.

The police directed the stranger to the Lincoln Heights station where Hammer was held. He left and was not heard from again.

On February 20, fifteen days after the Skeele kidnapping, the accused couple stood for a preliminary hearing in superior court. Refusing to enter a plea, Luella Hammer stood mute as the judge entered a double plea of not guilty and not guilty by reason of insanity. The court appointed three psychiatrists to examine the woman prior to the court date to determine if she was sane.

Van Dorn, in a reversal of his stated intent, followed his lawyer's advice and pleaded not guilty, as well. The judge slated the trial for March 9, before the bench of superior court judge William Tell Aggeler.

Two events of no little import, however, placed a kink in the court schedule. On March 4, Franklin D. Roosevelt was sworn in as president of the United States. Two days later, on March 6, in an effort to halt a nationwide run on banks, the new chief executive declared a bank holiday. His decree effectively shut down the nation's financial machinery. The crisis clogged the courts and necessitated postponement of the kidnapping trial until April 5.

"The continuance was made," acknowledged the *Times*, "because of the congested condition of the court calendar."

By the end of the month, three-quarters of the nation's banks reopened. The crisis was on the mend, and the Skeele kidnapping trial was able to proceed as scheduled.

Despite her assertions to the contrary, the court appointed psychiatrists declared Hammer sane. Displeased by their prognosis, however, she stated that she intended to stand trial on the original court-mandated plea of not guilty by reason of insanity.

The jury was selected with uncommon efficiency. In a matter of hours, nine men and three women were chosen to hear the case. Later in the day, the court called Mrs. Skeele as the state's first witness.

"The 65-year-old woman told a story of a night of terror in a prison house where she was taken bound hand and foot, gagged, blindfolded, and her ears stuffed with cotton," recited the *Times* with dramatic effect.

Drama, however, was not evident in Mrs. Skeele's voice. Instead, she described her harrowing experience in a calm, straightforward recitation. She told the jury about the telephone call alleging an automobile accident and her husband's hospitalization:

> I telephoned to my son Franklin telling him of the report, and then prepared to accompany the driver when he arrived.
>
> Soon the doorbell rang and I opened the door. There I saw the defendant Van Dorn. I went down the walk with him to a coupe standing at the curb. Van Dorn entered the car with me and had some difficulty in starting the motor. When it started a woman stepped around the car and took the wheel, driving away.
>
> They started the car down the hill. Van Dorn suddenly placed his hands over my mouth. I fought him bitterly, but he succeeded in gagging me and threw a blanket over my head. He told me that he would use chloroform unless I went quietly. I fought for some time and finally found the handle of the car door, which I opened and one foot touched the ground as I tried to escape.
>
> He jumped out and threw me back in the car between them and put the blanket back over my head. By that time my strength was gone. We rode on and arrived at a house, entering a side door. I heard the clock strike ten, ten minutes after we entered.

It was then that they bound Mary's hands and feet, stuffing her ears with cotton. However, the stuffing did not produce its desired effect. Through a long and sleepless night, the victim heard muffled voices and the unsettling sound of a revolver's hammer clicking on empty cylinders.

In the morning, Mary was given a breakfast of toast and coffee and, much to her astonishment, was told by her kidnappers that they would take her home providing she agreed "not to make a rumpus." At lunchtime, they gave her a bowl of tomato soup, and they made the same promise. All the while, they kept her confined to a bedroom and the blindfold remained in place.

Apparently, during the night, Hammer and Van Dorn reasoned that they were somewhat less-than-proficient kidnappers. They sensed that men in dark suits seen about the neighborhood were detectives, and neither had the courage to check the money drop to see if the ransom had been paid. Perhaps, if they took Mrs. Skeele home, she would tell folks she was on a lark and her kidnapping was a playful hoax. Surely, if they let her go, law enforcement authorities would realize they were not really kidnappers.

Much later, under the cover of darkness, the abductors led Mary to their car. "They drove about for about an hour," she told the court. Shortly before eight o'clock, the automobile stopped, the abductors removed her blindfold for the first time in twenty-four hours, and released their victim. She recognized familiar surroundings and knew at once that she was in her own neighborhood. In a few minutes, Mrs. Skeele rang her own doorbell.

On more than a few occasions, Luella Hammer's behavior interrupted court proceedings. She laughed aloud, made odd clucking sounds, and waved her arms over her head. Either the interruptions were calculated by a sane woman trying to convince the jury of her insanity, or they were the outbursts of a woman suffering a form of mental illness.

When trial resumed the following day, Earl Van Dorn asked to address the court. Granted permission, he rose to his feet and, without hesitation, declared that he wanted to change his plea to guilty. Judge Aggeler accepted the plea and instructed a bailiff to escort Van Dorn from the courtroom to his jail cell.

"As the import of the situation dawned on Miss Hammer," chronicled a *Times* reporter, "the woman moaned and cried aloud in the courtroom, creating such a disturbance that an adjournment was

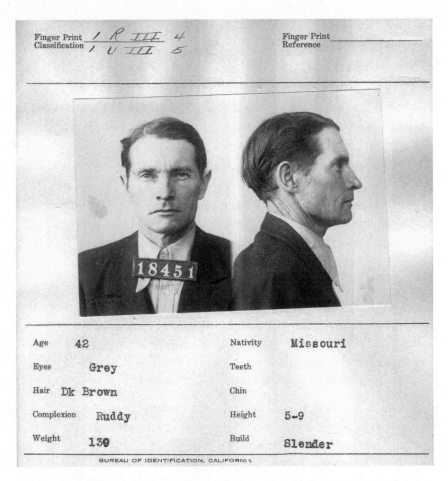

| Finger Print Classification | 1 R III 4 | | Finger Print Reference | |
| 1 U III 5 | | | | |

Age 42   Nativity Missouri

Eyes Grey   Teeth

Hair Dk Brown   Chin

Complexion Ruddy   Height 5-9

Weight 130   Build Slender

BUREAU OF IDENTIFICATION, CALIFORNIA

Figure 8.4 California state prison record card, Earl Van Dorn.
California State Archives

taken while attendants from the county jail hospital were called to quiet her. Failing, the trial was put over until [the following day]."

Reporters from other papers who witnessed the scene said the accused woman "collapsed," and they characterized her behavior as "hysterical."

The judge appointed two psychiatrists to examine Hammer and to report the following day concerning her present mental condition. Consequently, when court resumed the next morning, the psychiatrists were the first witnesses called. Both told Aggeler the woman was sane.

In closing arguments, Hammer's lawyer, Nathan O. Freedman, insisted that his client was mentally unbalanced. At the same time, he embraced Van Dorn's testimony that Hammer had no part in the abduction. Freedman's generous naivete was in vain.

On April 10, the court sentenced Van Dorn to a term of ten years to life. Moments later, they led him from the courtroom to begin his journey to Folsom Prison.

Later that afternoon, the jury convicted Hammer of kidnapping Mary Skeele. Characterized as a stunning example of an open-and-shut case, the jury deliberated for less than an hour.

Since Hammer had pleaded not guilty by reason of insanity, state law mandated that the jury determine her sanity during a second phase of the trail.

The sanity hearing commenced the following day, when four alienists testified that the convicted kidnapper was sane. Each man agreed that Hammer was feigning insanity—that her courtroom antics were a ploy to convince the jury she was of unsound mind.

Three county jail matrons disagreed. Since the beginning of her incarceration, her behavior was erratic, they testified. She imagined that they had placed sound detectors in her cell to record not only her speech, but her innermost thoughts as well. The matrons observed the inmate in animated conversations with herself, her hands in constant motion.

Hammer's brother-in-law, a North Dakota banker, testified that at one time she owned six houses. Each sat idle, however, because of her irrational refusal to rent them. He also told of disjointed and nonsensical conversations that led him to believe she was insane.

For the second time in as many days, the efficient jury reached an expeditious verdict. Hammer was sane.

"The woman, constantly attended by a deputy sheriff, accepted the verdict quietly, continuing to make meaningless motions with

Age	76	Nat.	Calif
Eyes	BLUE	Teeth	Fair
Hair	Bon	Chin	Ro
Complexion	Fair	English Height	5-3
Weight	115	Build	Med

Figure 8.5 California state prison record card, Luella Pearl Hammer.
California State Archives

her hands," reported the *Times*. "As she was led from the courtroom she hummed a tune and waved good-bye to the group of curious spectators who had remained to hear the findings of the jury."

On April 17, Judge Aggeler imposed on Hammer a sentence of ten years to life, and remanded her to San Quentin Penitentiary. As the judge pronounced sentence, the convicted woman began laughing hysterically, screaming and applauding.

Aggeler was unmoved: "The actions of the defendant … are further proof in my judgment that she is feigning insanity."

The following week, Hammer was taken by train to San Quentin. "She just yelled all night," complained the deputy sheriff who escorted her. "She kept the passengers awake, running up and down the Pullman corridor."

Whether sane or not, Luella Pearl Hammer would not pay the price of her folly quietly.

Chapter 9: To Snatch a Priest

I was standing on the sidewalk in front of my home when I saw a light touring car draw up to the church and stop," recalled Mary Bianchi, an observant neighbor who lived across the street from the church. "A man of small stature turned out the lights of the machine, got out, and walked to the pastor's house. He wore a soft hat pulled down over his eyes, and [driving] goggles. As he approached the house he drew the collar of his overcoat up about his face."

Inside the rectory—it was a large, two-story structure adjacent Colma's Holy Angels Church—housekeeper Marie Wendel heard a rap at the door. The caller was a stranger who told Wendel he needed to see Father Heslin on an urgent matter. The short man wearing a dark suit, whom she described as "considerably excited," mumbled in a foreign accent something unintelligible about "a death call."

Wendel summoned the priest. He listened patiently as the man hastened through his story: A relative lingered near death. Last rites must be given at once. They should leave immediately.

The priest asked the man to wait while he went to the church to retrieve appropriate sacraments. He returned in a few minutes, told the stranger he was prepared to accompany him, and followed him to the automobile, parked curbside. As they got into the car,

Wendel overheard bits of conversation, including the mention of San Pedro Road.

Bianchi observed the scene from her vantage point across the street: "It was about five minutes after nine when they drove off." Noting that the stranger failed to turn on the vehicle's headlights, she watched as they headed toward the Pedro Mountains.

Rarely did Father Heslin leave the parsonage at night, and Wendel worried about the driver's ability to negotiate a heavy fog blanketing the landscape. "I was very tired," she recalled, "but I decided to wait and get the father a bite to eat when he came back from his cold, wet drive."

The housekeeper busied herself with make-work chores. Ordinarily, on the few occasions the priest was out at night, Wendel waited up for him. "When eleven o'clock came, I was so very weary that I thought I would go to bed." Father Heslin, she reasoned, would return soon. Should he be hungry, there were ample leftovers for a snack.

It was August 2, 1921.

By 6:30 the following morning, Wendel was up and about. She recalled:

> I made the fire and put the coffee on. Then I thought I would ring the church bell … for the seven o'clock mass. I started out, but decided to rap on [Father Heslin's] door for fear he had overslept after his hard night ride. I rapped at the door, but got no reply. Then I rapped again and finally opened the door to call in. When I saw his bed was untouched, I was very much alarmed.
>
> I did not know what to do at first. I thought I would get the car and go and look for him, for I was sure that he met with an accident on the road. Then I remembered the car was in the repair shop.

Stranded and helpless to act, she telephoned Monsignor James Cantwell, a close friend of Heslin's, at diocese headquarters in San

Francisco. He, too, feared the priest had met with an accident and suggested Wendel notify the police.

She did. She gave authorities a description of the vehicle and told them of hearing talk about the San Pedro Road.

Colma constable Silvio A. Landini was all too familiar with drivers who challenged soupy nights and, consequently, failed to negotiate curves obscured by fog. He ordered a thorough search of the cliffs skirting the snake-like road into the Pedro Valley between Colma and Half Moon Bay. It was possible that the priest and his mysterious driver had plunged to injury or death at some treacherous point on the highway. He told his deputies to search ravines and creek bottoms along the mountain road.

Lawmen, parishioners, and concerned citizens came together in a massive search effort. When, after two days, the search yielded no tangible results, peace officers reluctantly conceded that foul play was a possibility.

All the while, a startling development had been kept under wraps. When it became apparent that silence was no longer useful, authorities released the information to the media. On August 5, California newspapers rolled off the presses with a garish display of shocking headlines. Perhaps most sensational was that of the *Oakland Tribune*: "Missing Colma Priest in Chains in San Mateo Hills—Tortured as Kidnappers Wait Delivery of Ransom."

A ransom letter—partially typewritten, partially scrawled—ranked among the most bizarre ever produced by a ransom-seeking kidnapper. Dated August 3, the day after the priest's disappearance, and mailed special delivery to Archbishop Edward J. Hanna at St. Mary's Cathedral in San Francisco, it read, in part:

> Act with caution for I have father Heslin of Colma in bootleg cellar, where a candle light is left burning when I leave and at bottom of candle are all the chemicals necessary to generate enough poison to gas to kill a dozen men and as he is fastened with chains you will see that he is in a very bad way and if I am arrested or bothered in any way I will leave him just where he

is and in two hours from the time I leave him he will be dead
for the candle will not burn more than an hour and a half after
I leave him for I cut it that length.

 If any door is open to this cellar by anyone except myself
it will ignite a bunch of matches and upset a can of gasoline
on top of him and the entire police force and all your damn
knights would not be able to get the chains off him before he
would burn to death.

"Knights" was a reference to the Knights of Columbus, then
meeting at a convention in San Francisco. Several members of the
organization volunteered to search for the missing priest, and a few
speculated to reporters about Heslin's disappearance.

The chilling missive demanded ransom in the sum of $6,500—"in
fives, tens, twenties, fifties, and hundreds, but none higher than
hundreds." The kidnapper gave detailed, if somewhat convoluted,
instructions for delivery of the money, but seemed fixated more on
his willingness to commit murder. Should the delivery person look
suspicious, "he will be tagged with a hand grenade, as I have six of
them ready for treachery ...."

The writer implied that service in France during World War I
stripped his conscience of any reluctance to kill:

 [I]f anything arouses my suspicion I will leave him to die
right where he is. I had charge of a machine gun in the Ar-
gonne, and poured thousands of bullets into struggling men
and killing is no novelty to me, besides it will be your own
bunch that will kill him if you do not do just as you are told.

Another note containing additional instructions would follow,
wrote the kidnapper. He concluded by suggesting that when the
victim was exchanged for ransom, a doctor ought to be included in
the party: "Had-to-hit him four times and he is unconscious from
pressure on the brain so better hurry and no fooling."

Surely, the rambling note was the product of a diabolical mind.
"The letter is weird in the extreme and yet there runs through it a
serious and even sinister note that saves it from being ridiculous,"

wrote the *San Francisco Chronicle*. "It differs materially in many respects from the ordinary 'crank' letters with which the police are thoroughly familiar. All in all, the police authorities are convinced the missing priest is in grave danger, and every effort is being put forth to discover his whereabouts."

Two handwriting experts carefully scrutinized the letter and both agreed, "The writer is a fanatic who harbors animosity toward the Roman Catholic Church." Neither man believed that ransom was the principal motive behind the kidnapping. They indicated as well that block printing at the bottom of the letter "is a script often used by demented persons." The letter was composed on "a cheap grade of bond," lacking any watermarks. "The sheets are half-sheets, white and of the same grade known in offices as 'second sheets.'" Type style, font size, and the space between letters were strong indications that the typewriter was a Corona.

Authorities had reason to theorize that Father Heslin was a random victim chosen, perhaps, at the last minute. The kidnapper had typewritten the first sentence of the ransom letter—"Act with caution for I have father Heslin of Colma in bootleg cellar …."— except for the words *Heslin* and *Colma*, which were scribbled in pencil after the note was completed.

A week prior to his kidnapping, Heslin had transferred to Colma from a parish in Turlock. He was largely unknown in his new parish. The notion of the priest making enemies in a week's time seemed unlikely. Some authorities speculated the perpetrator was holding the San Francisco diocese for ransom, and the priest was only a surrogate victim.

If indeed the choice was random, that fact would put to rest other emerging theories. Constable Landini, for instance, theorized early on that robbery might have been a motive. Apparently, Heslin purchased several thousand dollars worth of Liberty Bonds during the late war, and he was known to own oil stocks. Authorities found neither bonds nor stocks among the priest's possessions at the rectory.

A theory attributed to San Francisco chief of police Daniel O'Brien was more elaborate. Father Heslin, so the story went, left the parish house to administer the last rights to a gangster of "foreign birth." The man rose suddenly from his deathbed and gasped out a murder confession. Gang members and relatives of the dying man feared the priest would report his confession to the police. Consequently, they kidnapped him.

Committed to a gangster theory as well, Constable Landini was convinced that Heslin was held in an "underworld resort," a "well-known Italian roadhouse" between Colma and Salada Beach. The constable assembled a raiding party of fifty officers. His effort netted a cache of illegal liquor—Prohibition was the law of the land—and a number of "girls" of "the nightlife." It did not produce clues relative to the kidnapping.

Not surprisingly, sightings of the kidnapped priest were as numerous as theories. Within an hour after the time Father Heslin left the rectory, someone spotted a priest near Mission San Jose. In the company of four men, he was in an automobile traveling at a high rate of speed.

The next day, another observer spied a priest, "in all probability, Father Heslin," struggling in an automobile near San Luis Obispo. "Two men were holding a third, dressed in a priest's habiliments, who was making a furious effort to escape from the machine," reported the *Chronicle*. "A second automobile, carrying two men, kept close to the car in which the priest struggled."

On the day of the Mission San Jose sighting, another sighting came from Mayfield (Palo Alto) in Santa Clara County. The next day, the priest appeared at Montara, in San Mateo County. Other sightings included Napa and Lake Alta in the Sierra Nevada.

Four men told authorities they repaired an automobile in which Heslin was a passenger. It was a case of mistaken identity. So were the other sightings.

Monsignor Cantwell took a call from an unidentified woman in possession of "inside" information about the kidnapping. She said Father Heslin was a prisoner in a cave near a ranch in the Portola Hills. A search of the cave revealed a crackpot caller, but no priest.

Leads abounded, but none held any substance.

The *San Francisco Examiner* was correct when a reporter noted, "The running down of numberless clews brought not the slightest indication of [Heslin's] whereabouts."

The coast guard was alerted and agreed to keep a careful watch on the surf "in the belief that if murder has been committed it would be revealed by the washing of the priest's body upon the shore."

Meantime, Archbishop Hanna instructed all priests in the diocese to urge their parishioners to communicate at once the slightest bit of information that might be useful to law enforcement authorities.

Heslin's kidnapping entered its fifth day when residents of Colma held a town meeting "in the plain little schoolhouse." Implying that lynching would be difficult to avert, a *Chronicle* reporter wrote:

> There was a curious grim intensity about the meeting. Bronzed men, who looked as if they might have driven in from neighboring truck farms, sat with their work-gnarled hands resting on their knees and gazed straight ahead of them with determined eyes. The city lawyer who faces a jury made up of men with eyes like those knows that glittering pyramids of words will be of no avail.
>
> The spirit that has Colma in its grip is not the hysterical excitement that manifests itself in mob demonstration. It is quiet, and it is the more significant because it is quiet.
>
> The abductors of Father Heslin will have to reckon with all Colma, and the reckoning will not be an easy one.

On August 10, Archbishop Hanna received yet a second ransom note. "Don't be surprised to get this," it read. "It is to tell you Father Heslin is not dead. Neither is he injured yet. Fate has made me do this. Sickness and misery has compelled my action. I must have money. Please forgive this act if you can. Have $15,000 cash ready. You will hear from me very soon."

"Examination of the pen-printing," declared a police handwriting expert, "convinces me [the letter] is worth no more than a passing thought." Professing certainty of his analysis, the expert stated that, "The character of the writer is shown to be of a nature so weak and jellyfish-like that he would never have the requisite nerve to abduct any grown person, let alone a husky priest like Father Heslin."

In fact, San Francisco police detectives had written the letter with the archbishop's knowledge, in an effort to draw the kidnapper out. It proved unnecessary.

It is altogether possible that news reports of a $5,000 reward offered by priests of the San Francisco diocese for finding Father Heslin dead or alive were not lost on William A. Hightower. During the afternoon of August 11, the unemployed baker left his room at the Grand Southern Hotel on Mission Street and found his way to St. Mary's Cathedral. It was Hightower's notion to pay a drop-in visit to the archbishop. Not surprisingly, he was told that the prelate was in a conference and could not be disturbed.

A talkative sort, Hightower got to chatting with Ernest J. Hopkins, an *Examiner* reporter who was on a vigil in the archbishop's anteroom, feeding on morsels of news. During the course of a lively conversation, Hightower opined that the kidnapped priest was dead—and he knew where the body might be buried.

Sensing that he was about to scoop every newspaper in California, Hopkins took Hightower in tow and escorted him to the *Examiner* newsroom. City editor William M. Hines and San Francisco chief of police Daniel O'Brien joined them there—perhaps the most important people this odd man had ever met.

Nevertheless, it was Hightower's show from beginning to end, and he played the leading role with appropriate vitality.

The Saturday following Heslin's kidnapping, recounted Hightower, he bumped into Dolly Mason at the corner of Ellis and

Mason streets. Dolly, a 24-year-old "woman of the night life," was an acquaintance he made while working briefly in Salt Lake City. She was a "girl" who bobbed her hair, painted her lips, and rouged her cheeks, rolled down her stockings and wiggled to the rhythm of hot jazz, and willfully violated the Volstead Act in backdoor speakeasies. In a voice made breathless by excitement, this exciting young woman told him a bizarre tale.

A foreigner, "probably a Greek," came to her room in an advanced state of intoxication. While being "entertained," he babbled drunkenly about his hatred of all things Catholic, and about death and dying and killing. He showed her

Figure 9.1 William A. Hightower.
California State Archives

a revolver and, said Hightower, "she pretended to shrink from it in fear."

"You do right to be afraid of that gun," the foreigner said. "It has taken human life."

Thinking that his "incomplete and broken revelations" might have to do with the kidnapped priest, Dolly boldly asked him where he buried the body.

"He isn't alone," was the Greek's abstruse reply. "I've a man watching him all the time—a man who cooks flapjacks."

Dolly was unable to glean more from his "wandering brain."

Disjointed as the story was, Dolly's recitation of the foreigner's tale intrigued Hightower. He recalled a recent trip to the Colma region. Suddenly, the image of a roadside signboard "bearing a

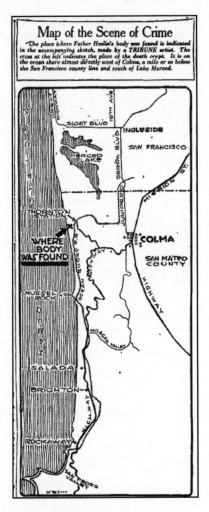

Map of the Scene of Crime

"The place where Father Heslin's body was found is indicated in the accompanying sketch, made by a TRIBUNE artist. The cross at the left indicates the place of the death crypt. It is on the ocean shore almost directly west of Colma, a mile or so below the San Francisco county line and south of Lake Merced.

Figure 9.2 Map of crime scene.
Oakland Tribune, 1921

picture of a man frying flapjacks" was vivid in his memory. "It might not be a real man who is watching that body," said Hightower to himself. "It might be a picture on a signboard."

The next day, Sunday, Hightower rented a Ford and drove out the Pedro Valley Road in search of the flapjack man. He found the signboard west of the roadway, just below a deserted railroad stop once called Thornton Station. Believing the priest was buried nearby, he made an intensive search.

Hopkins, the *Examiner* reporter who latched onto Hightower, described the area:

Toward the end of the Pedro Valley road, as it drops twisting down the hillside to Salada Beach, there is a spot where the road crosses the abandoned tracks of the Ocean Shore Railroad.

Westward from the road is a hollow of sand dunes, ceaselessly wind-whipped and broken by clumps of stunted gorse.

The edge of a line of cliffs is 250 yards from the highway at this point. The cliff, 150 feet high, overlooks the beach. [There is a] spot where the upper edge of the cliff had caved, leaving a level bench some 20 feet long and 12 feet in width. The floor of this bench is 10 feet below the upper lip of the cliff, and the inner wall is overhung, leaving a recess at the bottom.

Peering over the rim of the cliff, Hightower's eye was drawn to the low-lying bench. There, he saw a man's black scarf lodged by the wind into a crack in the cliff. After a moment's hesitation, he swung his legs over the sandy wall and dropped down ten feet to the shelf floor.

His effort found reward almost immediately. Lying in the sand was a .45 caliber cartridge. He poked about the sand with his fingers and brought out a piece of gunnysack stained with blood.

"That was enough for one day," said Hightower, overtaken by an eerie feeling. "I wanted to get away from there. I didn't feel like looking any further."

He took the .45 cartridge and the bloody bit of gunnysack and returned to his room at the Grand Southern Hotel.

Hightower told his listeners that he "pondered the matter thoroughly" for three days, believing more and more that Father Heslin's body was buried at the site. He made what he called "a single-handed search of San Francisco rooming houses" in an effort to locate Dolly Mason, but with no success. The young woman had remarked earlier that she might go to Portland, and Hightower assumed she had.

By August 11, the day this newsroom drama played out, the amateur sleuth's desire to learn more was "overwhelming." He took the streetcar to Colma and walked to the beach. Retracing the steps taken on his previous outing, he located the flapjack signboard with no difficulty and lowered himself over the sandy wall. The spot was undisturbed. He poked around and found more cartridges. The black scarf was still wedged into a crack and he left it there.

Apparently, his "overwhelming" desire to learn more quickly deserted him. He climbed back over the wall, returned to the streetcar stop in Colma, and headed for St. Mary's Cathedral in San Francisco. Naïveté led him to assume that Archbishop Hanna would welcome his intrusion. The archbishop was not so inclined.

Oddly enough, it did not occur to Hightower to notify the police about his discovery.

If a strange man sitting in his anteroom seeking an audience did not interest the archbishop, Chief O'Brien was more than pleased to accommodate Hightower and to meet with him in the offices of the *Examiner*. Not only did he sit patiently though the man's lengthy tale, he volunteered automobile transportation to the area Hightower described. As a matter of fact, the chief offered to drive his own vehicle, and the talkative stranger would be his special passenger.

Before leaving the *Examiner* building, O'Brien telephoned Colma, making arrangements with Constable Landini to join the party.

Fortunately, O'Brien drove a touring car large enough to accommodate Hightower, the city editor, a photographer, a staff writer, and reporter Hopkins.

"Threading the twisting curves of the Pedro Valley road through the drizzling fog, the party reached Thornton station and the flapjack advertisement shortly before 11:00," wrote Hopkins with the kind of sensational flair *Examiner* readers expected:

> Here Hightower took the lead. The others ploughed in his wake through quicksand and ghostly sand dunes, in a darkness that was lighted only by the dim phosphorescence of the sea.
>
> It was a fitting place for ghosts to flit by night—a fitting place for a murderer's deeds. The gale dashed sand in the eyes, and blew speech away before it could be heard. Through stunted black gorse that blotched the shadowy sand it sang like a murderer's wailing laughter.

The party expected one of three outcomes: an honest mistake, a hoax, or a grisly discovery.

Hightower scrambled over the wall. "This is the place," he called back.

The men negotiated the wall one by one, passing down the shovels. Hightower and George Lynn, the *Examiner* staff writer, began to dig. "The flare of lights revealed, just where the base of the sandy wall began to curve inward, the telltale marks of a pickaxe," observed Hopkins. "The earth was so soft that it came away readily to a mere scooping stroke of the shovel."

"Something's here," shouted Lynn.

Hopkins took the shovel and promptly discovered that a gentle thrust was met with dull resistance. "An instant later, a three-inch square of cloth was uncovered at the bottom of a conical hole," he wrote. "Landini lit a torch of paper and we knelt and peered into the hole."

In another moment, the constable's shovel uncovered a man's hand. The spadework stopped at once. After a brief conference, O'Brien, Landini, Hines, and Hightower returned to the chief's automobile and sped to a nearby farmhouse. There they rousted an artichoke farmer from his bed and commandeered lanterns from his storeroom.

Ten minutes later, the outcome was certain—and grisly. "The pitiful figure of the dead Father Heslin was brought to view among the gaunt shadows cast by the lanterns and the kneeling figures of the men," penned Hopkins.

Preliminary identification of the rapidly decomposing body was made by the clerical collar about the neck and a religious emblem attached to a gold watch chain. They found a bill of lading from the Southern Pacific Railroad, a pastor's railroad pass, auto repair bills from Turlock in his pocket—and, preserved in a red Moroccan leather case, bread and wine, the sacraments taken to a dying man who did not exist.

Sensibly, O'Brien ordered that all activity cease, that the corpse remain undisturbed until daylight. Seven men tramping about the area in the black of night could unwittingly destroy valuable evidence.

En route back to San Francisco, the entourage stopped nearby at the Mystery Castle, a deserted mansion atop a bluff overlooking Salada Beach. Its notorious history and close proximity to the

Figure 9.3 Dr. Galen Hickok, Mystery Castle.
San Francisco History Center, San Francisco Public Library

gravesite made officers wonder if there existed a connection to the Heslin murder.

A few months prior, a man calling himself Dr. Hickok was locked away at San Quentin. The man, whose checkered past included theft of a physician's license, operated the castle as a private hospital in which illegal operations were performed on young women in distress. Prior to Hickok's incarceration, law officers dug up the grounds surrounding the structure in search of bodies. None were found.

The men inspected the castle's interior and searched the grounds. Their examination revealed nothing germane to the case.

After their arrival at the Hall of Justice, Landini and O'Brien, along with several detectives who had been called from their beds, went into conference. The newspapermen went about their business.

Despite the late hour, the officers and reporters abandoned any notion of sleep. There was much to ponder, much to discuss. The night dragged endlessly, or so it seemed.

Meanwhile, Hightower slept soundly—in a heavily guarded cell in the city prison. For all his willing glibness, the unemployed baker had made himself the prime suspect in a gruesome murder.

Hopkins used the lull to gather his thoughts and scribble notes fashioned into dramatic prose. The completed copy appeared on the front page of the morning *Examiner*:

Was the man—calm, unemotional, cynical—who had led us straight to that spot in perfect darkness, in reality a fiend with [a] murder-spotted soul, driven by some morbid urge to return to the scene of his crime, bringing—of all people on earth—the police?

William A. Hightower had seemed to know too much. That was the outstanding fact about [him]. How much did Hightower really know?

He had known much—his actions showed that; he had given certain explanations, but in the light of day they seemed increasingly far-fetched. He was a strange man. How much did he know?

At dawn, police returned to the gravesite. Close examination revealed $80 in folded "greenbacks"—punctured by a bullet hole— inside the priest's pocket and $4.75 in silver coin. They also found a knife, fountain pen, pocket ruler, a case containing eyeglasses, and a bloodstained handkerchief.

Clearly, robbery was not the motive.

Lifted carefully from its sandy grave, the body was placed on a litter and carried to an ambulance belonging to the San Mateo County coroner's office. Men from nearby farms gathered near the road and watched in silence as the priest's remains were taken away.

Meantime, in the city prison, Hightower was shaken awake by a guard. Dressed and fed, he was turned over to Detective Captain Duncan Matheson and taken by automobile to his Mission Street hotel room. There they joined Detectives Tom Curtis and Phil Lindecker, who were sifting through Hightower's belongings.

They discovered the blood-soaked piece of burlap and .45 caliber cartridges Hightower claimed to have stumbled onto at the gravesite. They also found a late model Savage rifle, three boxes of bullets, a butcher's knife, a tent, and an assortment of newspapers. Each paper was earmarked at the story of Father Heslin's disappearance.

But one item—it was an astonishing find—stood out from the others. It was an ominous-looking device, fashioned of wood and steel, and held together by nuts and bolts and screws and wires. Hightower called it his "Infernal Machine."

Described by the *Chronicle* as "diabolical in its ingenuity and one of the most deadly things ever conceived," the Infernal Machine would simultaneously fire ten shells loaded with buckshot. The shells fit into short iron pipes set in a base of plaster of Paris. It utilized nails as firing pins, controlled by powerful springs. If placed on the ground, the iron pipes—the barrels—of the weapon were elevated. When fired from this position, the shot would strike its target waist high from a distance of twenty feet, with a radius of coverage equal to the width of an average roadway. The device could be fired from a remote location by pulling a string attached to the firing apparatus.

A volley from the Infernal Machine, declared the *Examiner*, "could mow down a platoon of advancing men."

Questioned by Matheson, Hightower explained that he was an inventor. He had designed the machine during the war for use by the army, but it failed to impress a committee of experts.

Not content to leave it at that, Hightower sought to impress the detectives with his knowledge of firearms, explosives, and deadly chemicals. Then, for inexplicable reasons, he told officers that he carried the Infernal Machine to the San Pedro Road. He intended to test fire the device and observe its action, but conditions less than ideal caused him to abandon the test.

Matheson wanted to see the proposed test area, and he insisted they leave immediately. The would-be inventor led them to a spot one mile above Colma on the San Pedro Road. It was on the direct route to Father Heslin's burial site.

Boasting about the machine's capability, Hightower told a tale about Father Brady, a parish priest in Oakland, who was well-connected to freedom fighters in Northern Ireland. He lugged the device across the bay and Brady watched as Hightower demonstrated its prowess. However, for reasons mystifying to the inventor, the priest was unimpressed.

It was a tale Hightower should not have told. A simple inquiry revealed that the Oakland parish never had a priest named Brady.

Caught in an obvious falsehood, Hightower was unperturbed. He misspoke, he told detectives. He had demonstrated the Infernal Machine to Father Murphy at Sacramento.

Murphy had no memory of a man named Hightower and no one ever spoke to him about such a weapon. Apparently, Hightower possessed an odd talent for self-incrimination.

It was a simple matter for police to theorize a practical use for the Infernal Machine in the Heslin kidnapping. Hightower, so the theory went, intended to place the device at a spot designated for the ransom delivery. To effect his getaway after the money drop, the machine would be set up to fire a lethal volley at any officer or group of officers who followed in pursuit.

The net closing around Hightower was tightening hour by hour as detectives learned that he was more than casually familiar with the area in which the body was discovered. In his initial conversation with Chief O'Brien, he mentioned long-abandoned Thornton Station and the location where tracks of the Ocean Shore Railroad crossed over the roadway.

In 1906, the now-defunct Ocean Shore Railroad employed Hightower as a cook for construction crews while laying track in that very location. His familiarity with Thornton Station was not coincidental.

The same year, immediately following San Francisco's catastrophic earthquake, Hightower was one of countless people who scavenged the rubble of fallen buildings in search of valuables. Like others involved in this unscrupulous activity, he needed a hiding place for his loot. Familiarity led him to the same area near Salada Beach, and there he buried a trunk containing "treasures."

As fate would have it, however, he was unable to reclaim his loot. Try as he did, he could not locate the hiding place. Consequently, his quest to find the trunk led to frequent excursions to Salada Beach.

His story about the intoxicated Greek and the flapjack sign weakened considerably when Archibald Haskin, advertising manager of Albers Brothers Milling Company, told authorities that there were eight such signs in San Mateo County alone. Throughout California, more than 400 flapjack signboards looked down on motorists traversing the state's roadways.

Recall of a flapjack sign as an identifying marker for a specific location required a degree of familiarity not acquired in a passing glance.

An enterprising detective learned that the suspect rented an automobile—the Ford version of a touring car—on the evening of August 2. He left the garage about 6:30, and returned the automobile sometime prior to 1:00 A.M. Father Heslin's kidnapping occurred a few minutes after 9:00.

Hightower admitted renting the Ford—the admission figured in his alibi—but insisted that he left the rental agency at 4:30 in the afternoon and returned the automobile at 11:00 that night. He and a woman companion, Doris Shirley, used the Ford for an outing to San Jose, he said.

If, indeed, he spent the evening with Doris Shirley—if, indeed, Doris Shirley existed—she might be the suspect's saving grace. Aside from her, he was at a loss to name a single person who could vouch for his whereabouts from the time of the kidnapping until the following morning.

Charles Le Febre and Vincent Biretta, proprietors of Le Febre Motor Car Sales Company, told authorities that Hightower hired six or seven cars over a period of six weeks. With the exception of a single Hudson, the cars rented were Fords.

"He seemed to be such a nice fellow that I refused a deposit from him," said Le Febre, alluding to the night of the kidnapping. "I thought he was all right."

"Hightower was always pleasant and looked and acted like a well-to-do business man," added Biretta. "He seemed to have plenty of money."

At a Corona typewriter store on Market Street, an alert detective learned that Hightower had recently returned a machine rented on July 12. Preliminary tests indicated the typewriter had produced the ransom note. The detective transported the machine to police headquarters for expert analysis.

A search of Hightower's belongings produced a cache of letters and passionate poems written to women. In one poem, composed for a seventeen-year-old girl, he wrote, "My tongue is not trained to the language of love."

Intriguing as the poems and letters were, their content was not important. It was important, however, that a typewriter was used. During an era when few men were familiar with the operation of these laborsaving office devices, Hightower proved competent in their use.

Several residents of Colma claimed to have seen Hightower in town on Tuesday afternoon, just hours prior to the kidnapping. Then, on Wednesday afternoon, Bruce Rutherford and William Shackleford were heading north from Half Moon Bay when Hightower "hailed" them from the roadway near Hickok's Mystery Castle at Salada Beach. The men gave him a ride to San Francisco. Their statement placed the suspect near the gravesite the day after the kidnapping.

Officers returned Hightower to the Hall of Justice where he underwent withering interrogation by Matheson and other detectives, as well as by San Mateo district attorney Franklin A. Swart.

"This is a hell of a way to treat a person," Hightower lamented. "I've helped you. You're a fine bunch of fellows to browbeat me in this manner."

Born near Waco, Texas, in 1878, the 43-year-old suspect complained of a life "devoid of adventure" and "spectacular romance." He was, he said, a "jack-of-all-trades" who had gone to work in the family cotton patch while still a child. He learned to cook and bake and, for a time, followed "the life of a sailor." Later, he drifted about the country, stopping wherever opportunity beckoned.

On two occasions, he owned his own business. Between 1909 and 1913, he operated a bakery in Clovis and another in Bakersfield from 1915 to 1920. His specialty was pastries and cakes and he enjoyed a large patronage. Former employees described him as a fair man to work for, but they invariably noted certain eccentricities in his personality.

In 1910, he married Ethel Bowers, a young woman with 160 acres of Fresno farmland in her dowry. The marriage went sour and the couple separated.

An inventor by avocation, Hightower tinkered with a variety of devices designed to kill and maim. In addition to the Infernal Machine, he invented a "rotary-compound machine gun." Hoping to see it mass-produced for war use, he demonstrated it before a panel of experts. Like the Infernal Machine, it failed to win approval.

The day following discovery of the body, the San Mateo County district attorney charged Hightower with the murder of Father Heslin.

"The chain of circumstantial evidence against Hightower was welded link by link," reported the *Chronicle*. "Virtually every hour brought forward some new circumstances or some established fact that, in the minds of authorities, fixed his guilt."

"There is no doubt that we are making out a strong case against Hightower. He is a very bright man, and is shrewdly working to protect himself, but slowly he is being pinned down," opined

Isadore Golden, an assistant district attorney. He added that the suspect's story about Dolly Mason "has nothing of the ring of truth to it. He becomes more and more confused as he is questioned. I feel that before long he will be in a frame of mind to tell exactly what he knows."

Noting that Hightower's "answers and explanations" were less than adequate, Golden characterized many of them as "patently ridiculous."

When asked to repeat the story about Dolly Mason and the drunken Greek, Hightower astonished investigators with an altogether different tale. This time there was no mention of a buried body, but, instead, buried booze.

"Dolly thought the Greek was a bootlegger. She tried to pump him as to where the booze was buried and he spoke of a cave [at] Salada Beach," Hightower told authorities with a straight face. "When Dolly told me this I thought 'here is a chance to get some booze.'"

Considering its inflated cost and great demand during Prohibition, uncovering a cache of liquor would have been a highly profitable stroke of luck. Nevertheless, interesting as the story was, it was an utter contradiction of Hightower's original tale.

"Hightower is a very cool, calculating individual," said district attorney Swart.

> The man is guilty beyond … a doubt. His every word and action since we began questioning him shows that. He is a bright fellow—one might almost say brilliant—and he knows it. He is taking great pride in matching his wits against ours, but his story is weak, very weak. There are any number of points on which we know he is lying. Not only do we know it, but we can prove it.
>
> He is one of the most remarkable fellows who have ever come to my attention. He tells the most improbable stories and tells them in a glib way, evidently sincere in the belief he

is fooling us. The man has convicted himself out of his own mouth.

As district attorney of San Mateo County, Swart explained why he had Hightower held in the San Francisco city prison. "We would not dare to take the prisoner and lodge him now in any jail in the vicinity of the crime. The people of San Mateo County are too thoroughly aroused over this crime."

Matheson, the detective in charge of the investigation, was convinced of Hightower's guilt. Nevertheless, he hypothesized that the suspect acted in concert with an accomplice, probably the drunken Greek. Nor did the chief of detectives think it was Hightower who called at the rectory on August 2, driving away with Father Heslin. Bianchi, the observant neighbor, described the driver as short of stature. Hightower was six feet tall. The caller, said the housekeeper, spoke with a foreign accent. If anything, Hightower possessed a nearly imperceptible Texas drawl.

The detective was confident that police would find the alleged accomplice. "We expect to locate that man and have him under arrest before Friday night," he said.

"There is no doubt as to his guilt," concluded Matheson. "We have it on him and there is no possibility of his escape."

"While the police and other authorities are firmly convinced as to Hightower's guilt," penned a *Chronicle* reporter, "the question as to the real motive behind the crime still is a mooted one. Chief O'Brien and Captain Matheson agree the ordinary motive back of the kidnapping is the desire for money, but into this case insistently has crept from the beginning the possibility of hatred engendered by religious beliefs. If money was the sole object, it is reasoned, why did the kidnappers pick on a poor priest? On the other hand, the hatred theory is somewhat borne out by the fact the man eventually was murdered without any real attempt at collecting a ransom."

Meantime, an intensive search was underway for Dolly Mason, the inebriated Greek, and Doris Shirley.

A detective was stationed at the general delivery window of the Seventh and Mission streets post office, where the accused claimed Dolly Mason received her mail. In fact, postal authorities were in possession of an unclaimed letter written to Mason by Hightower. No one fitting the woman's description came by to claim it, but not until Hightower granted permission would postal authorities release the letter to detectives.

"I believe there is something in what that drunk told you," the suspect wrote the elusive woman. "I am beginning to think it might have something to do with the priest. See me at once when there is a reward offered."

Authorities believed that Hightower wrote the letter in an effort to bolster his alibi should he be connected to the murder. They surmised that he planted it specifically for their perusal.

Police in Sacramento experienced a moment of excitement when they located the first of several Dolly Masons. However, this woman looked nothing like the description offered by Hightower. She received an apology for time wasted.

At Santa Rosa, police records revealed the arrest of a woman known as Dolly Mason in 1916 on a charge of plying men with liquor and robbing them. However, the Santa Rosa Dolly was a 45-year-old, and Hightower's Dolly was 23.

Yet another Dolly Mason had spent sixty days in an Oakland jail in 1917 on a charge of petty larceny. She, too, was an older woman.

While the search for Dolly Mason continued unabated, the *Oakland Tribune* strongly suggested: "The woman is no more than an invention of Hightower's imagination."

Dismissing Doris Shirley proved more difficult. According to Hightower, he met her in Sacramento and she accompanied him to San Francisco. Investigation revealed that they lived together for a week at the Larne Hotel, located at Ellis and Mason streets. Oddly enough, it was the very corner at which Hightower claimed to have had the "drunken-Greek-flapjack conversation" with Dolly Mason.

On July 31, Hightower and Shirley took a room at the Hotel Senate on Turk Street. They were registered until August 4, when Hightower moved to the Grand Southern Hotel. Apparently, Shirley moved to the Hotel Marymont at Jones and O'Farrell streets.

Upon their arrival from Sacramento, Shirley sought work as a waitress and Hightower looked for a cook's position. Hearing word that Hickok's Mystery Castle was available, the man's entrepreneurial side emerged. Overgrown with weeds and in disrepair, the place was deserted and the rent was cheap. Hightower remembered it from days past and decided to have a look.

He rented a Ford from Le Febre, and he and Shirley, so he claimed, drove to Salada Beach. They toured the unkempt castle and wandered about the thorny grounds, discussing the plausibility of turning the place into a roadhouse and hiring out-of-work moving picture actresses as entertainers. Nothing came of the idea and Shirley struck out on her own.

A lead to the woman's whereabouts materialized when officers learned of a trunk shipped from Hotel Marymont to the B. B. Transfer Company. The police confiscated the trunk, which was slated for shipment to Santa Rosa.

Hopeful as they were, authorities admitted disappointment when a locksmith opened the trunk. It contained clothing and nothing more.

A clerk at the Hotel Senate told investigators that "Mrs. Hightower, as I knew her, was an attractive, little woman, young and neatly dressed. She did not speak to anybody [at] the hotel in my hearing and seemed to be a respectable woman. I should say that she was about 22 years old."

If indeed Shirley and the accused slayer were lodging together as late as August 4, the implication of her presence in Hightower's company on August 2, the evening of the kidnapping, was apparent.

Police badly wanted to chat with Doris Shirley.

The *Chronicle* found Hightower's movement between hotels curious: "The excellent character of the hotels Larne, Senate, and Grand Southern adds mystery to the intentions of Hightower. The management in all three establishments say that he never showed any word or action that he was not a man of excellent caliber. The hotel clerks in all three places are schooled in the identity of people of the nightlife and none of them could tell police that Hightower had any dealings with men or women of the underworld."

Having written something categorically positive, the newspaper was quick to add a negative. During his stay at the Larne, Hightower was suspected of visiting a *demimonde* at a nearby hotel, the writer claimed. "The woman is now being sought."

If so, the effort went unnoticed. The search for the *demimonde* received no further attention in the newspapers.

During a lull in his interrogation, Hightower requested a private meeting with Fred Hall. A Bakersfield mining investor and financier of no small repute, Hall was well connected politically. He owned a working ranch and had once employed the accused murderer as a cook. The men had been acquaintances for a decade. Police hoped Hall's presence might induce a confession. It did not.

"Hightower," said Hall, "you know you wrote that [ransom] note."

"I don't know a thing about it," replied the accused. "Do you think that I could be guilty of a crime like that?"

"I not only think you could—I know you are."

"So, you think I killed the priest? Well, I don't much care what happens. It doesn't make much difference to me. I'd about as soon be hanged as live another forty-three years as I have lived."

After the meeting, Hall told authorities that Hightower was "erratic" and "fully capable" of murder. He characterized his former employee as "crazy, cruel, and diabolical."

More important than his opinions, however, Hall revealed Hightower's "implacable hatred" of the Roman Catholic Church, and his detestation of all things related to Catholicism. He said he based the statement on many conversations over the years. It refuted, flatly, Hightower's claim of profound respect for the church.

"I'll tell you," concluded Hall, "this man has one of the keenest brains I have ever come in contact with."

Charles Le Febre, the Ford dealer, arrived at the Hall of Justice to identify the prisoner. He easily identified Hightower, and he rebutted Hightower's claim that he rented a vehicle at 4:30 in the afternoon on the day of the kidnapping.

From the beginning, Hightower insisted that he and Doris Shirley left the city at 4:30 for a leisurely drive to San Jose. They dined in a restaurant there and returned to San Francisco, arriving at 11:00 P.M. Hightower stated that not once during the roundtrip did he drive the automobile at more than fifteen miles per hour.

The auto dealer said the story was nonsense. Hightower drove off the lot at 6:30 and did not return the vehicle until sometime around 1:00 in the morning. William Forest, his mechanic, corroborated the statement.

Hightower backpedaled. It was cloudy in San Francisco, he asserted, and he was not certain of the exact time. He did not explain the relationship between clouds and clocks.

He reversed himself again when a former associate from Utah refuted his statement that he had never "thought of or engaged in anything of a criminal nature." In fact, so Hightower admitted, he planned a blackmail scheme in which he attempted to recruit his accuser.

No sooner had Hightower denied being in the vicinity of the gravesite than the young sons of Mike Dolan, a San Francisco police officer, contradicted him. They told of their exploration of the area and of having seen Hightower in July on the San Pedro Road adjacent the gravesite.

As layer upon layer of evidence accumulated, the *Chronicle* perceived a "change in the theory" of authorities. "Heretofore, it has been assumed there were two ... kidnappers. It is entirely possible, they now assert, Hightower was unaided. They are convinced he carefully prepared the [burial] ground at least a month in advance. He was seen many times in the vicinity of the grave early in July."

"We are closing in on him," mused Swart. "He is alert and crafty. He has prepared his alibis carefully, but he unquestionably is breaking under the strain. He still is proud of his ability. He sometimes balks at our questions, and in a little notebook makes notes of his objections. He is manifestly pleased with his ability to act as his own lawyer."

In an eyebrow-arching statement, San Francisco district attorney Matthew Brady said Hightower was legally entitled to a hefty portion of reward money offered by a variety of entities for finding Father Heslin. Martin Madsen, secretary to Governor William D. Stephens, bridled. If found guilty, Hightower would not see a plug nickel from the California treasury.

Colma constable Landini commented:

> Hightower has known entirely too much from the start. When he and I were below on the ledge digging for the body of Father Heslin in the spot pointed out by him, I warned him to be careful not to shove the shovel in too hard or far as it might damage the [body's] face so as to prevent recognition.
>
> "The face isn't there," he declared. "I'm digging at his feet."
>
> Several minutes later, when we had dug out the sand, we found the feet in the exact spot pointed out by him.

Landini shared Chief Detective Matheson's belief that Hightower was not the man who called at the rectory and drove away with the priest. Beyond that point, however, their theories conflicted. Landini was convinced that the man who summoned Father Heslin into the night was an innocent dupe doing the killer's bidding— "that the slayer not only did away with the priest but, to cover up his tracks, slew the man who knocked at the door of Father Heslin's home in Colma."

His hypothesis left room for the assistance of an accomplice. If Hightower kidnapped the priest in cahoots with a partner, the partner was slain to avoid being paid his half of the ransom money.

Landini was searching for a second body.

An *Examiner* reporter watched as an army of men under the constable's direction denuded the landscape near the burial site. He wrote in florid prose about "a stench—the stench of a decomposing human body—rising in a lonely spot not far removed from where the corpse of the slain priest was hurriedly buried." The "death fumes" rose across "the wind-swept Salada Beach wilderness."

The digging continued the next day and the next, and then it stopped—and the newspaper stopped writing about "death fumes" and "a second awesome revelation at hand."

They found no decaying body and the odor of "death fumes" apparently dissipated. Still, Landini was relentless. He insisted that, if necessary, he would "plow down the mountain and dig up the whole countryside."

Hightower had been behind bars two days when an unexpected caller visited the Hall of Justice. Sergeant Arthur H. De Guire sat at his desk inside the anteroom fronting Chief Detective Matheson's office. At 8:15 in the morning, a "well-garbed brunette with big brown eyes and milk white-skin" opened the door. The young woman was "clinging to the arm of a sleek young man."

"I understand that the police want me," she said simply. "I'm Doris Shirley."

De Guire whisked the long-sought woman inside Matheson's office where the detective was in conference with Assistant District Attorney Golden. Offered a chair, the "quiet brown-eyed girl" crossed her legs revealing a "well turned ankle." She promptly lit a cigarette. Lee Putnam, her escort, lit a cigar and each puffed calmly as officers asked probing questions.

Shirley explained that she had spent the previous week in Fresno with Putnam, her "sleek" fiancé. She was aware of the murder only

Figure 9.4 Mrs. Doris Putnam, nee Shirley, with new husband, Lee Vincent Putnam. *California State Archives.*

in passing: "I picked up a newspaper yesterday and saw that I was being sought by the police. Lee and I left Fresno at eleven o'clock last night and arrived here early this morning. We didn't even stop for breakfast, but went straight to police headquarters."

During the next sixty minutes, she dealt a "smashing blow" to the suspected slayer's alibi.

Shirley did not come to San Francisco from Sacramento, as Hightower claimed. Rather, the two came as a couple from Salt Lake City. It was there, not in Sacramento, that she became acquainted with the accused.

She knew no such woman as Dolly Mason, and she had never heard a story about a flapjack man and a drunken Greek. Because Hightower told police he brought Mason from Salt Lake City to San Francisco, Shirley suspected the other woman was a composite character created in the suspect's fertile imagination.

Yes, admitted Shirley, she had been Hightower's *inamorata* and had lived with him at several hotels. She was astonished, she said, when she learned that he was the prime suspect in a kidnapping-murder. She was not, however, privy to his private business.

No, she did not drive with Hightower to San Jose the night of the kidnapping: "The only automobile trips I ever took with him were sometime in the latter part of July. We never went as far as San Jose. One time we drove—rather I drove him—nearly to Burlingame, and on another occasion we rode out to the beach. Those are the only two automobile trips we took. I never drove down toward Colma or any other place in that direction with Hightower."

On the evening of Father Heslin's disappearance, when Hightower claimed he and Shirley were in San Jose, she was in downtown San Francisco. As a matter-of-fact, the accused drove her to the Imperial Cafe at Seventh and Market streets where she dined alone. She told officers that she and Hightower walked from the Hotel Senate to a Ford dealer where he engaged a rental car. They drove off in the vehicle about 6:30, and he dropped her at the restaurant. Hightower told her he had business to attend to from which he expected to make a "big sum of money." He offered no details.

After dinner, Shirley bumped into Putnam, an Oakland cafe entertainer whom she had known in Denver. They "walked the street" for some time, then went to a motion picture and vaudeville show at the Pantages Theater. She did not see Hightower again until after midnight when he returned to their room at the Hotel Senate.

So taken were Matheson and Golden by Shirley's story that "they carefully shielded her from a swarm of newspaper reporters." After she "shot Hightower's alibi to smithereens," as Golden put it, the officers took her and Putnam to a nearby restaurant and treated them to a belated breakfast.

When told that the young woman had "given the lie" to his scenario of August 2, Hightower said, "I have no desire to contradict the lady. She is a good little girl and I still love her."

After breakfast, the police returned Shirley and Putnam to the Hall of Justice where they underwent another round of questioning. Placed in separate rooms, each came through "with flying colors," according to the *Tribune*. Doris admitted having tried "the byways of the underworld," but insisted it was a passing phase she regretted. Officers were convinced she was telling the truth, that she knew nothing about the kidnapping and murder.

By the conclusion of the second round of questioning, the *Chronicle* noted that Shirley "tore to shreds [Hightower's] intricate defense."

Then something unorthodox, if not improbable, occurred. A scene played out worthy of a silent film star, and no less preposterous than many silver screen plots. The Santa Clara authorities escorted Shirley and Putnam, principal attractions at the Hall of Justice, to a waiting automobile with "the greatest secrecy possible." With San Mateo County district attorney Swart at the wheel, "a mad dash" commenced through city streets. The attorney "zigzagged" across town in an effort to "throw off" reporters following in "hot pursuit."

Swart maneuvered the vehicle at lightning speed "down the peninsula to Redwood City." Pulling up to the courthouse, "the trio ran up the stairs and into the clerk's office." There, by pre-arrangement, Mrs. Joseph Nash, San Mateo county clerk, met with the couple. Never mind that it was Saturday afternoon and the office was closed, Nash prepared the paperwork attendant to a marriage license.

Moments later, Judge Ray Griffin, "known far and wide as 'the marrying judge,'" burst into the room. With formalities quickly attended to, Griffin "entered upon his duties." Redwood City chief of police C. L. Collins and deputy sheriff Stanley Woods acted as witnesses and Swart gave the bride away.

Twenty-four-year old Doris Shirley—Edna Carroll, she said was her real name—was joined in matrimony to 27-year-old Lee Vincent Putnam.

By the time frustrated reporters caught up with the entourage, Mr. and Mrs. Putnam had left by taxi to an unnamed destination. No one who witnessed the ceremony would admit to any part in it.

The pressure on Hightower never relaxed. While Shirley and Putnam underwent questioning, officers escorted Roy Ganey to the suspect's cell. The young man was a former sailor who had worked with Hightower on a construction project near Ogden, Utah.

"What are you doing here?" Hightower demanded, almost hysterically. "What do you want? Who are you? Who do you represent?"

"I have come here to tell the truth," Ganey replied quietly.

Officers asked Hightower if he knew Ganey.

"No, I don't know him. I don't know him."

Ganey's story was simple and direct. Hightower was the talkative cook for a construction gang, and he tried to befriend the younger man. With much bravado, he told of kidnapping a Chicago millionaire's son and collecting ransom money.

"Did you every tell Ganey that?" demanded a detective.

The suspect's answer was, at best, unusual: "I don't remember."

Under the anxious eye of Constable Landini, digging at the gravesite recommenced and workmen removed tons of earth. No second body surfaced. However, pieces of evidence found in great number included personal items belonging to Father Heslin.

Hopkins, the *Examiner* reporter whose ostentatious prose described the murder victim's unearthing, gained another opportunity to test his rococo vocabulary: "From deep beneath the sand at the side of Father Heslin's dark grave on the cliff-edge at Salada Beach came forth the revealing sunlight of truth."

No one paid much attention to a tent found in Hightower's hotel room until Landini's army of shovelers dug up floor planks stained by blood, cinch blocks, and tent pegs with remnants of top string attached. Coupled with pieces of lumber already found, the new discoveries constituted the "complete equipment for erecting a tent."

The tent from Hightower's room was re-examined. Missing were cinch blocks and tents pegs. String found at the dig matched the string found with the tent.

It was damaging evidence.

When the tent was unfolded, a sign written in Hightower's hand—all in capital letters—was found attached to the roof slope. Its succinct message read, "TUBERCULOSIS."

An insidious disease for which there was no sure treatment, doctors told sufferers to seek sunny climates. Countless thousands did. During the early days of the twentieth century, California and Arizona advertised aggressively as sanctuaries where abundant sunshine often cured the disease in weeks. There was no truth in the claim, but it brought health-seekers infused by hope.

A disproportionate number of World War I veterans were afflicted with tuberculosis. Veterans hospitals were few, and all were overcrowded. In large numbers, men traveled West seeking sunshine. But times had changed. Derisively called lungers, they were unwanted and increasingly shunned by a fearful population. It was common to see "no lungers allowed" in advertisements for rooms, apartments, and eating-places.

Tubercular tent communities rose up on the outskirts of cities and towns. Lunger were regarded with fear and loathing, and only the most daring would approach within shouting distance of one. Therefore, when Hightower affixed the dreaded word to a sign atop a tent, no further warning was necessary. Without argument, people kept their distance.

Hopkins echoed the tenor of the times when he asked, "What was the best way to insure swift and fearful retreat on the part of any who might draw near? What word perfectly spells 'fear' to the minds of all those who can read? Hightower could have done no better had he ransacked the dictionary. He wrote the single word: 'TUBERCULOSIS.'"

Discovery that a tent had been erected at the burial site gave rise to several theories. Knowledge that it went up over plank flooring led lawmen to conclude that it was part of a bizarre plan to hold a priest—perhaps any priest—hostage during ransom negotiations with the diocese. The sign, of course, would keep the curious at bay.

Authorities reasoned that Hightower erected the tent days, perhaps weeks, prior to the kidnapping. Surely, everything was in place by August 2, the night he abducted Father Heslin. It was likely that the victim was driven there directly from the parsonage—and never left.

Yet another theory suggested the impracticality of holding a hostage in a tent. Its canvas walls were by no means soundproof, and the difficulty in securing a prisoner—even in chains—in such a structure was apparent. It was possible, so the theory went, that the limitations imposed by the kidnapper's arrangement compelled him to murder the priest early on.

Hightower had a ready explanation for the tent's use. One day in July, he "flirted with a girl" he met on the street. She told him that she and some friends were planning a picnic to the beach and invited him to join the party. "I told her I had a tent and would take it along," he said.

On the appointed day, Hightower rented a Ford and drove to the beach with his tent in tow. The group intended to use it as a changing room, but it was too windy to put it up. Consequently, they spread it over the sand and used it as a covering from which to sun themselves.

When asked the name of the "girl" who invited him, Hightower's recall escaped him. Nor could he remember the names of the other "girls."

Asked why he tacked a tuberculosis sign to the tent, the accused slayer shrugged and said, "I don't know."

On August 13, the diocese conducted a pontifical requiem mass for Father Heslin in St. Mary's Cathedral in San Francisco. As thousands of spectators lined the sidewalk fronting the ornate structure, some four hundred priests and prelates followed the black casket into the cathedral. Archbishop Hanna delivered the eulogy, characterizing the fallen priest as a "martyr of the church."

Concluding a long day of interrogation, Detective Matheson issued a statement declaring his belief that Hightower was guilty of kidnapping and murder, that he had no accomplice, that Dolly Mason was a myth, and that the tent found in Hightower's room had been erected at the burial site in preparation for Heslin's killing.

Early the next morning, Matheson and four heavily armed plain-clothes detectives whisked Hightower from his cell in the city prison. They escorted him to a waiting automobile for a journey to Redwood City, the San Mateo county seat. There, the county jail would be his home through the duration of his trial.

"Captain Matheson had spent considerable time planning the trip," wrote the *Chronicle*. "He avoided the usual route of travel on Sundays, taking the South Side drive. Matheson said that Hightower repeated to him several times that he was feeling good, was enjoying the ride, and that he hoped things would turn out all right."

There were no incidents and they encountered no automobiles along the way. However, just as Hightower trudged up the stairs to the jail, a woman approached the party. She looked at the prisoner, then at Matheson, and said, "I hope they hang him, Captain."

The "holiday crowd" that converged on the beachfront burial site that day likely contributed to the lack of automobiles on the route between San Francisco and Redwood City. Police made no provisions to seal off the area and, according to the *Chronicle*, some 2,500 automobiles—forty-two cars every ten minutes—converged on this barren stretch of sand.

"With a holiday on their hands and ideal weather for touring, entire families from San Francisco, Colma, Daly City, San Mateo,

Redwood City, and points even further south, piled into automobiles and drove to the site of the tragedy," reported the newspaper. No mention was made of the crowd's potential to destroy valuable evidence. "Heavy, high-powered machines, indicative of wealth, as well as small, cheap cars, were parked along the highway in a line half a mile in length."

Most folks stopped just long enough "to plod over the soft sand to the cliffs for a cursory view, after which they returned to their cars and drove off." However, many "amateur sleuths" set to work, "digging for clews in [the] sand near the crypt."

They paid keen attention to the flapjack sign as well, and groups of thrill-seekers stopped at the Mystery Castle to peer through windows and poke about its weed-strewn grounds.

Considering the punctilious attention given crime scenes today, it seems preposterous that authorities were so lackadaisical. However, the climate of investigation was altogether different during the early 1920s. Forensic science was largely unknown and the level of investigatory sophistication was, at best, rudimentary.

Hightower's first evening behind Redwood City bars was spent in chitchat with county jailer James P. Coleman. Hightower spoke about his childhood and whippings he endured for various infractions. Then he said, "There is something the matter with my head. Guess I have been thinking too much recently. Do you know, I get the queerest notions sometimes. When I get to thinking it seems like my head begins to expand and it keeps on growing until I feel every minute like there is going to be a big explosion. It has bothered me now for a long time. Most times I think clearly, but it seems like lately it has been getting worse and I can't seem to remember things well. I wonder if I'm going crazy."

Authorities wondered if he was setting the stage for an insanity plea.

A mild sensation ensued when an envelope lacking a return address was opened in the *Examiner* newsroom. In it was a photograph identified by the anonymous sender as Dolly Mason. When shown the photo, Hightower declared, "That's her. That's Dolly." He noted, however, that Mason was a blonde; the woman in the photograph was a brunette.

Publication of the image produced leads sufficient for *Examiner* reporters—they coveted their interloping role as clandestine detectives—to track the woman to an Oakland lodging house known to shelter prostitutes. What followed was, apparently, an odd coincidence.

The woman in the photograph did on occasion use the name Dolly Mason. Even before newsmen flushed her out, her physical resemblance to Hightower's delineation of his mystery woman drew attention.

"The very first time a description was printed of the girl to whom Hightower says he talked, I told my girl friends that that was an identical description of me," said a breathless Dorothy Gifford.

Described as a "child of the butterfly life" and a "familiar figure along incandescent Powell Street," the twenty-five-year-old Gifford swore out an affidavit that she had never laid eyes on Hightower.

She said his story of a street-corner conversation about a flap-jack signboard, a drunken Greek, and a buried body was ridiculous—"a creation of his imagination without any foundation in fact." Gifford claimed that such a meeting was impossible because she "never engaged in conversation while standing on the street."

When taken before Hightower, the prisoner pulled a face and said, "I never saw her before." He added that "the Dolly Mason I knew had a harder face and more vampish eyes."

Never mind its silliness, the *Examiner* was getting mileage out of a nonstory. Despite denials from both Gifford and Hightower, and only passing interest expressed by law enforcement authorities, the newspaper scribbled several thousand words about the woman and splashed its columns with lurid headlines. Half a dozen photos of the attractive young woman, striking a variety of poses, drew full-page coverage. Apparently, she savored the attention.

After the photo session, Gifford returned to Oakland, where police promptly arrested her for vagrancy. Oakland officers said her name was Wanda Smith, and Wanda did indeed engage in conversations while standing on the street—mostly with strange men.

While the *Examiner* wrote dramatically about rumors of lynch parties forming in San Mateo and Santa Clara counties, and of extra guards posted inside and outside the jail to protect Hightower from mob violence, the *Chronicle* looked on askance. "Redwood City went about its business in the usual way," it noted with calm dispassion. "There was no gathering near the county jail."

When jailer Coleman went home for lunch, Hightower and twelve other prisoners, all trustees, remained unattended. The *Chronicle* noted that "there was not a single peace officer in the county jail."

District Attorney Swart swiped at the *Examiner* when he said, "These mob and violence stories printed in certain papers are not to be credited."

Even more dramatic than the *Examiner*'s fatuous claims was a confrontation that occurred in Swart's office the following day. Housekeeper Marie Wendel and neighbor Mary Bianchi arrived from Colma to identify the accused murderer.

"My God, it's him! It's the man who took Father Heslin away. The face, the features. Oh, I …!" wailed Marie Wendell.

Wendel stretched clenched fists toward Hightower as she gasped out words of identification. Then she collapsed almost at his feet.

Revived by officers, the housekeeper endured sixty minutes of intense questioning. Her identification remained unshakable:

> His every look betrays him. The same face, the same features, the same sharp profile, the same voice, the same eyes; all those tell me unerringly he is the man.

I sensed his presence before he was halfway in the room. He has almost a woman's voice. I would know him among a thousand men. There is something about his presence, about his actions, as well as about his appearance that makes me know.

It is not my opinion; it is my absolute conviction, my abiding knowledge that this is the man.

When Bianchi saw Hightower, she rose from her chair and stared at him. Then she sank back, shuddered convulsively, and covered her face with her hands. "It is the same man," she declared. "I could not be mistaken. It is not just that he looks like the man who came for the good Father, it is in very truth that same man. You need not fear a mistake. There is none. This man is the very man I saw that night, and none other."

Later, Hightower told investigators, "I'm through. I'm done. I've been unlucky all my life and my judgment has been worse than my luck. I suppose you will hang me."

To a *Tribune* reporter, he said, "The newspapers already have me hanged, drawn, and quartered. I have faith in juries, but I have little hope of acquittal."

Then he made the kind of astonishing statement that was becoming his trademark:

I have such a high regard for the Catholic religion and the Catholic priesthood that I would be willing to be tried by a jury of Catholic priests. I am assured of my own innocence, but I cannot expect a fair trial because of the ignorant prejudices of the public mind.

But I am not worrying. That is because I have only myself to worry about, and I am pretty tired of myself. I have had myself for a long time now, and it really hasn't been much use. It will be rather a relief to be rid of myself.

On the strength of the Wendel-Bianchi identification, the search for an accomplice was abandoned. Authorities were now convinced that Hightower acted alone. The single hold-out was the ever-digging

Constable Landini who persisted in his insistence that the culprits numbered two.

On the morning of August 17, a coroner's inquest convened at city hall in Daly City. Dr. John R. Clark, autopsy surgeon, testified that death could have resulted from either or both of two traumas—severe blows to the head or two bullet wounds to the body. Clark found the skull fractured in several places, with bits of bone driven into the brain. The more damaging of two bullet wounds penetrated the abdominal cavity and passed through the right lung. The doctor was convinced that Father Heslin was struck by a heavy object, possibly a pickaxe, and shot almost simultaneously.

Hightower was not named in the inquest's verdict, which was the district attorney's intention. Swart was disinclined to introduce testimony beyond what was necessary to establish the fact that the priest met a violent death. As a trial lawyer, he appreciated the pitfalls of revealing too much too soon.

Shortly after midnight, Dr. J. A. Larson—he was a Ph.D., not a physician—brought his sphygmomanometer and his boss, chief of police August Vollmer, from Berkeley to Redwood City. The chief was there as an observer. The device measured respiration, pulse action, and blood pressure. A crude forerunner of the lie detector, they used the sphygmomanometer to conduct a "scientific soul test."

Larson, a former psychology instructor at Harvard, attached something called a pneumograph to Hightower's chest. By means of a small writing point, the pneumograph registered the suspect's respiration on smoked paper from one brass drum to another. A second instrument called a chronograph recorded lapse time between questions and answers.

While Hightower was wired to this odd-looking apparatus, Swart questioned him for more than an hour. At the conclusion of the test, Larson reported the "suspect was covering up important facts on every crucial question that was asked."

When the district attorney asked point-blank if Hightower murdered Heslin, the smoky paper recorded "violent agitation."

If the folks from Berkeley were unimpressed by Hightower's veracity, his audacity appalled silent screen idol Mary Pickford. He wrote the actress a lengthy missive in which he reminded her of a letter he wrote at a moment when she and husband Douglas Fairbanks had gotten bad press notices.

"I cannot remember the name of the secretary that answered [my letter]," wrote the jail inmate, "but she informed me that you would be sincerely appreciative of the beautiful and encouraging things that I said."

Hightower reconstructed a few sentences from the mawkish, idolizing letter written long before, and told Pickford that he was "an idealist" who could not have committed the crime for which he was accused. He told the film star that his previous letter would be invaluable in establishing what a swell fellow he was, and he asked her to search for it among her valued treasures.

Pickford, who employed a small army of young women to read the bags of mail sent to her each day, had never laid eyes on Hightower's adoring post. However, his latest communication was brought to her attention and she promptly turned it over to the police.

While Mary Pickford was not a woman capable of influencing the accused slayer's future, Doris Shirley was. Much to the chagrin of the San Mateo County's district attorney, the young woman's past was emerging as something less than sweetness and light.

From her home in Denver, Lee Putnam's mother made it clear from her home in Denver that she disapproved of the marriage: "I believe the Shirley girl married my son as a matter of protection." She noted that Putnam had been "confined in a sanitarium for mental treatment," and she suggested that Shirley had played on his sympathies.

"If my son's new wife is implicated in the case, she will receive no aid from us," said the mother.

In fact, Putnam's young wife was well known in Denver. Edna "Mickey" Carroll, alias Doris Shirley, came to the Mile High City from Minneapolis after her lover Ralph E. Cavanaugh died by gunshot in an apparent dispute over bootlegging profits. Before she left Minnesota, her court testimony put three men behind bars.

In Denver, she hooked up with Thomas J. Coleman and became the alleged "Queen" of his bank bandit gang. During the previous April, Coleman's gang divested three messengers of the Stockyards National Bank of $23,000. Eleven days later, the authorities captured Coleman. They credited the capture to Mickey Carroll's extravagant spending of robbery loot.

Coleman and three companions pleaded guilty, ostensibly to save Mickey from prosecution, and all were sentenced to life in prison. Carroll pledged that she would live out her life "true" to Coleman. Instead, she went to Salt Lake City and bedded down with Hightower. Growing weary of him, she bumped into Putnam—her old acquaintance from Denver—and became his bride.

The revelations did not ease Swart's job. In was necessary that he have complete confidence in the young woman's truthfulness, and he drilled her unmercifully about her unsavory past and her relationship with the accused kidnapper-murderer. While they were honeymooning under subtle surveillance in a mountain hideaway at county expense, attorney Swart paid the couple frequent visits.

Apparently, the young woman with a shady past was winning him over. According to the *Chronicle*, "Swart has said that he is impressed with the frankness and sincerity of Doris Shirley. He is of the belief that the woman is trying to play absolutely fair with him."

Checkered as Shirley's first quarter century had been, the story she told authorities proved consistent and unimpeachable. Apparently, Swart was an able judge of character. Moreover, the confidence he placed in the young woman was manifest when Hightower's preliminary hearing commenced on August 19.

Under the utmost secrecy, Hightower transferred from the county jail at Redwood City to San Bruno. In the tiny, red-brick town hall fronting the unpaved highway, Justice of the Peace Ellis C. Johnson waited. The hearing was kept such a secret that no more than thirty people—mostly witnesses, law enforcement officers, and reporters—were in the room.

Ignoring expert advice, the accused acted as his own attorney. He was no match for Swart, and did himself no favor. Kept largely in the dark about the massive pile of evidence weighted against him, Hightower was clearly stunned by his predicament.

According to reporters, Hightower "went into the court smiling, serene, confident. He came out grave, perturbed, shaken. He pleaded 'not guilty' to his arraignment, waived his legal rights to postponement of preliminary examination, and faced his accusers apparently secure in the conviction that his alibis could not be broken down."

He was mistaken.

The court called witness after witness, each challenging the truthfulness of Hightower's assertions. As was reported, he was confronted by peers who, "in hushed voices, unfolded one damning fact after another—facts which one and all were diametrically opposed to his oft-repeated statements concerning his whereabouts, his comings and goings. Then came the psychological moment for which District Attorney Franklin K. Swart had waited and prepared. He called the name—'Mrs. Edna Putnam.'"

Hightower knew the authorities had questioned Doris Shirley. He knew nothing more. He was confident that she remained his *inamorata*—an impressionable young woman caught in his deceitfully romantic web. Certainly, she, of all people, would stand by him and bolster his alibis.

She did not. The *Chronicle* reported:

A comely young woman in the rear of the courtroom made her way slowly toward the witness stand in response to the summons. The accused man did not even turn his head. To him, the name Putnam was unknown, a name—nothing more.

Slowly, almost languidly, the suspect raised his head until his emotionless eyes met those of the witness—it was Doris Shirley.

The girl told her story. It was an old story—told by a young girl. It was a tale not pleasant to hear, but it commanded itself as being true. It was a story which literally tore to shreds every vestige of the alibi upon which the prisoner evidently had based his highest hopes of ultimate acquittal.

When the witness finished her testimony, Swart asked if the defendant had any questions. As Swart later recalled: "The man at the table tried to speak. He raised his hand to his throat, opened and closed his lips once, twice, and then in a voice fraught with tenderness, a voice so low the witness had to learn forward to catch the words, he asked three questions. The answers were not the answers he sought. Long and earnestly, he gazed at the witness, and then in the same low voice murmured, 'Your memory is woefully short, little girl.'"

Shirley refuted every claim made by the accused. Just as she had stated earlier to investigators, she testified that she came with the defendant from Salt Lake City, not Sacramento. She knew nothing about his Dolly Mason-flapjack-sign-drunken-Greek tale. She had never met nor heard of Dolly Mason. She was with Hightower on August 2, when he picked up a rented Ford at 6:30, not 4:30 P.M. She did not drive with him to San Jose, but dined alone at a Market Street restaurant where he dropped her. She went to a motion picture and vaudeville show with Putnam and did not see the accused slayer again until after midnight.

Following Shirley's testimony, Swart rested his case. The court turned to Hightower. The defendant declined to testify and he called no witnesses.

Judge Johnson looked squarely at the accused killer. In a voice made solemn by an unpleasant duty, he informed Hightower that he would be remanded to superior court to stand trial for first-degree murder.

Hightower's expression was blank.

On the return trip to the lockup at Redwood City, the defendant turned to Swart and said:

> I was surprised in a way at Doris, but then they are all alike. You take a baby with a doll. Even a baby knows that the doll is not human; it knows that the doll is full of sawdust, but it likes to be fooled. So does every woman.
>
> I have held in my arms many a pretty girl. They all fall for my line although they know in their hearts that I am pulling fast stuff. They all love to hear it. Doris was no exception, but she disappointed me.

Despite the stoic demeanor presented to Swart, Hightower was anything but calm. He paced his cell, shouted unpleasantly at guards, refused his evening meal, and interlaced the name Doris with bursts of profanity. After a fitful night's sleep, he awakened worn and haggard. He picked at his breakfast, then asked for and received a typewriter. He spent the day composing a statement for public consumption. Hightower wrote: "It seems to me that there is more than a suspicion of inconsistency in the theory that a man is innocent until he is proved guilty, when the press and public un-hesitatingly judge him guilty until he is proved innocent, and make no effort to find proof of his innocence."

Certainly, this self-serving argument sought public sympathy. While its thesis contained no new insight, it did point accurately to a fundamental flaw in human nature and the vacuity of newsroom ethics. Determining Hightower's guilt or innocence was a function of the court system. In an ideal society, the press would adhere to a rigid code of objectivity and public judgment would be held in abeyance until completion of the judicial process.

It was not an ideal society.

Hightower's statement continued: "There has been arrayed against me the prejudice of the press and public, together with the talent and resources of two great counties. While in my defense not one penny has been spent, not one witness has been called …."

The writer asked the public to "withhold its judgment until some faint whisper may be heard from my side of the case."

Compelling as his polemic was, it did nothing to pacify public outrage at his alleged crime. Neither did his most recent assertion that a look-alike was responsible for all his problems.

During a routine interrogation, Swart showed Hightower a photograph taken the previous winter in Golden Gate Park by a *Chronicle* photographer. Men seated on benches were playing checkers, and one of the players was unmistakably the accused killer.

"That's not me," cried Hightower excitedly, declaring that he was not in San Francisco during the winter. He pointed to his face in the photo and said, "That is my double. That is the man so many people have thought was me. That is the fellow these people have seen about the beach and other places. That's the reason they have all identified me."

Swart, of course, asked him where he was during the winter. Remarkably, Hightower could not recall.

Reinvigorated by a new alibi that a double was responsible, the accused man told his jailer he was hungry. "What would you like?" asked Coleman.

Without hesitation, the prisoner replied, "I will eat a salad, roast beef, a baked potato, bread and butter, some tea with cream and a slice of mince pie."

San Mateo County fed its prisoners well.

The unhappy reality of Hightower's preliminary hearing may have convinced him that acting as his own attorney was a fool's errand. When he made it known that he was searching for counsel, no shortage of attorneys vied for his attention. It was, after all, a high profile case certain to generate copious amounts of publicity.

San Francisco lawyer William F. Herron applied for the job in a roundabout way. Of his own volition and against the accused man's wishes, he filed a writ of *habeas corpus* in the district court of appeals. The petition claimed that Hightower was being held under duress at Redwood City and that district attorney Swart kept him incommunicado and without legal representation.

The writ met with the prisoner's wrath. Hightower liked Swart and considered his treatment fair. Nevertheless, Herron filed the writ and it made its way to the perusal of a three-judge panel.

Meantime, Hightower spent four hours in conference with Bakersfield attorneys Glenn Aldrich and Franklin Heck. It was their mission to assess both the accused and the case against him and to report their findings to E. J. Emmons. A former state senator, Emmons was a high-powered and picky lawyer out of Bakersfield who wanted nothing to do with a case unless he was certain he could prevail in court.

Oddly enough, it was Fred Hall, Hightower's former employer, who sought to engage Emmons. Hall was convinced of the accused slayers' guilt, and he told him so. Nevertheless, he was an eminently fair and decent man who wanted Hightower to have the best counsel available.

Late on the afternoon of August 26, guards handcuffed Hightower and took him across the street to the San Mateo County courthouse for his arraignment before Judge George H. Buck. Surprised by his lack of representation—Emmons was still pondering a decision—Buck appointed Redwood City attorney Albert Mansfield as counsel for the defendant. He explained that Hightower had the right to replace him with an attorney of his own choosing.

Efficient as the proceeding was, unfinished business remained. The judge ordered the defendant to return to court on September 6, when a plea would be entered and a trial date set.

A few days later, and much to his chagrin, Hightower was taken to San Francisco to answer Herron's writ of *habeas corpus*. Before appellate judges William H. Waste, John E. Richards, and William H. Langdon (later chief justice and justices of the California supreme court, respectively), the accused was asked if he had been afforded the opportunity to obtain counsel.

"Yes," he replied. "Mr. Swart has never tried to keep me from getting anybody I wanted. He insisted at all times that I get an attorney. I have been treated at all times with much greater consideration that I had any right to assume I would get."

It was not the kind of statement ordinarily made by a defendant about his prosecutor.

With uncommon swiftness, the court exonerated the district attorney of holding the defendant incommunicado and of preventing him from receiving counsel. It found the defendant was held in Redwood City by "due process of the law." Herron's writ was dismissed and Hightower was remanded to the custody of the San Mateo County sheriff.

Despite his annoyance with Herron, when E. J. Emmons at last agreed to defend him, Hightower followed his advice and allowed him to appoint the "writ-happy" attorney to the defense team. He retained Mansfield, the public defender, as well. Mansfield had been born and raised in Redwood City and was intimate with the surrounding areas. He might prove a useful asset to the defense.

Soon, grumbling came not from Hightower, but from his attorneys. After a lengthy session with the defendant, Mansfield told the *Examiner* that Hightower was as communicative "as a clam with lockjaw."

Emmons came to town during the first week of September. "Business engagements" prevented him from meeting with his client, but he did find time to chat with the press. "I shall defend him with all my ability," he said, adding the obligatory statement that Hightower could not be guilty of "this heinous crime."

Emmons returned to Redwood City on September 6 and accompanied Hightower to Judge Buck's court. To no one's surprise, the prisoner pleaded not guilty. Buck ordered the trial to commence on October 3, and Emmons promptly returned to Bakersfield. Before his departure, however, he appointed W. W. Laidley as a fourth member of the defense team.

As the trial date rapidly approached, a brief drama played out. J. Harry Dunlap, a private detective of dubious reputation hired by the defense team, swore out a complaint against David Bender for the murder of Father Heslin. Bender, recently arrested in San Francisco, had escaped from the Maryland State Penitentiary, where he was incarcerated for killing a Baltimore policeman.

Prior to Bender's escape, and just a few days before Heslin's kidnapping, the convict proposed to another inmate that they "do a kidnapping job and make some big money." The inmate declined the offer and subsequently reported it to authorities.

The private detective sought an arrest warrant for Bender on suspicion of kidnapping and murder. Defense counsel Herron backed him up. "I honestly believe that Bender is the murderer of Father Heslin," he said.

Unmoved, Swart called the effort a "hoax." Colma justice of the peace Ellis Johnson agreed and refused to issue the warrant. However, he did issue a warrant for Dunlap's arrest. Authorities took the private detective into custody and charged him with perjury.

When Hightower's murder trial opened Monday, October 3, the *Examiner* told its readers that "the legal tactics may be as brilliant as the case is extraordinary. Unless all forecasts fail, the trial will stand among the classic battles of Western courts. Nothing is lacking to make a masterly courtroom drama."

At least, so the *Examiner* hoped.

By nine o'clock, curious spectators filled the courtroom beyond capacity. Every seat was taken and the overflow crowed was turned away. Consequently, hundreds of people loitered about the premises. Armed guards surrounded the courthouse and tension was high. When they led Hightower across the street from the county jail, deputies cut a swath through a dense mass of excited onlookers.

No sooner had court convened than chief defense counsel Emmons asked Judge Buck for a postponement. Swart jumped to his feet. He reminded Buck that the defense was given ample time to take depositions and summon witnesses. Emmons, Swart said, had agreed, and he had asserted that "no effort would be made to delay the trial. I am surprised that counsel for the defense has seemingly forgotten this agreement."

"There will be no continuance granted at this time," ruled the judge. He turned to the defense. "Are you ready to proceed?"

With mild sarcasm and more than a hint of pomposity, Emmons replied, "We must, perforce, do so."

Prospective jurors heard and responded to the usual questions. Had they read press accounts of the investigation? Had they formed opinions about guilt or innocence? Were they opposed to capital punishment? Perhaps most important, they were asked if their verdict would be influenced by the fact that the murdered man was a Catholic priest.

Citing the complexity of the case, Emmons said he would make a "strenuous effort" to assemble a jury possessed of "high mental equipment."

A *Los Angeles Times* reporter sent north to cover the trial noted the defendant's demeanor: "Hightower sat beside his counsel listening intently to the interrogation of veniremen, but apparently with composure. His complexion [was] pale, and a fringe of graying hair on an otherwise bald head made him seem several years older than his 43 years. As he accompanied officers back to his cell he whistled a cheerful tune."

Late the following day, the court seated a jury of eight men and four women. The judge turned to prosecution and defense attorneys and said, "Gentlemen, you will be as direct in your questioning of the witnesses as you can. I do not want any delay. I will pass on objections without discussion."

According to the *Tribune*, Buck was considered "the speediest judge in the state." He was not fond of histrionics or bombast and he intended to conduct an efficient trail.

Swart opened the prosecution's case with a recitation of the Father Heslin's abduction and murder. He repeated Hightower's story about Dolly Mason, the flapjack sign, and the drunken Greek, and he related how the defendant led police and reporters to the gravesite.

Called as a witness, San Francisco police chief O'Brien told the court, "Hightower was not the least bit excited when the hand of the priest was uncovered," nor when the body was unearthed a few minutes later.

Newspaperman George Lynn corroborated the chief's story and described Hightower's intimate knowledge of the gravesite area.

On the following day, Hightower heard a dozen witnesses testify in a chain of circumstantial evidence with which prosecution intended to prove him guilty of murder.

Three police officers told about discovering the Infernal Machine in the defendant's hotel room. They described its terrifying capability in great detail. The same men and two others connected Hightower with ownership of a pistol that fired bullets the same caliber as those found in the body of the murdered priest.

Other witnesses testified that they saw Hightower near the gravesite at Salada Beach as early as July 11, again a week later, and on August 10. A detective repeated the defendant's admission that he took the Infernal Machine to the roadway near the flapjack sign for what culminated in an aborted test.

Ford dealer Le Febre testified about Hightower's rental of an automobile on the night of the kidnapping. The prosecutor pointed to inconsistencies in the defendant's story about the hours of the vehicle's rental and return.

The trial was in its fourth day when Swart called Doris Shirley to the witness stand. She was a principal drawing card for spectators and reporters. An audible buzz was heard when the attractive young woman made her way through the courtroom.

Without variation, she told the story she had originally told San Francisco police—the story she reiterated at the preliminary hearing. She did not drive with Hightower to San Jose. He dropped her at a restaurant and she dined alone. After dinner she went to the Pantages Theater with Putnam. She did not see the defendant again until he returned to their hotel room well after eleven o'clock.

The story was told in a "half-audible voice" and with "rigid self-restraint," wrote the *Examiner*. "Her skin, white as death, showed rapid flushes that chased themselves out of sight. She feared the cross-examination by Herron. And it came."

The defense attorney's questioning fell short of the newspaper's ominous supposition. Herron tried to shake her memory about dates. He failed. Then he tried to rattle her recall about times. He failed.

"You needn't go any farther," admonished the efficient judge.

Herron tested her memory about vaudeville acts at the Pantages. She remembered one called "Greenwich Villagers," but could not recall other names. The attorney pressed.

"You needn't go farther on that," said the judge.

She passed his test on the dates she and Hightower had moved from one San Francisco hotel to another. "Why did you leave San Francisco to go to Fresno?" he asked next.

"For the reason of getting away from Mr. Hightower," she replied.

The attorney asked about her recent mountain hideaway honeymoon at county expense, and he asked why police placed her and her new husband under surveillance. When she started to answer, Judge Buck cut her off. "That's enough of that," he said.

Herron ticked off a list of aliases she had used in various cities and asked her what she did for a living during her sojourn in Salt Lake City. "You needn't answer that," said the judge.

Finally, Herron asked her if she had testified in other murder trials. "You needn't go into that," growled Buck. "We are trying this case."

The lawyer paused. Then he sighed. "That's all," he said, deflated by the narrow boundaries imposed by Buck.

The young woman offered a kind of half-smile and left the stand.

It was not the withering cross-examination anticipated by experienced trial watchers. Nor did Shirley meet their expectations and crumble under pressure. The *Examiner* was correct when it noted that the crowd "had come to see a battle royal, but was deprived of its Roman holiday."

Notwithstanding spectator disappointment, newspaper pundits scored a victory for Shirley and a loss for Hightower's defense. With the same unanimity expressed following her appearance at the preliminary hearing, the California press told readers that Doris Shirley demolished the defendant's most important alibi.

Immediately following adjournment, Emmons sought the court's permission to ask Shirley and her husband for a private interview. Judge Buck replied that he would not interfere. Swart, given little choice in the matter, agreed.

Early in the evening, defense counsel Mansfield accosted the couple in the lobby of Redwood City's Hotel Sequoia. Shirley looked the lawyer in the eye and told him that what she said in court was all she had to say. She denied the interview.

In a blatant display of bad form, the same lawyer expressed to a *Chronicle* reporter growing frustration with his client: "Hightower has told me more than once that he would hang first before he would bring trouble to any woman. Furthermore, he has not always told us the full details of certain things we have asked him."

Mansfield revealed that during Herron's cross-examination of Shirley, Hightower scribbled several notes to the lawyer. "Let her alone," read one.

As the trial wore on, experts identified the typewriter rented by the defendant as the machine that produced portions of the $6,500 ransom note. Handwriting experts identified Hightower's hand as the instrument responsible for scribbling other portions of the ransom note.

Edward O. Heinrich, consulting criminologist and professor at the University of California—often called "the Wizard of Berkeley"—applied his expertise in geology to identify samples of sand found on the tent and other objects in Hightower's hotel room. He told the jury that the samples were identical in quality to sand found at the Salada Beach gravesite.

Heinrich examined Hightower's pocketknife as well: "I made a careful microscopic examination of the knife. On the big blade I found two small specimens of cotton fiber. I magnified one of these samples many times and then photographed it."

He showed the court photographic enlargements and pointed out that the cotton fibers on the pocketknife were an exact match with fibers taken from cord found on boards at the burial site. In addition, the fibers matched exactly with cord fibers found in the defendant's hotel room.

The *Examiner* dismissed Heinrich's findings as "typical Sherlock Holmes evidence." In fact, the Berkeley professor was on the cutting edge of an emerging discipline later defined as forensic science—and he would later earn worldwide recognition for his efforts.

Marie Wendel, parish housekeeper, climaxed the prosecution's case when she took the stand, pointed at Hightower, and identified him as the "goggled stranger" who drove away with the Colma priest. "There is the man who came for Father Heslin," she insisted.

As court drew to adjournment on October 10, the state rested its case.

The next day, Emmons, the highly touted Bakersfield attorney, committed a dreadful miscalculation. He called Hightower to the stand to testify in his own defense.

"Hightower talked too much," noted the *Chronicle*. As a matter of fact, "he talked so much that even Judge Buck attempted to stop him on several occasions." Emmons, his own lawyer, "implored him time after to time" to cease his monologues and "answer questions in monosyllables."

But Hightower was on a roll. "With the ease of an 'old salt' spinning yarns," quipped the *Examiner*, "Hightower took courtroom and jury into his confidence at the rate of 400 words a minute."

The defendant admitted that he lied to the police in San Francisco, that he lied to District Attorney Swart, and that several times he substituted the name Dolly Mason for Doris Shirley.

"I am a baker by trade, but an inventor by inclination," he told the jury:

> I have been interested for many years in women of the night life. I have been for them and have always aided them whenever I could. There is a Dolly Mason. I knew her first in Bakersfield about five years ago. She is in San Francisco. I do not know her address and I would not tell it if I did.
>
> I admit I lied to Captain Matheson. I admit I lied to Mr. Swart. I lied to protect Doris Shirley Putnam.

Hightower, his voice purring with fond nostalgia, waxed eloquent about romancing Shirley in Salt Lake City: "I had seen her in various places and I asked, 'Is that pretty little brown-eyed girl running around loose? Does anybody own her?'

"They asked me, 'Do you want to be introduced to her?'

"And I answered, 'I certainly do.'"

Emmons, his face reddening, exploded. Scarcely able to contain himself, he told his own client that he was out of order. He tried to redirect the defendant: "You said you had been told of facts which Miss Shirley wanted to hide. What were they?"

Hightower astonished both his attorney and the court when he replied, "They couldn't be dragged out of me with red-hot irons."

Try though he might, the furious Emmons could not keep his client on topic and could not stop his rambling discourse about Shirley:

> We had intended to rent a house when we came to San Francisco. In Salt Lake I heard of a fine mansion that could be rented for $50 a month. That certainly sounds interesting in these times. I wish to say that this was not to be a house of prostitution—if the district attorney cares to go into that.
>
> We stopped at the Clunie in Sacramento. We then came together to San Francisco. She thought detectives were watching her. At times, we used an assumed name to throw these detectives off the scent.
>
> I first went out and looked over the Mystery Castle at Salada by myself. I thought it was not suitable for our purposes, but wanted Doris to give her opinion. So I drove out there and she was not interested, so we didn't examine the place further.

Despite his incessant chatter about Shirley, he did not neglect a persistent denial of his involvement in the kidnapping and murder of Father Heslin. He meandered back to the subject repeatedly. He restated the litany—Dolly Mason, a flapjack sign, a drunken Greek—he had told and retold so many times that much of the public knew the story by rote.

> I had worked in the vicinity of Salada Beach many years ago, and as there are only a few flapjack signs around Colma, I got the idea in my mind that whatever it was that was buried was hidden in this vicinity. It was more to please Doris than anything else that I switched from a small machine to larger one to take her riding. I wanted her to come with me one night and hunt for the buried treasure or whatever it was that the stranger had told Dolly Mason about. Doris, if she has a mind to, can tell you that I did hope to find something worthwhile.
>
> I made several visits to Salada to hunt for caves. I did not know what I was looking for, but I had a hunch that I would find something. When I read in the papers that a priest was

missing, I had an idea that it might be his body that was hidden and that this was what the stranger meant in his drunken state when he told Dolly Mason about having killed a man and having something of great value buried with a man watching it who was cooking flapjacks.

Being a cook, I knew the connection between hot cakes and flapjacks. I went out to look for the cache more to please Dolly Mason than anything else.

The defendant concluded his rambling discourse by denying "knowledge of anyone who had been concerned in the murder of Father Heslin."

When at last, Hightower ran out of things to talk about, his defense team uttered a collective sigh. The defendant, opined the *Chronicle*, "tangled himself in a fatal net."

Other defense witnesses were called, but the effort was all for naught.

In his closing statement, Swart told the court that the evidence against Hightower was "overwhelmingly conclusive." He asked the jury to render a verdict of guilty.

Closing for the defense, Herron insisted that the circumstantial evidence against his client "did not prove guilt beyond a reasonable doubt." Charging that Doris Shirley lied about Hightower, he asked, "Are the virtuous women on this jury going to hang a man on the perjured testimony of a painted denizen of the night life?"

At 2:07 on the afternoon of October 13, the court remanded Hightower's fate to the jury. Not two hours later, at 3:53, jurors returned to the courtroom and pronounced the defendant guilty of murder. Surprisingly, however, jurors forsook the hangman's noose and recommended life in prison.

Hightower took the verdict calmly, chewing gum all the while. "Well boys, I guess you won't see me for some time," he quipped to reporters.

Two days later, the convicted slayer was taken to San Quentin. According to his escort, San Mateo County sheriff Michael Sheehan, Hightower "assumed an expectant air, as though his appearance would be the occasion of a formal reception."

It was not. The single formality was to strip him of his clothing and his identity. Garbed in penitentiary stripes, the killer officially became Prisoner No. 35458.

The convict dressed himself in penitentiary stripes for forty-three years, nine months, and eight days, all the while proclaiming his innocence. On May 20, 1965, following twenty-seven unsuccessful appearances before the parole board, Hightower was released from prison.

When reporters questioned him about the murder of Father Heslin, he brushed their questions aside: "The past is past. I am looking forward to the future. I've got a lot of living to do."

Hightower was 86 years of age.

Peggy True's Infatuation

In 1915, as a young girl of 17, Peggy True gained fame in San Francisco when her play, *The Beast Man*, enjoyed a successful run. But her fame was fleeting. She made an unhappy marriage and wrote nothing more of consequence. In 1920, True was committed to St. Luke's Hospital suffering from a nervous breakdown, a nonspecific euphemism for any number of mental disorders.

Prior to the Heslin affair, Hightower became infatuated with the young lady—from afar. Although strangers, he commenced writing a series of letters composed over a period of months, and received by her at St. Luke's.

The first letter went unanswered. Undaunted, Hightower sent flowers. Still, there was no reply. He sent candy, then fruit and more letters. Included in his postings was an abundance of romantic poetry. Finally, there came a proposal of marriage—and Peggy True became angry.

She sent a stinging rebuke to the offensive correspondent. She reminded him that she was a married woman and told him his conduct was indecorous.

Oddly enough, Hightower was encouraged by her anger. Calling her his "dream girl," he wrote that he would "furnish you with the necessary funds to go to Reno and get a divorce, if you wish to observe the conventions. Otherwise do not consider your husband as a barrier. If you do not wish to get a divorce I can readily do away with the barrier which your husband forms."

Apparently, it did not occur to her that his crude suggestion might imply a willingness to murder her spouse. Now, having read in the newspapers about Hightower's alleged orchestration of a kidnapping and murder, True had second thoughts. She contacted the police.

Officers paid her a visit and she gave them a bundle of letters. One letter in the batch held particular interest for investigators.

In it, Hightower told True the story of a man who created obstacles to his invention of a machine gun. The man died.

In his letter, Hightower stated: "He certainly had my consent to climb the golden stairs, and I was much tempted to assist him in making the start on that climb, but did not see any way clear of doing it and still be able to obey the Eleventh Commandment or would certainly have expedited his exit."

The Eleventh Commandment, he explained, was, "Thou Shalt Not Be Found Out." He added, "It takes all the sting out of the other ten, and is the only one that I am going to worry about any more, for a person is a fool to try to do their best when all they get is the worst of it."

Hightower's braggadocio to San Mateo County district attorney Franklin K. Swart that women always fell for his "line" may have possessed a ring of truth. After Peggy True gave incriminating letters to the police, a *San Francisco Chronicle* reporter accosted her.

"I should be quite willing to take the witness stand in behalf of William Hightower," she told the astonished scribe, "as I believe that he is entirely incapable of such a revolting crime."

The reporter pressed the young woman for an explanation, and she said, "I have never met Hightower, but from the tone of the letters he sent me, I certainly feel that such a crime is completely foreign to his nature."

When the slayer's trail opened in Redwood City, the one-hit dramatist was there. Each day she competed for standing room with "the feminine crowds that were wedged at the back of the courtroom tight as posies in a French bouquet." One afternoon, as officers escorted Hightower from the courtroom, True cried out his name and threw herself at the defendant. Startled deputies were obliged to restrain her.

Apparently, the playwright's infatuation with the accused slayer was boundless. She dismissed the jury's guilty verdict by saying she would believe it when she "heard the word from his own lips."

She was not given the opportunity. Peggy True and Hightower never met.

Chapter 10: The Aviatrix and Her Gigolo

Beyond a dwindling number of 1930s aviation aficionados, Marjorie Crawford is a largely forgotten figure. There was a day, however, when the gifted young aviatrix shared headlines—if ever so briefly—with Amelia Earhart, Ruth Elder, Bobby Trout, Marvel Crossen, and other notable women flyers.

Years prior, when Earhart glimpsed her first "flying contraption," she said, "it was a thing of rusty wire and wood and looked not at all interesting." Then World War I began and a dramatic transformation in American aviation took place. In the blink of an eye, what had been a novel experiment became bold reality. Awkward flying machines became sleek airships, and sputtering motors gave way to increasingly sophisticated engines capable of reaching astonishing speeds in excess of 100 miles per hour. Flying was magical, and the wild blue yonder captivated the American public.

When Charles Lindbergh flew nonstop from New York to Paris in 1927, the young airmail pilot won global renown and became an American icon. In less visible settings, countless engineers, and the jaunty pilots who flew their winged creations, worked with vigorous diligence to enhance the speed of aircraft, increase their flying radius, and produce more reliable "aeroplanes." Still, regardless of the impressive advancements that occurred in aviation science, flight was still in its rudimentary stage.

Much to the chagrin of traditionalists, the notion of soaring high into the sky dazzled women as well. During an era when women were valued largely for their ability to attract the opposite sex, make babies, cook meals, and tend to other domestic chores, a unique sorority of "flying sisters" emerged. By 1930, the United States boasted some 200 licensed female pilots. Fifty-two of the women, more than 25 percent of the total number, made their homes in California.

Nowhere in America were flying conditions more ideal than in Southern California, where competitions and exhibition flying events drew countless thousands of enthusiastic spectators. When women pilots were featured in the events, the crowds increased exponentially.

Exhibition flying, or "stunting," as its practitioners called it, was much more than flyers showing their stuff for an enthusiastic public. It was the means by which pilots honed the skills necessary for survival. Despite myriad improvements in engineering, flying was not for the weak of heart. The Curtiss Jenny, standard of the army and one of the most reliable planes in the air, was far from safe. "Never forget that the engine may stop," read its owner's manual, "and at all times keep this in mind."

Countless times a pilot in mid-flight experienced a motor gone suddenly dead. Putting the aircraft on the ground and living to tell about it demanded enormous skill, as well as nerves of steel. Many pilots did not survive the experience.

Flying fields were dangerous as well. Will Rogers once quipped that an airfield was "a tract of land completely surrounded by high-tension wires and high chimneys, adjacent to a cemetery."

Rogers' definition was not far from the mark.

Yet danger was part of the thrill of flying. It was also the drawing card that brought countless spectators to early air shows.

In June 1929, an "exhibition flying by artificial light" and "the first hangar dance in history" drew some 4,000 onlookers to the inauguration of Glendale's Grand Central Air Terminal. The event featured "a variety of planes from the smallest and oldest to the newest and largest," and, in addition to daring flying stunts, it offered vaudeville on an outdoor stage.

Marjorie Crawford, a 21-year-old Texas transplant and popular flying ace was among the participants that day. Just recently, Marjorie made headlines for a record-breaking nonstop mid-air refueling flight in a giant, tri-motored Albatross. Notwithstanding her youth, Crawford was gaining notoriety among the nation's press-getting women pilots.

Certainly, it was no disadvantage to her career that this fierce competitor was a stunning young woman. She was, as an ex-husband described her years later, "rough and tough with the face of an angel—a beautiful blonde angel—and a figure, Amen!"

Beauty combined with exceptional skills made her an ideal subject for newspaper photographers and headline writers. Marjorie's distinctive, if not altogether quirky, personal life gave reporters much to scribble about.

As the young flyer set records, generated news copy, and collected considerable prize money, Homer Weber, Marjorie's former flight instructor, claimed a proprietary interest in her earnings. He sought a court injunction to clip her wings, stating that she owed him $1,373 for use of his airplane, and he insisted that she was under contract to fly for him exclusively.

Should Marjorie be grounded, her attorney argued, it would "invalidate her pilot's license" and "interfere with her career." Not wanting to shoulder responsibility for either outcome, the judge concluded that grounding her would be "an act of great injustice." He denied the injunction.

Soon after the judge's ruling, Marjorie nearly grounded herself. Through no fault of her own—mechanical failure was to blame— she crash-landed. As luck would have it, however, she walked away from the wreck, none the worse for the wear.

Figure 10.1 Aviatrix Amelia Earhart, fourth from right, and peers pose at award ceremony in Los Angeles. Left to right: Louise M. Thaden, Bobbie Trout, Patty Willis, Marvel Crosson, Blanche W. Noyes, Vera Dawn Walker, Earhart, Marjorie Crawford, Ruth Elder, and Florence Lowe Barnes.

Underwood Archives

   Marjorie was not so lucky a few days later when, as a passenger in Olive McDowell's automobile, the young flyer became victim of a nasty fender bender. Five weeks in the hospital were required to mend a broken ankle and a dislocated hip. Annoyed at her grounding by a nonflight related accident and, of course, losing income, she sued McDowell for $25,000. Her luck returned and she won the suit.

   Lucky as Marjorie was, she was chronically unlucky at picking husbands. At a birthday bash celebrating her twenty-second year, she met William Wellman. In quick time, she fell in love with this dashing World War I flyboy, Hollywood *bon vivant*, and director of the fabled motion picture *Wings*. Moreover, he fell in love with Marjorie.

Nevertheless, there existed complications. Wellman was married to former Ziegfeld Follies beauty Margery Chapin, and Marjorie was married to Carl Crawford, a professional polo player. Wellman's dilemma found a tidy solution when Chapin announced that she was in love with Wallace Harvey, an entrepreneur oilman. How the polo player reacted to his wife's disaffection went unrecorded.

So well did the aviatrix navigate the air into a profitable career that she spurned a judge's alimony award when she divorced Crawford. "My client is able to support herself and does not need alimony," her gruff lawyer told the surprised jurist.

Days after leaving divorce court, Marjorie was compelled to quash rumors that she and Wellman were secretly married. "What are you trying to do," she asked an inquiring reporter, "make bigamists out of us?" Marriage to Wellman, she explained, was not possible until her divorce from Crawford was final, and that process would take a year. She was quick to add, however, that "the very next day, we will be married."

And they were.

In December 1931, the two flyers flew to Yuma, Arizona, and were joined in matrimony by a justice of the peace. Following the simple ceremony, Marjorie made an announcement that startled both her fans and the burgeoning aviation industry. She was hanging up her wings to become a housewife. "I intend to devote myself to my home and to writing on aeronautic subjects," she told surprised reporters. "I am especially keen about encouraging women to fly, for any girl [who] can drive an automobile can pilot a plane."

Forthwith, the young aviatrix withdrew from competitive flying. Still, she did not cover her wings in mothballs. Marjorie and her new husband—he was a pilot of no mean skill—spent considerable time among the clouds.

A memorable flight occurred the morning after a strenuous argument—Wellman characterized it as a "dogfight"—when the agitated couple took to the air with Marjorie at the controls. She kept the plane on the runway until the very last moment, and then veered into the air almost vertically. Said Wellman, "My gut did strange maneuvers it had never done before."

For a solid hour, Marjorie put the plane through twists and turns, diving, soaring up and down and around, and at breakneck speed. Unnerved as he was, Wellman forced a stoic expression and never uttered a word. That night, however, he slept in the guestroom.

Tempers had yet to cool when at breakfast Marjorie served him a half grapefruit. As they ate in stony silence, an impulse struck Wellman to "squash that grapefruit in her lovely face." He did not, but the temptation was keen in his memory when he filmed *Public Enemy*. In a scene made immortal by Wellman's sudden inspiration, the director instructed James Cagney to squash a half grapefruit in Mae Clarke's face during a breakfast-table argument.

From the beginning, the Wellman-Crawford liaison was rife with turbulence. Midway into its first year, they separated, and then divorced after fifteen months of marriage. Marjorie claimed mental cruelty. She told the court that she objected to risqué jokes told by her husband in mixed company, that he did not treat her women friends with the kind of courtesy she "deemed becoming," and he often swore at her. She did not mention that she often swore at him, as well.

The moment the divorce was final, Wellman flew to Las Vegas with 20-year-old Dorothy Rae Coonan. There, the freckle-faced Busby Berkeley dancer became his third wife. Following close on his heels, Marjorie took her third husband—but not before a bewildering drama played out in public view.

Readers of the April 3, 1934, issue of the *Los Angeles Times* saw a familiar photograph of Marjorie Crawford beneath a startling headline: "Woman Tells Kidnap Story."

Danny Dowling, variously described as a "motion picture dancer," "Hollywood man-about-town," and "film colony gigolo," languished unhappily in a Yuma, Arizona, jail cell while Marjorie poured out a tale of woe to Los Angeles police detectives.

Dowling, well-fortified by liquor, came to her Hollywood home Friday evening, May 30. He brushed past the maid, entered Marjorie's dressing room, and held the young beauty at gunpoint. Having captured her undivided attention, he forced her into her own automobile and drove her to Yuma—to get married.

Figure 10.2 Danny Dowling,
motion picture dancer.
Underwood Archives

While escorted from the Yuma lockup back to Los Angeles, Dowling protested vigorously, telling law enforcement authorities that Marjorie's story was poppycock. Nevertheless, the retired aviatrix filed a formal complaint, charging him with kidnapping and with two counts of assault with a deadly weapon. When Dowling learned of the complaint, he burst into tears.

"I have loved her ever since I met her," he said between sobs. "I would not have harmed her in any way. It is true that we have had a few minor quarrels but we always made up. She accompanied me voluntarily to Yuma and had she wished to leave the car at any time, I would not have interfered. She had numerous opportunities to leave if she had wished to do so."

Marjorie, said to be in tears when she signed the complaint, spoke through her attorney. His client, the attorney stated, was "through with Dowling and has no wish ever to see him again."

Dowling was arraigned in municipal court, with his bail set at $5,000. Unable to raise such a sum, he was incarcerated in the county jail to await his preliminary hearing.

When the hearing began April 19, the defendant's lawyer read two "burning love epistles" to the court, written to Dowling by Marjorie. One addressed him as "Sweet child;" the other opened with "Good morning, Darling." Both concluded with "Oceans of love." While she readily admitted writing the letters, the young woman insisted she had severed her relationship with Dowling a week prior to the alleged kidnapping.

Certainly, terms of endearment indicated a level of affection on Marjorie's part. Still, the body of one letter may have indicated motivation of an altogether different kind on Dowling's part. "I am sending you all I can spare and I hope it will be enough," penned Marjorie. "It seems money is hard to get these days," she concluded, reminding him that she was not immune to the vagaries of the Great Depression.

Ann Stewart, Marjorie's maid, testified that Dowling pushed his way into Marjorie's home, removed a revolver from a bathroom drawer and tucked it into his pocket. "If anybody in this house makes a false move," said the intruder, "I'll put a bullet in him."

Marjorie's story offered an important variation. She told the judge that Dowling pointed the pistol at her and said he would kill her unless she accompanied him to Yuma for purposes of matrimony. With no choice in the matter, she joined him in a lengthy drive across the desert. She made no attempt to escape, so she testified, because her abductor made a point of brandishing a revolver in a menacing manner.

At Yuma, they registered at a hotel where she feigned illness and took to bed. Meanwhile, Dowling arranged for the delivery of a marriage license to the suite and forced her to sign it.

After a while, she convinced her kidnapper to search for a drugstore and fetch an ice bag for her head. While he was away, she called the hotel desk and told the clerk she was the victim of a kidnapping. When Dowling returned to the suite, Yuma police officers greeted him.

Later, under cross-examination, both "bedroom" and "bathroom" issues slipped prominently into Marjorie's testimony. So "delicate" was her story, wrote a *Times* reporter, that both jury and courtroom spectators listened "amid dead silence," lest they miss a word.

When Dowling insisted she accompany him on the road trip to Yuma, "I told him I wouldn't go anywhere in those clothes," she told the judge. "And he said 'Change them then,' and followed me into the dressing room. I said, 'You might at least turn your head,' and he did."

At Yuma, they engaged a suite with both bedroom and bathroom. "Did you take a bath while there?" asked the defense attorney.

"Yes, I did," replied Marjorie. "It was awfully hot."

"Did Dowling help you?" he queried next.

"Well, he took off my blouse and skirt, but I did the rest."

Dowling vigorously denied kidnapping Marjorie. In fact, he insisted that he accompanied her to Yuma at her own request. She was ill and her doctor had ordered her to a warmer climate. En route to their destination, she became irrational. He was certain the illness clouded her judgment and compelled her to make up the entire story. The man-about-town asserted, however, that a serious bone of contention between them was her propensity to make up tall tales. As much as he loved her, he thought Marjorie might be a habitual liar.

Dowling made what the *Times* characterized as "startling statements" when the lawyer redirected his questioning to bedroom and bathroom issues. "She was feeling ill and I called a doctor who gave her an opiate after she refused breakfast," testified the accused abductor. "Later, I returned and, after taking a bath, wakened her and told her to take one. When I entered the bathroom she was in the tub with her head hanging over the edge so I gave her a bath, got her nightgown out of the grip as she told me, put it on her, and saw her crawl into bed."

From her place at the prosecutor's table, Marjorie displayed disagreement by shaking her head vigorously from side to side. The defendant looked at her and said, "As God is my judge, I gave you a bath."

According to the *Times*, Dowling's bedroom-bathroom testimony "left the courtroom gasping" and caused Marjorie to suffer "a fainting collapse."

After Marjorie and courtroom spectators regained composure, the defense counsel asked Dowling if he had spoken with his accuser during the noon recess.

"I did."

"Did you caress her?"

"I kissed her, if that's what you mean."

"Is it true," injected the prosecution, "that you grabbed her arms, forced her to the wall, made her listen to you, and then kissed her and left?"

"I did not. I love that girl and she loves me. I've loved her every minute since I met her."

Two Arizona highway patrol officers stationed at the Arizona-California border testified in Dowling's behalf. Sergeant William J. Dunn told the judge that when he asked to see the defendant's driver's license, Marjorie reached across Dowling and handed the officer her license. "Dearie," she said, "I have mine."

Corporal Bruce Duncan said Marjorie told him, "We're going to Yuma to get married."

Frederick Orr, a Yuma truck driver, saw Marjorie's car parked in front of a drug store for some fifteen minutes. She was alone in the automobile and appeared to be waiting for someone. He thought she was a movie actress and waved to her. She smiled at him and returned the wave.

"She didn't seem to like Dowling very much," Robert Gibson told the judge. "She said he is just a gigolo." Gibson was the Yuma hotel clerk who reported the alleged kidnapping to police. Marjorie later hired him to drive her in her automobile back to Los Angeles.

Apparently, the judge embraced Marjorie's claim that Dowling was a gigolo who had tried his hand at the snatch racket. After weighing all the testimony, he ordered the celluloid *danseur* to stand trial in superior court on charges of kidnapping and aggravated assault.

Then in early May, an astonishing thing happened. Marjorie and her alleged kidnapper requested a conference with the judge. Smiling and giggling, the giddy couple revealed their elopement to Wellton, Arizona, where a justice of the peace married them on May 3. Ironically, they used the very license Marjorie claimed Dowling forced her to sign at Yuma.

The judge did not smile or giggle. His face reddened. Then he exploded. "Someone may be charged with perjury," he seethed.

Later, acting on a defense motion to dismiss the charges, the judge acknowledged that portions of Mrs. Dowling's story seemed improbable, yet evidence was sufficient to warrant prosecution. He denied the motion to dismiss and scheduled trial in superior court beginning June 5.

The giddy newlyweds were stunned. California law mandated that because Marjorie had instituted the charges against Dowling prior to their marriage, she would be compelled to testify against him.

After postponement and much haggling, the judge reconsidered. If, by chance, the court found Dowling guilty, the judge's ruling

Figure 10.3 Marjorie Crawford during divorce proceedings from Danny Dowling, October 15, 1934. *San Francisco History Center, San Francisco Public Library*

might look exceedingly foolish to a panel of his peers in appellate court. Consequently, on July 16, he dismissed all charges.

Harry Carr, the *Times'* acerbic columnist, gazed on the affair with a jaundiced eye:

> Having worked the gag to the limit for all the publicity it seemed to yield, Marjorie Crawford managed to bounce back onto the front pages by marrying the man she accused of kidnapping.
>
> It is about time that Hollywood people with exhibitionist complexes were told where to head in.

Two months after the Dowlings' blissful wedding, Marjorie announced through her attorney that she had filed for divorce. In October, the retired aviatrix dabbed her eyes with a handkerchief as she told a judge about Dowling's cruelty. On one occasion, wrote the *Times*, Dowling "slapped her severely because she refused to give him all the money she had in the bank and turn over to him her stocks and bonds." On other occasions, he threatened to blow her brains out with a revolver and disfigure her face with acid.

Apparently, the dancer possessed odd habits.

Dowling made the papers again in late August 1935, upon his release from jail after serving twenty-five days on a liquor violation. The undaunted gigolo anxiously awaited finality of his divorce from Marjorie so he could marry Betty Lee, his former dancing partner.

In time, Marjorie Crawford faded from view, her name relegated to a footnote in early aviation history.

Chapter 11: George Palmer Putnam & the Hollywood Nazis

When John Putnam settled in Salem, Massachusetts, in 1642, happenstance gave emergence to a rising dynasty whose family name would resonate with prominence over the course of three centuries. From middle-class New England stock came ministers, lawyers, physicians, ship captains, military officers, politicians, gentlemen farmers, and—most enduring of the legacy—men who published books chronicling the times in which they lived.

Among early family members, Israel Putnam is, perhaps, the best remembered. Born at Salem in 1740, as a young man he migrated to Connecticut and served the crown as a major in the French and Indian wars. But Putnam was a radical whose loyalty rested with the colony, not with its British keepers. In 1766, when Parliament's arbitrary Stamp Act created a crisis among colonists, Putnam was a vociferous dissenter in the Connecticut General Assembly, and he became a founder of the treasonous Sons of Liberty. When open rebellion erupted, he was at the forefront of the fray.

After the Battle of Lexington, Putnam led the Connecticut militia to Boston and was appointed a major general in the Continental Army. He was a principal figure in the Battle of Bunker Hill and, later, he commanded troops in New York pending the arrival of George Washington. Irascible and often embroiled in controversy, Putnam was not among Washington's favorite generals. The two were frequently at odds, especially regarding tactical matters. Sadly, a stroke cut Putnam's career short in 1779.

Grandnephew of the illustrious general, the first George Palmer Putnam was born at Brunswick, Maine, in 1814. The son of a dedicated tippler possessed of a literary bent, George developed an early and insatiable taste for books. George's mother left his father in 1826, resettling in New York City; her young son, an unenthusiastic apprentice in his uncle's Boston carpet store, wrote letters to her complaining about his "literary starvation." Then, in 1830, the 15-year-old lad booked passage on a schooner to New York Harbor. With ambition that belied his inexperience, he answered a "Boy wanted" ad posted by a Manhattan newspaper. From that inauspicious beginning, he set upon a profession in publishing that would both revolutionize and institutionalize the printed word.

By 1838, the year he joined forces with John Wiley, 24-year-old Putnam was a New York City bookseller. Under the name Wiley & Putnam, his horizon expanded from retail sales to publishing. A decade later, after scuttling the partnership, Putnam was publishing books under his own name written by William Cullen Bryant, Thomas Carlyle, Francis Parkman, Samuel Taylor Coleridge, James Fenimore Cooper, Nathaniel Hawthorne, Washington Irving, and Edgar Allen Poe. At the same time, *Putnam's Magazine*, long a mainstay among the young nation's periodicals, flourished.

Following the Civil War, sons George Haven—called "the Major," he had been a Confederate prisoner of war—John, and Irving joined the firm. When the founder died in 1872, G. P. Putnam's Sons was born. Demonstrating a sense of literary foresight comparable to their father's, the sons published such luminaries as Joseph Conrad, William Henry Hudson, and John Galsworthy. In special partnership with Theodore Roosevelt, the firm published his *Naval War of 1812* and, some years later, his multi-volume *The Winning of the West*.

During the Putnam firm's heyday, what had long been a largely localized and decidedly unprofitable activity became a highly organized, nationalized, and commercialized enterprise. The methods for the writing, manufacturing, selling, and even the reading of books changed forever.

In 1930, George Haven, who guided the firm, died. The deaths of Irving and John followed, and G. P. Putnam's Sons merged with another publishing house. The father-son tradition came to an end, and even the patriarch's grandson and namesake, a company vice president, moved on.

It would be intriguing to know how the founder would have regarded his grandson. When the firm was merged, *Time* magazine wrote that "The departure ... [of] ... George Palmer Putnam [II] was almost as newsworthy as the deal itself. In the past decade, he has made himself conspicuous on the publishing scene. He is a man with the dangerous combination of literary ability, business acumen, [and] energy."

What *Time* meant by "dangerous" is anyone's guess. It is almost certain, however, that had the grandson not inherited a fortune, he would have built his own. G. P., as he was known to intimates, was tall, lean, strikingly handsome, intellectually gifted, fiercely competitive, and endowed with an uncommon flair for generating publicity.

Born in Rye, New York, in 1887, Putnam developed an early affinity for books about the great outdoors and the exploits of daring young boys. He endured boredom at an exclusive boys' school in Connecticut, and was uninspired by a short stint at Harvard. Much to his family's chagrin, he set out for California, nursing the notion of mining for gold and striking it rich. He did not strike gold and, probably at his father's insistence, he enrolled at the University of California at Berkeley. He found the university no more inspiring than Harvard had been. After a single term, the young man packed his bags for Bend, Oregon, a town of some twelve hundred people, a dozen saloons, and more than a dozen gambling dens and bordellos.

When the local mayor fell to his death from the window of a whorehouse, Putnam offered himself as a candidate and became the town's chief executive. Meantime, he established the *Bend Bulletin* newspaper. Displaying a natural flair for journalism and no regard whatever for the conflict of interest created by his acerbic pen, he delighted in writing about the town's foibles. His tenure as publisher/editor/mayor was marked by flamboyance and controversy.

During the summer of 1908, while on a climbing expedition in the Sierra, he met Dorothy Binney, a young woman whose adventuresome spirit paralleled his own. She was a Wellesley graduate, and her father was an inventor and co-owner of the company that manufactured Crayola crayons. The couple was married in 1911, and Dorothy followed the youthful mayor to his home in Bend.

In time, however, small-town life grew tiresome. After voluntary service as a lieutenant of field artillery in World War I, Putnam, by then the father of two sons, returned to New York where he entered the family business. As the author of four published books—two about Oregon, one about his adventures in Central America, and another about his war experiences—he joined the firm with an eye fixed on authors, or would-be authors, who shared his enthusiasm for bold adventure.

Like millions of Americans, Putnam was fascinated by the fledgling aviation industry and the courageous pilots it spawned. He published rocket enthusiast Frank Guggenheim's *The Seven Skies*, as well as *Winged Defense*, authored by controversial General William "Billy" Mitchell, head of the newly established Army Air Corps. He put into print *Skyward*, Lieutenant Richard E. Byrd's account of his celebrated flight over the North Pole. To promote the book, Putnam parked Byrd's plane at Wanamaker's department stores in Philadelphia and New York. Thousands of visitors, many seeing an aeroplane up close for the first time, were awed by the aircraft and purchased freshly inked copies of the flyer's book. But Putnam's *coup de maitre* came in 1927, when he published *We*, Charles Lindbergh's blockbuster biography and account of his transatlantic flight.

Putnam's marriage to Binney dissolved in a Reno divorce in late 1929. Two years later, on February 7, 1931, he married aviatrix Amelia Earhart. Theirs was an unconventional but happy marriage punctuated by Earhart's ever-growing list of accomplishments. Tragically, her final adventure, a flight around the world ended in her disappearance in the Pacific, a mystery that has never been solved.

Following Earhart's disappearance, Putnam did not return to his rambling four-acre Rye estate. It held too many memories of Amelia. Shippers packed his belongings and he put the Rye property on the market. Nor did he return to the New York publishing industry. G. P. Putnam's Sons had merged, new faces were about, and the founder's grandson sought a new beginning. He relinquished his vice presidency and with renewed optimism, he set off for Los Angeles.

By the late spring of 1939, Putnam was ensconced in a palatial home on Valley Springs Lane in North Hollywood. There, in an in-house office, he presided over his new venture, George Palmer Putnam Publishing.

"I came back to publishing because I love it," he told a reporter. "Maybe I'm like the fireman who won't retire. He scampers after flames. I chase manuscripts. Right now I'm convinced plenty of good ones exist in California."

On his fall publication list were books about a Hollywood stunt girl, a film colony doctor, a reporter, a radio singer, and a woman judge. It was typical Putnam fare—light books for mass consumption.

If, however, anyone sought proof that Putnam was back in his stride, the fact was evidenced by the alacrity with which he brought out his first book—and by the sensational nature of the book itself.

Putnam was getting his bearings and settling into his new routine when an unfamiliar face—"a gentleman"—appeared on his doorstep.

"Would you like to handle a strange, powerful story?" the man asked.

"Certainly," replied Putnam, taught by experience that if the story was a dud, the waste can was just a toss away. "What is it?"

The stranger revealed that he was in communication with a German, an anti-Nazi, who had the "scheme and plot and data" sufficient to provide the "background" for a starkly realistic novel. For "obvious reasons," he said, the German—a woman—did not wish her name to become known. Nor did she have the skill to write the book herself. They would need a ghostwriter.

On inquiry, the gentleman told Putnam that the proposed novel's title was *The Man Who Killed Hitler*.

During the late 1930s, the world was a dangerous, volatile place. Politically attuned Americans watched with a censorious eye as Reich Chancellor Adolf Hitler orchestrated broad measures of ugliness across the European landscape.

In the early days of February 1938, Hitler seized control of the German army and appointed Nazis to key positions. It was but a prelude to what has come to be called the *Anschluss* when, two months later, Germany invaded and then annexed Austria. From Vienna, occupation forces promptly issued an ominous edict that all Jews must flee the country.

In September, British prime minister Neville Chamberlain predicted that Europe would enjoy "peace in our time," after putting his signature to the Munich Agreement. Incredibly, it sanctioned Nazi annexation of Czechoslovakia's Sudetenland. Much of the free world roundly, and rightly, denounced Chamberlain.

On November 9, Nazis arbitrarily slaughtered thirty-five Jews, arrested thousands more, and destroyed Jewish synagogues, homes, and businesses throughout Germany and Austria. In what has come to be called *Kristallnacht*, so named for the sound and sight of breaking glass, 30,000 Jews were rounded up and shipped to concentration camps.

The New Year, 1939, commenced with Hitler's proclamation to the German parliament demanding the extermination of all European Jews. Then, just days before the enigmatic stranger knocked at Putnam's door, Hitler and Italian dictator Benito Mussolini forged a military and political alliance between Germany and Italy that was to be known forever afterward as the Axis.

The world teetered on the brink of the abyss, and Putnam—he was no political novice—knew it. In a split second, even sans knowledge of the plot, this astute promoter grasped fully the sales and publicity potential of a book envisioning death to the Führer.

Using the gentleman stranger as intermediary, Putnam was sent in swift order a scenario from the German woman who insisted she remain anonymous. Then he hired a ghostwriter, who also remained anonymous.* Hastily written, in his rush to take it to press, the publisher forbade rewriting or careful editing of the manuscript. Not surprisingly, it showed.

By early April, *The Man Who Killed Hitler* enjoyed prominent display in the nation's bookstores. While praise for the novel was by no means universal, some reviewers liked it—a lot. Paul Jordan-Smith, literary critic for the *Los Angeles Times*, was among them.

"The story has enough power to keep you in a fever of excitement," he wrote. "It awakens a profound sympathy, probes out all your compassion, commands your respect, surprises you, and never offends your reason. In brief, it is a story told with restraint, artistry, and deft cunning."

Gushing as Jordan-Smith's review was, it was not representative and book sales languished. Famed Hollywood gossip columnist Hedda Hopper gave the book a plug when she mentioned that Putnam intended to send Hitler an autographed copy. The United Press picked up the story and quoted Putnam as saying, "I am mailing a copy of the book addressed to Adolf Hitler, Esq., [in] care of the German Embassy, Washington, D.C. It will be a birthday present, and will be accompanied by a nice letter."

---

*It was later revealed that Dean Southern Jennings, a San Francisco newspaperman and author of pedestrian fare, like *The Intimate Casebook of a Hypnotist* and *Valla: The Story of a Sea Lion*, was responsible for the writing. German actress Ruth Landshoff-York created the scenario.

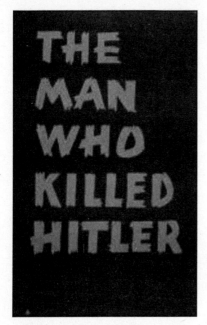

**Figure 11.1 Cover of Putnam's
1939 book,**
The Man Who Killed Hitler.

Whether he actually sent the "birthday present" to Hitler is unknown, but newspaper stories about it may have sold a few books to curious buyers. "If Hitler fails to read it," wrote *Times* columnist Lee Shippey, "he will miss an extremely interesting piece of fiction."

A few days after the Jordan-Smith *Times* review appeared, Putnam made headlines again. This time, however, the headlines were not in the newspaper's book section but on the front page: "Threat Made on Putnam's Life. German Letter Advises Halting Publication of 'Hitler' Book."

On the afternoon of April 19—the novel had been in bookstores less than a week—a letter written in German was brought to Putnam by special delivery mail. He had the missive translated and disclosed its contents: "If you have any regard for your future safety, stop publication of this book at once," read the ominous note. "The arm of Greater Germany reaches far and we have no desire to continue warning you. If you are wise you will do what we tell you because something can happen to you, and your future may be extinguished. The great work of the Fuehrer cannot be stopped by enemies. Heil Hitler."

Putnam reported the letter to authorities but told the press he was not worried about the threat. However, his concern heightened somewhat when, the next day, he received two death threats by telephone. In both instances, the voice spoke in heavily accented English, and each caller threatened his life if he failed to withdraw the novel from bookstores immediately.

According to Putnam, he did, indeed, worry when, on April 22, an even more sinister death threat arrived by special delivery. Contained in the envelope was a bullet-riddled copy of *The Man Who Killed Hitler*. "Eight bullet holes mangled the small book," reported the *Times*.

A letter, made up of words cut from newspapers and magazines and pasted to a sheet of white paper, accompanied the book. "Mr. Putnam, you're a criminal," it read. "You failed to read future. Bullet wound would be fatal to YOU! If you don't abandon the book THE MAN WHO KILLED HITLER. Take no chances of a bloody killing if you want to live. Your opportunity awaits you. Take it or leave it. Germany defies the World! Los Angeles Nazis, heil!"

"I am not frightened," Putnam told a reporter. "But I am curious. Very few people carry out threats of this type. However, I am not going to be at home for a few days. It seems wiser."

Apparently, after the would-be killers shot a book to pieces, their interest in Putnam waned. Three weeks passed with nary a word heard from them. Then, on May 14, their silence was broken—or so it was assumed—when headlines blazed on the front pages of Sunday papers across the country: "George Palmer Putnam Kidnapped," wrote the *New York Times*. "Seized by Nazi Sympathizers."

Sometime between 5:00 and 6:00 Saturday evening, Josephine Berger, the publisher's secretary, had informed her boss that Rex Cole telephoned a request that Putnam come to his home at 7:30 for an important meeting. Cole was a literary agent and close friend. "It turns out that his was a faked call," Putnam told reporters, "but I didn't know it at the time."

As Putnam report, at about 7:20 he went to the garage:

> ...to get my car and drive to Cole's. I was just about to step into the machine when two men jumped out from behind a partition at the rear of the garage. I didn't have a chance to look at them closely but one of them seemed to be rather small and the other one was tall.

One of them grabbed my arms. They spoke a few quiet words to each other. Then they put something over my head, which I think was a flour sack …. At the same time something was jammed against my side. It might have been a finger or a pencil but it felt enough like a gun muzzle to me so that I didn't struggle.

They were very courteous. They told me to get in the car and shoved me through the door. All three of us sat in the front seat. The keys were already in the machine and they drove me away in my own coupe.

With one abductor behind the wheel and the other guarding the prisoner, they pointed the publisher's expensive automobile toward Bakersfield, some 100 miles north of the Putnam estate.

The two men conversed with each other in German. I couldn't understand a word they said. Then they changed to English and one of them asked who furnished the information for the book I am publishing. They tried to find out the identities of the authors but I refused to tell. I told them I didn't know. Then they lapsed back into German.

On the outskirts of Bakersfield, the driver turned onto a bumpy road. Within a few minutes, he stopped the automobile and told Putnam to get out. "We walked a ways through soft dirt. My arms had been bound behind me during the drive but my legs were left free."

They led him into a building under construction and "they took the sack off my head. It was very dark. Then they fastened my arms and legs with tire tape and stuck strips of tape across my mouth. They were firm about their actions, but very courteous and they made no threats."

Putnam was left to his own devices and the kidnappers disappeared in his automobile. "I don't know how long I lay there, but it must have been at least two hours. I could see an auto going by now and then. I kept straining to work lose the tape over my mouth and finally it slipped off. I heard some people coming to their home nearby and called for help."

Figure 11.2 Putnam reenacts his kidnapping for reporters.
San Francisco History Center, San Francisco Public Library

Neighbors Roy and Henrietta Walker heard Putnam's pleas for assistance. They rushed to his aid, untied his arms and legs, and notified law enforcement officials. Bakersfield was "sealed off" and police and sheriff's deputies organized a manhunt for the kidnappers.

After undergoing much questioning, Putnam returned to his Hollywood home, where police posted armed guards. There, for some five hours, he repeated his tale to detectives and reporters alike.

At last, reportorial courage was summoned and the question that burned against each reporter's pen was asked: "Did Putnam realize that the whole business smelled like an elaborate hoax?"

The publisher bridled. "If anyone wishes to claim this is a publicity stunt for the book, *The Man Who Killed Hitler*, let him say it to my face," quoted a scribe for the *Chicago Daily Tribune*, "and I'll give him a forceful demonstration that it is not."

Threats of a thrashing aside, it is instructive to note how many times and in how many interviews Putnam mentioned the title of his book.

"The whole experience was much too painful and too realistic and too elaborate to be a publicity stunt," he continued. "After all, I scarcely would have ruined my trousers and driven myself all the way to Bakersfield, there to lie in the cold, trussed in a painfully cramped position, just for the sake of a publicity story."

Not long after Putnam's rescue, his expensive coupe was located a mile and a half from the building in which he was left bound and gagged. Acting on information supplied by a talkative dogcatcher, officers found the car near a combination dancehall-swimming pool. The "machine" had been "vigorously scrubbed" of fingerprints, much to the disappointment of investigating officers. The only items of interest found were lipstick-smeared cigarette butts in the ashtray. A couple of well-placed questions, however, established that the smoker was a married woman Putnam was courting.

Nor were the myriad fingerprints found in Putnam's garage helpful in solving the kidnapping riddle. Most belonged to him, and some belonged to one or the other of his doting secretaries.

A Bakersfield cab driver told police he had picked up a "blue-eyed, blond-haired" German who asked about the kidnapping—before it occurred. The operator of a Hollywood filling station claimed two well-dressed Germans driving an expensive automobile asked, just prior to the abduction, for directions to the Putnam estate. Nothing came of either story.

Putnam sought FBI assistance in solving the case. Apparently, the bureau politely declined. The district attorney's office turned up its nose and refused to join the investigation. When the kidnap victim's lawyer asked the Kern County grand jury to investigate, he was informed that the grand jury "does not hear cases in which the police have no evidence of a crime."

The kidnapping played out in the nation's press over a period of five days, and then the story simply vanished without a trace. Editorializing under the headline "California Fantasy," the *Washington Post* may have had the final word:

> Mr. George Palmer Putnam denies that his recent harrowing experience at the hands of Nazi kidnappers was a publicity stunt. About a month ago, the name of Mr. Putnam appeared as publisher on the title page of an anonymous work called *The Man Who Killed Hitler*. Despite the considerable sum invested by Mr. Putnam in advertising it, this book has had, up to now, no earth-shaking success. The idea that sales might perk up a bit if something could be done to cause mention of the book on the front pages of nearly all the newspapers in the land seems, of course, a very logical one. But rarely, if ever, does anything occur in the proximity of Hollywood according to the rules of logic.
>
> Thus, by its very illogic, the behavior of the kidnappers who lured Mr. Putnam from his home, carried him 100 miles away and left him bound and gagged, but not too tightly, in an abandoned house, but not too far from rescuers, seems credible. Something as magnificently irrational as that is precisely what might be expected of Nazi enthusiasts who come under the mesmeric influence of the Southern California climate.

In a remarkable lapse of scrutiny, an intriguing event had occurred a decade prior in New York that escaped the attention of both California law enforcement officers and members of the press following Putnam's alleged kidnapping. During the latter part of July 1929, three men, all political prisoners of Italian dictator Benito Mussolini, escaped from a penal colony on the island of Lipari near Sicily. The trio made its way to Paris and from that stronghold of quasi-liberalism, they made headlines across the globe.

Emilio Lussu, trained in law, was a social democrat elected to the Italian parliament in 1921. A founder of the Sardinian Action Party and a vociferous secessionist, he was considered one of the nation's most radical anti-Fascists.

Said to be among the most charismatic of anti-Fascist intellectuals, Carlo Rosselli abandoned a professorship in political economics to establish an influential underground newspaper. Mussolini considered him the regime's most dangerous enemy, and he sentenced him to the penal colony on the island of Lipari for subversion.

Francesco Nitti was the nephew and namesake of an exiled former Italian premier. A teacher, Nitti was sentenced to five years at Lipari for aiding anti-Fascist exiles in activities considered detrimental to national interests.

According to a *New York Times* report, their daring escape from the penal colony—Nitti characterized Lipari as Italy's Devil's Island—caused such uproar that Mussolini himself was directing the investigation

Putnam was quick to seize what he viewed as a sensational opportunity. Toting a book contract in his attaché case, he sailed the Atlantic. He remained in Paris until he had what he wanted—Nitti's signature on the contract and a completed manuscript. The persuasive publisher even had an introduction written by the exiled former premier.

"The book will be published in New York and London soon after the new year," announced the *Times*, adding that Nitti's exposé would appear in English, Italian, French, German, and Spanish editions. Putnam, obviously, had committed to a costly undertaking.

A week prior to his scheduled return on the steamship *La France*, Putnam visited the company's London office. There he received two letters, each dated December 29, each posted from Paris.

One letter was typewritten in Italian. "We have read newspapers here that you will publish the work of Francesco Nitti about his escape from Lipari. But this must not be done. Fascism will not tolerate such an offense. We and our New York correspondents will know what to do. All the wretched police in New York will not be able to prevent your establishment from being blown into the air with two bombs. We have already warned Fascists in New York. For your own safety and security, you must not publish Nitti's book. We know how to gain our objective."

The letter was signed, "The Fascists of Paris."

The other letter was written in English in pen and ink: "So you will publish a book against Mussolini and Fascism wrote by the idiot Nitti, nephew of the big pig Nitti. And what do you know of Italy? You think a dirty man escaped from jail can judge Mussolini, the most great man in the world, and his formidable success? Certainly not! Then who pays you to insult my country by publishing a book that can only disgust everybody? It is time to stop the damned propaganda of traitor anti-Fascists to which you give the help of the Putnam company."

The letter was signed, "A Black Shirt."

Contacted by the *Chicago Daily Tribune*, executives in the New York office shook a collective head. Putnam had said nothing about Fascist threats. Never mind that one note threatened to "blow into the air with two bombs" the company's headquarters, the publisher neglected to enlighten the home office about its possible obliteration. Then, after the threats were revealed, no one at the publishing house thought it necessary to bother the police department.

On January 3, as Putnam prepared to sail home, he received two more letters threatening his life. While disinclined to take the threats "too seriously," noted the *Times*, he took the precaution of notifying Scotland Yard.

Putnam was back to work in his New York office when he received two additional letters from alleged Italian *Fascisti* living in Paris. One was written in French, the other in Italian. The more sinister of the two contained a sketch of a black hand decorated with Fascist symbols: a dagger, a pistol, and a coffin. The letter also had a message: "Warning to the pig who publishes the book of the other pig, Francesco Nitti, against Italy and the great man Mussolini."

This time Putnam turned the notes over to the New York City police department. Then he called the *New York Times*. "Mr. Putnam," wrote a dutiful reporter, "said that the threats would not stop publication of the book."

They, of course, did not. The presses were rushed and Nitti's "tell all" exposé, *Escape*, enjoyed prominent display on bookstore shelves by the end of January.

At a time when America was reeling from the stock market crash, when unemployment lines were burgeoning in cities across the land, and when a major depression was unraveling the nation's economy, it seems that a book about a penal camp on an island few had ever heard of would be an unlikely seller. In fact, Nitti's anti-Fascist tome sold remarkably well.

Not surprisingly, no bombs exploded at Putnam company headquarters.

Whether by design or happenstance, Fascist death threats and a Nazi kidnapping generated worldwide publicity for George Palmer Putnam's books that no amount of money could have equaled.

Figure 11.3 Amelia Earhart and George Putnam arriving in Hawaii.
Underwood Archive

GEORGE & AMELIA

George Palmer Putnam's *coup de grace* came in 1927. On a gray day in May, Charles Lindbergh, an obscure airmail pilot, lifted into the sky over Long Island, New York, and took off on a flight for Paris. Americans joined the world in a long-held collective breath. Newspaper columnist Will Rogers, famous for irreverent humor, wrote, "No attempt at jokes today. A Slim, tall, bashful, smiling American boy is somewhere over the middle of the Atlantic ocean, where no lone human being has ever ventured before."

Thirty-three and one-half hours, and 3,614 miles later—the greatest distance ever flown nonstop—some 150,000 French citizens ballyhooed the successful landing. In the blink of an eye, Lindbergh became the most talked about man in America, a development that was not lost on publisher Putnam.

As he told James Bassett, columnist for the *Los Angeles Times*, "I paid Charles Lindbergh $100,000 cash for the manuscript to *We* [the pilot's biography and story of the trans-Atlantic flight], and gave him $100,000 more in royalties."

The day *We* was released, one New York bookseller moved more than 1,000 copies. In fewer than sixty days, the slim volume sold upwards of 200,000 copies—sales figures unmatched at the time. Putnam knew what he was doing, and the Lindbergh literary coup made the publisher a celebrity in his own right.

In the year following Lindbergh's flight, eighteen aircraft set course over the Atlantic for European destinations. Three succeeded in crossing its formidable waters; the others did not. Fourteen people perished. Three of the dead were women. Failures and fatalities notwithstanding, the great trans-Atlantic adventure lured countless pilots—and women flyers were among those afflicted most acutely.

Amy Guest, daughter of a Pittsburgh steel mogul and a pilot of no mean skill, was among them. But at fifty-five, Amy was out of shape and overweight, and she was an unlikely candidate for such a grueling and unpredictable undertaking. When the family got wind of her ambitious plan, they applied pressure to force her withdrawal.

She did withdraw, but she refused to abandon the notion of a woman flying the Atlantic. "Find me someone," she instructed an aide. "Someone nice who will do us proud. I shall pay the bills."

Putnam, now sporting a well-deserved reputation as a keen promoter of aviation, entered into the search. The woman he found was a highly skilled aviatrix then employed as a social worker in Boston. Her name was Amelia Earhart.

He telephoned her at work and inquired vaguely if she might be interested in doing something "aeronautic" that could be risky. She hesitated, wary that the caller was a bootlegger seeking a pilot to fly contraband liquor. Putnam assured her that the enterprise was legitimate and he asked her for references. She asked Putnam for references. At last, they agreed to meet.

After details of the proposed flight were unveiled and Earhart expressed her enthusiasm, he asked her, "Why do you want to fly the Atlantic?

She looked her interviewer in the eye: "Why does a man ride a horse?"

"Because he wants to, I guess."

"Well then," she said.

Then, after months of preparation, agonizing delays, and reams of publicity generated by Putnam, the *Friendship*—an orange-and-gold Fokker aircraft—broke through a cloud of heavy fog to put down on the coast of Wales. Never mind that the plane was piloted by Slim Gordon and Bill Stulz, and Earhart was little more than a passenger—a woman had, at last, flown the Atlantic.

Only later was it learned that the *Friendship's* inelegant landing, slightly off course, was occasioned by a dangerously empty fuel tank.

Amy Guest, delighted by the achievement, met the trio at Southampton, and so did thousands of Britons, who had eyes only for Earhart. The London *Times* characterized the flight as "a woman's triumph," and anxious reporters scribbled down virtually every word that spilled from Earhart's lips. The reception was equally clamorous when she returned to the United States. Quickly nicknamed "Lady Lindbergh," Amelia became a household word.

Then, ensconced in a study at Putnam's Rye, New York, estate, Earhart set upon the task of composing a book—*20 Hrs. 40 Min.,*

Our Flight in the Friendship—that her host would publish to great acclaim.

She and Putnam's wife Dorothy became fast friends, but the uncommon affection displayed by her husband toward their houseguest did not go unnoticed. For myriad reasons inevitably attendant to the dissolution of a marriage—certainly, Earhart was one of them—Dorothy went to Reno, then the nation's capital of quick divorce. She charged that after eighteen years of marriage, she and Putnam were "incompatible"—that he "failed to live up to the requirements of a dutiful husband." Not surprisingly, the complaining wife failed to mention the existence of a boyfriend whom she married a month after the divorce was final.

On February 7, 1931, a *Washington Post* reporter found himself in the sleepy village of Noank, Connecticut. There he penned the headline, "Versatile Publisher, Explorer Weds Transoceanic Aviatrix in Quiet Ceremony ...."

In a remarkable letter written to her future husband just prior to the wedding, Earhart expressed her "reluctance to marry ... that I shatter thereby chances in work which means so much to me." She continued:

> I shall not hold you to any medieval code of faithfulness to me, nor shall I consider myself bound to you similarly.
>
> Please let us not interfere with the other's work or play, nor let the world see our private joys or disagreements. In this connection, I may have to keep some place where I can go to be myself now and then, for I cannot guarantee to endure all the confinements of even an attractive cage.
>
> I must exact a cruel promise, and that is you will let me go in a year if we find no happiness together.

Later, using a flyer's metaphor, Earhart characterized the marriage as a "partnership" with "dual controls."

For the first and, perhaps, only time in his life, the gregarious Putnam placed his ego in check and took a back seat, at least publicly, to his more famous wife. He kept watch of her schedule, shielded her from unwanted crowds, protected her from excitable reporters, and—whether graciously or not—assumed responsibility when something went awry. He appears to have been a doting husband, devoted to his wife's interests.

In May 1932, Earhart did what no woman had done, and what only Lindbergh had done at all. She soloed across the Atlantic, putting down her Lockheed Vega in a surprised farmer's field near Londonderry, Ireland, after scuttling her original destination because of fuel and weather concerns. However, no one—except the badly disappointed residents of Le Bourget, France—cared a whit. Her flight, an astonishing fifteen hours and eighteen minutes, bested Lindbergh's by more than half.

She roomed at the U.S. embassy in London, received congratulations from the King of England, visited the Prince of Wales at St. James's Palace, found herself entertained by the House of Commons, and attended the races, escorted by Lady Astor, where George Bernard Shaw sought her out. "Her glory sheds its luster on all womanhood," gushed the London *Sunday Express*.

Earhart was, unquestionably, the most celebrated woman in the world.

Luster aside, the gifted aviatrix did not rest on her laurels. Later that summer, she became the first woman to fly nonstop across the United States, from Los Angeles to Newark, accomplishing the flight in nineteen hours and five minutes. She shattered the previous speed record, which had been set by a man.

In January 1935, she flew from Hawaii to Oakland, California, becoming the first woman pilot to fly solo across the Pacific Ocean. In May, she flew nonstop from Mexico City to New York City, arriving at her destination in fourteen hours and nineteen minutes.

Along the way, she was showered with honors and awards.

The following year, and much to her satisfaction, she was appointed a traveling—what else?—faculty member and aeronautics advisor at Purdue University.

Then, early in 1937, Earhart announced that she would attempt to circumvent the globe. In March, she aborted her first round-the-world flight when, on the second leg of the journey, she crashed during takeoff at Honolulu.

Earhart returned to the mainland and prepared for another attempt. On May 21, 1937, at 3:50 in the afternoon, she and American aviator Fred Noonan took to the sky from Oakland, California, in a specially outfitted Lockheed Electra. This time she flew not to Hawaii, but to Miami, Florida. Confident that the cross-country flight had debugged the sleek new aircraft, Earhart set a southerly course with stops at San Juan, Puerto Rico; Caripito, Venezuela; Paramaribo, Dutch Guiana; and Fortaleza, Brazil. At each stop, they were greeted with enthusiasm and kindness.

The Electra soared over the Atlantic Ocean to the Red Sea and skirted the Arabian Coast to India. The route took them to Calcutta, Rangoon, Singapore, Java, and Port Darwin, Australia, then to Lae, New Guinea.

Obscure as it was to most Americans, Lae was home to more than 1,000 Europeans and served as headquarters of Guinea Airlines. Consequently, a three-thousand-foot-long airstrip and a first-class communications system greeted the flyers.

Staying over in Lae's new hotel, Earhart made a prearranged call to the *New York Herald Tribune*. "Everyone has been as helpful and cooperative as possible," she said, adding "hot baths, mechanical service, radio and weather reports, [and] advice from veteran pilots here."

They stayed an extra day, went sight seeing, and retired early. At ten o'clock the next morning, Earhart and Noonan—carrying 1,100 gallons of gasoline, the Electra's maximum—took off for Howland Island, a mere speck of land 2,556 miles distant.

Pilot and navigator had been in the air twenty hours and fourteen minutes when the *Itasca*, a naval ship at sea monitoring the airplane's progress, heard Earhart's distinctive voice on the radio. Adhering to a frequent and well-disciplined routine, she gave the radio operator her coordinates and then signed off the air.

It was the last time anyone heard her voice. Much like a wisp of cloud vanishing beyond the horizon, Amelia Earhart and Fred Noonan disappeared.

At 21:45 Greenwich time, ninety minutes after Earhart's last radio transmission, and long past the time for her scheduled landing at Howland, the *Itasca* notified fleet command that the Electra was missing.

After an agonizingly slow beginning, a massive search effort was undertaken. No trace of the aircraft was found. Meantime, Putnam quartered himself at the coast guard station in San Francisco where, day and night, he monitored radio reports hoping in vain to hear his wife's voice. Days turned into weeks, and the months passed by. After more than a year, Putnam, with no small measure of reluctance, concluded that his wife was dead.

Chapter 12: The Perfect Crime

When nighttime strollers on the Berkeley campus of the University of California saw lights burning in the science laboratory, they knew at once that the shadow moving in the windows was Bliss Baker.

"My, how hard that boy works," said some. "No wonder he's an honor student," said others. "What an odd bird," said those not inclined to take college life so seriously.

In the parlance of the Jazz Age, Baker, a twenty-year-old senior, was a "flat tire"—a bore. It was 1925, and more than a few Berkeley students embraced with enthusiasm the liberated lifestyle of the Roaring Twenties. It was a free-spirited generation stimulated by economic prosperity and punctuated by mass-consumerism. Daddies bought students automobiles, which introduced an era of unrestricted mobility and backseat romance—which produced an unparalleled upswing in pregnancies. But never mind. Young folks were "hip to the jive."

Prohibition became federal law in 1920, and the demand for illicit booze exploded. So ubiquitous was the bootlegging industry that it paralleled the boom on Wall Street. Hip flasks, especially among young men, were a bodily appendage. The flask might contain "coffin varnish," the dregs of bootlegged booze, or "giggle water," a less lethal variety that reduced inhibitions and often set the stage for amorous adventures. Regardless of its contents, to be without a flask was to risk social censure.

In this era of hot jazz, hot-blooded flappers, and backdoor speakeasies, Bliss Baker was a "wet blanket," a "palooka" who moved outside the student body's trendy set.

Born to modest circumstances, Baker was the son of a San Jose laborer who could ill afford to finance his son's college education. Graduating from San Jose High School in 1922, the youngster was awarded a small scholarship and enrolled at the University of California. His mother and sister Pauline moved with him to Berkeley and the trio took a flat in the Glenn Apartments on Dwight Way. Eighteen-year-old Pauline enrolled at Armstrong Business College and the mother worked in a "cloak and suit house" to finance Baker's education.

He was an outstanding student who earned straight A's and ranked among the university's top achievers. In an effort to finish his undergraduate degree in slightly more than three years, he attended two sessions of summer school and enrolled in extra classes during regular terms. His graduation was slated for August 1925, and then he would sail for eastern Europe on a scholarship to study languages at a Prague university.

Academic excellence aside, Baker was not immune to foibles.

Early on, he worked in the university library. He was dismissed, however, for "improper possession" of seven books from the reserve shelves. A mistake, he said. Another blot on Baker's record occurred when he was a member of Berkeley's Company D of the National Guard. His stint ended when he was charged with failure to follow orders. A misunderstanding, he said.

Aside from membership in a small Slavic language club, Baker was largely aloof from Berkeley's vibrant social life. Now and then, he brought home extra money earned by tutoring Russian language students, but activities that took him away from his books were infrequent.

Still, Baker was an anomaly. Subject to flights of fancy, he lacked sophistication and mature judgment. Inexplicably, an untidy corner of his mind was cluttered with peculiar whims. Lately, the study of criminology had become an avocation, if not an obsession. Criminals, he determined, were uniformly dumb and officers of the law were not much brighter.

Russell Crawford, a childhood friend two years older than Baker, was cut from similar cloth. He, too, was an honor student, who had graduated from the University of Oregon at nineteen. Like Baker, he embraced the study of criminology as an avocation and, perhaps, with even greater zeal than his friend. There were, however, fundamental differences between the two. Baker possessed brilliance—he was a thinker. Crawford possessed cleverness—he was a doer. Baker was intellectually withdrawn. Crawford was gregarious and full of himself.

Clearly, however, the common thread that bound the two together was a lack of moral compass.

In addition to studying criminology, Baker and Crawford read, or misread, Friedrich Nietzsche—*Beyond Good and Evil* and *On the Genealogy of Morals*. Like countless others before them, they misconstrued Nietzsche's moral philosophy and embraced a convoluted notion of the philosopher's theory of man and superman.

They were, of course, supermen. They were the embodiment of the dominant male who should allow nothing to stand between himself and success—not law, and certainly not men of inferior intellect and lesser ability. Cruelty, distasteful as it might be, was wholly justified to attain whatever ends they sought.

In fact, Nietzsche came to Baker and Crawford not through courses in philosophy or passion for the works of notable philosophers. They discovered Nietzsche in wire dispatches from Chicago splashed boldly on the front pages of northern California newspapers.

Just months prior, teenagers Nathan Leopold and Richard Loeb were sentenced to life imprisonment by a Chicago judge. The young men were spared the electric chair by the compelling histrionics of legendary defense lawyer Clarence Darrow. He pleaded his clients guilty of a gruesome murder and then argued eloquently against the death penalty—for thirty-three days. His argument prevailed.

Leopold graduated from the University of Chicago at eighteen. He was an expert in ornithology and botany, and was fluent in nine languages. Loeb graduated from the University of Michigan at seventeen but was less intellectually gifted than Leopold. Nevertheless, his academic prowess, coupled with physical magnetism, imbued him with unbounded egotism.

Both came from wealthy families, lived pampered lives and cared nothing about right or wrong. After earnest disagreements, they established a fateful relationship based on a written contract signed by both. It stipulated that Loeb would become Leopold's lover and Leopold would join Loeb in fulfilling his long-held fantasy of committing the perfect crime. It was a bizarre trade-off.

Weeks were spent plotting a foolproof kidnap-murder. On a spring afternoon in 1924, they lured fourteen-year-old Bobby Franks into a rented automobile, where he was stabbed repeatedly. They stuffed rags in the boy's mouth, gagged him, and left him on the floor of the car to bleed to death while they stopped for a sandwich and waited for nightfall. After dark, they secreted the body in a culvert and then treated themselves to a full-course dinner.

Leopold called the Franks' home and told a terrified mother that her son had been kidnapped. He demanded a $10,000 ransom payment. Instructions for delivery, he told her, would arrive the next day. The second note arrived, but no ransom was paid. Discovery by a maintenance man of a child's shoe protruding from a culvert foiled the culprits' fantasy of committing the perfect crime.

In fact, the amoral teenagers were sloppy criminals.

Leopold and Loeb, who claimed an affinity for Nietzsche and considered themselves supermen—some newspapers blamed the German philosopher for Bobby Franks' murder—were considered "pikers" by Baker and Crawford. That a pair of exceptional scholars bungled what should have been an effortless crime offended their sensibilities. What they considered a paltry ransom demand amused them. The whole affair, they reasoned, smacked of blatant incompetence.

Hours were spent analyzing the Chicago crime and criticizing its perpetrators. At last, the young men realized that destiny had chosen them to commit the perfect crime. It was inevitable. After all, Nietzsche, they believed, had given them his blessing.

Baker and Crawford were atwitter with excitement. They agreed to meet nightly to plot their course. Berkeley's science laboratory was selected as their place of rendezvous. Theirs would be a crime constructed and orchestrated along rigorous scientific principles. Failure was impossible—unthinkable.

As Baker's rich fantasy life consumed more and more of his time, the dedicated scholar became less dedicated. Crawford, who supported a pregnant wife as a salesman for the Eureka Vacuum Cleaning Company, dedicated himself to irresponsibility. The would-be criminals/criminologists were joined at the hip.

A feature writer for the *Fresno Bee* noted that "the 'perfect crime' they planned involved the kidnapping of a wealthy person. This, they decided, offered the best means to obtain money. Murder was not a part of the project."

The plotters preferred "exquisite torture" or, at the very least, threats to commit "exquisite torture." It was their notion that a $50,000 ransom could easily be extracted from a wealthy person under threats of inoculating a kidnap victim with "disease germs."

Reconstructing a conversation that may have been apocryphal, the *Bee* writer described a diabolical scene:

Crawford entered the laboratory softly. Baker, tall, slender, with dark, intent eyes and astonishing hands was holding a test tube against the light. "It's all ready!" he cried.

Crawford asked what the tube held.

"'Germs!' answered the student. "Enough to scare a millionaire half to death and bring us the price of a trip around the world!"

"Baker flushed with triumph [and] the boys talked excitedly …."

Over the months, they studied and debated the fine points of kidnapping and extortion. With care and diligence, they laid out a scheme both were certain would demonstrate their genius and make them wealthy men.

Potential victims were given "scientific" scrutiny and long lists of positive and negative attributes were created. At last, the evaluation process culminated in the selection of Daniel C. Jackling and his wife, Virginia. Mrs. Jackling's sister Eleanor, the wife of Rudolph Spreckels, would play an ancillary role.

Born in 1869 in Missouri, Jackling was orphaned early on and taken in by relatives. He worked his way through college, graduated with a degree in mining and headed west during the boom at Cripple Creek, Colorado. By 1896, he was a mill superintendent at Mercur, Utah. Asked to examine potential copper property at nearby Bingham Canyon, Jackling urged mass mining and milling of the low-grade ore. In 1903, the Utah Copper Company was organized with Jackling as president. In time, the company became Kennecott Copper Corporation and Bingham became the largest open-pit copper mine in the world. Jackling's method of low-grade ore processing became the standard worldwide.

In 1915, the mining mogul came to San Francisco and married Virginia Jolliffe. The newlyweds fashioned the top floor of the St. Francis Hotel into a palatial home and the Jacklings settled into the city's business and social life. The couple's opulent lifestyle and lavish spending raised eyebrows even among the wealthy. Jackling traveled in a private railroad car and owned one of the largest yachts on the West Coast.

The Jolliffe sisters, all seven of them, married well. Eleanor's husband, Rudolph Spreckels, born in 1872, made his first million by the time he was twenty-six. Son of Claus Spreckels, the Hawaiian sugar magnate, Rudolph vowed to make his own fortune after he was banished from the family home following a quarrel with his father. He did. He competed with his father in the sugar market and made his own mark.

Figure 12.1 Daniel C. Jackling, president of Kennecott Copper Corporation.
San Francisco History Center,
San Francisco Public Library

In San Francisco, his adopted home, he developed extensive real estate holdings, owned controlling interest in a bank, and was president of the San Francisco Gas Company. Although he lost a palatial mansion in the 1906 earthquake and fire, he worked through the disaster and its aftermath as an anti-graft crusader. He vowed to destroy powerful political boss Abe Ruef and the machine that controlled city hall. Funding a lengthy investigation and subsequent prosecution, Spreckels put Ruef behind bars and became *persona non grata* in the process. He exposed too many well-placed San Franciscans. Woodrow Wilson offered Spreckels a diplomatic post, but the controversial reformer chose to remain in California.

Baker and Crawford did their homework well. They had learned who the keepers of San Francisco's fortunes were. They knew as well that Daniel C. Jackling would act decisively and without hesitation if he thought his wife had been kidnapped.

"Slowly and with the greatest care they worked out the details of their enterprise," wrote the *Bee*. "There was to be no slip-up."

In fact, the plan was startling for its simplicity. The phone line into the Spreckels mansion would be cut. After Jackling left for his office, a call would be placed to Mrs. Jackling telling her that Mrs. Spreckels had been taken to the hospital at San Mateo and was calling for her. While Mrs. Jackling was en route to the hospital, a random messenger would deliver a note to Mr. Jackling informing him that his wife had been kidnapped. The note would demand that a package containing $50,000 ransom be given to a cab driver waiting in front of the building. The unsuspecting driver would carry the package to a roadhouse where the clever perpetrators would take delivery—and live happily every after as well-to-do men who had executed the perfect crime.

It was a clean, simple, fail-proof plan—or so its authors thought.

At four o'clock Friday morning, June 25, 1925, Crawford shimmied up a telephone pole outside the Spreckels estate and cut the telephone wires. A reporter for the *San Francisco Chronicle* noted that "he used a pair of white cotton gloves so that he would leave no fingerprints, and tied the cut wires with a piece of hay rope so that passersby would not notice the severance."

Having several hours to kill, the plotters drove aimlessly in Crawford's car chatting smugly about the ease with which their first mission was being carried out. When planned scientifically, crime, they concluded, was child's play.

Daylight came, the hours ticked by, and then the moment arrived to put their carefully constructed formula to work.

Ample time was given for Jackling to arrive at his office on the eighteenth floor of the Hobart Building. Then the telephone rang in the opulent Jackling suite at the St. Francis Hotel. It was 10:45 A.M. when Virginia Jackling picked up the receiver. At the other end of the line was a sympathetic male voice.

"Mrs. Jackling?"

"Yes."

"It is my unhappy task to advise you that your sister, Mrs. Spreckels, has been hurt in a motor accident on the Pacific Highway. She is in the Mills Memorial Hospital at San Mateo and is asking for you."

Figure 12.2 Mrs. Virginia Jackling, left, and a friend at children's fundraiser.
San Francisco History Center, San Francisco Public Library

The *Bee* noted that "Mrs. Jackling was in a panic of excitement and worry. She tried to ask questions, but the wire was dead."

Then something happened that was not scripted in the Baker-Crawford scenario. As the would-be extortionists giggled with glee and complimented each other for their seamless performance, Mr. Jackling put down his coffee cup, set aside the morning paper, and looked with concern at his distraught wife. He asked her if the telephone call was bad news.

Virginia repeated the caller's message. Jackling, always calm in an emergency, offered consoling words and suggested that the caller may have overstated the urgency of the situation. Mrs. Spreckels may have suffered a bruise or two, probably nothing more.

Nevertheless, Virginia scurried about the suite directing her maid in preparations for the thirty-mile drive to San Mateo. She ordered the chauffeur to have her automobile ready, said goodbye to her husband, and started on her journey south.

Meantime, Jackling ordered his car to stand by, finished his coffee, and left for the office.

Unbeknownst to Baker and Crawford, their well-knit plan was unraveling already. Fully confident of success, however, they drove toward a telegraph office near the Hobart Building where they intended to hire a delivery boy. Just then, they spotted a Postal Telegraph messenger on the street. They pulled over and called him to the car. The youngster's eyes widened when Crawford offered him a dollar—no mean tip in 1925—to deliver a sealed message to Mr. Jackling. Impressed by the mission's importance—everyone knew who Jackling was—the lad readily accepted.

With that task completed, the conspirators called the Yellow Cab Company and ordered a taxi to go to the Hobart Building. Told it was a non-passenger pickup and delivery, the driver was instructed to park before the main entrance and wait for someone to approach the car with a package. Upon receipt, he was to take the package to Uncle Tom's Cabin, a roadhouse near Millbrae, and deliver it to a young man. So there would be no mistaking the proper recipient, the man would stand beside the road with his arms folded.

By any measure, the instructions were odd, but the taxi driver was accustomed to eccentricity.

At 11:10, twenty-five minutes after the telephone call to Virginia, the Postal Telegraph messenger entered the foyer of Jackling's office suite. In a breathless rush of words, the excited lad told C. A. Nickson, the mining man's secretary, that two strangers had paid him a dollar to deliver a personal message to Mr. Jackling.

Either it was very important, mused Nickson, or the senders were generous to a fault. He told the boy to wait and carried the message to Jackling's office. The copper magnate slit open the envelope and read an astonishing bit of prose composed months earlier in the Berkeley science laboratory: "Your wife, by the time you read this, will have been kidnapped. If you do not follow instructions as hereafter outlined, your wife will be exquisitely tortured."

The note ordered Jackling to make up a package containing $50,000 in twenty-dollar bills and deliver it to a Yellow Cab parked at the building entrance. It warned that should he fail to carry out the instructions in thirty minutes, "Your wife will be inoculated with the germs of loathsome diseases."

Jackling reacted to the ransom note with silent rage. How dare anyone think he would fall for such a naïve and obvious bluff? He stepped into a private office and telephoned San Francisco chief of police Daniel O'Brien.

"It was characteristic of Jackling that he told his story, incredible though it was, in a few words, so coolly and clearly that the official at the other end of the line instantly understood the whole plot," wrote the *Bee*. "In the few sentences that they exchanged, an entire counter-plot was arranged."

A moment later, Jackling received a telephone call from his bewildered wife. She was at the Mills Hospital in San Mateo. Her sister was not. So far as Virginia could determine, there had been no accident. Still, there was no answer when she called the Spreckels estate. What was happening?

In a calm, quiet tone, Jackling told her that the breakfast caller had been mistaken and not to worry about it. However, he asked that she return at once to their hotel suite and remain there. Over dinner, he would explain everything. He said nothing about the kidnapping threat or the ransom note.

Jackling took the elevator to the ground floor and crossed the street to the First National Bank—his brother-in-law, Rudolph Spreckels, was its president—and held a brief conference with the cashier.

Parked nearby, Baker and Crawford watched eagerly as the drama unfolded. Like boys on a lark, they were filled with giddy anticipation. When Jackling reemerged from the bank and approached the taxi, they let out a whoop. Then, filled with the scent of money, Crawford sped away from the curb and headed toward Millbrae and Uncle Tom's Cabin. The drama's final act—delivery of the ransom—was approaching.

As Crawford drove off, Jackling asked the taxi driver, "Are you waiting for someone?"

"Yes," he replied. "Have you a package for me?"

Jackling handed him the package and the man drove away carrying a metal box stuffed with shredded paper. As the cab moved into traffic, an unadorned automobile carrying four San Francisco detectives pulled in behind it.

For all his bravado, Crawford was losing his nerve. As they approached the roadhouse, he decided it would be safer not to park his automobile there. He suggested that Baker wait alone for the taxi. Should anything go wrong, he could play dumb. Crawford would drive a mile or so down the road. If the delivery was made successfully, the cabbie could drive Baker to Crawford's car.

Incredibly, it did not occur to Baker that Crawford was setting him up as the fall guy should the caper go sour. He agreed to the revised plan. Crawford dropped him at Uncle Tom's Cabin and drove away.

From a police perspective, the anonymous criminals were moments away from apprehension. What no one anticipated, however, was an unintended consequence of abandoning horses for motorized vehicles. As the taxi sped toward Millbrae, its unannounced police escort broke down—inelegantly. Had it not been for a passing motorist, Baker and Crawford might have lived out their fantasy of committing the perfect crime.

Sort of. Shredded newspaper in place of $50,000 had not played into their scenario.

A quick-thinking officer stepped into the roadway, waved his badge, and flagged down the driver of the oncoming vehicle. Seconds later, the surprised motorist was left gaping as the detectives sped after the vanishing cab in his commandeered automobile.

The taxi driver was well acquainted with Uncle Tom's Cabin. It was a notorious juice joint where illegal booze was cheap, and so were the women who offered their favors. Hauling drunks from one speakeasy to another was an unpleasant but unavoidable part of the taxi business. For that reason, it seemed incongruous to see a young man—he looked like a bookish college kid, freshly scrubbed and dolled up in a suit and tie—standing in the roadway, arms folded, in front of a rowdy roadhouse.

The kid waved him over and the driver stopped.

"Hello there, driver," said Baker, effecting business-like crispness in his tone.

"Hello."

"Do you know this sign?" he asked. Looking somewhat foolish, he folded his arms.

The driver had forgotten about the arm-folding signal. He shook his head. "No."

"No?"

"No."

"Well, have you a package?"

"Yes, but there's a $7.50 taxi charge and I want to be paid first."

"Well, drive down the road about a mile. I'll direct you, and you'll be paid there."

As Baker opened the door to step into the cab, the commandeered machine carrying four detectives careened in front of the taxi and threw on its brakes. Baker was snatched bodily by a pair of officers and thrust into the car, while the cabbie was taken into custody by the other two.

Shocked, the gifted young scholar promptly fainted.

Crawford, who may have witnessed the encounter from afar, quickly disappeared.

As the *Bee* commented wryly, the perfect crime "had developed astonishing imperfections."

Indeed it had. Baker, who thought himself invincible, was on his way to a private cell at the San Francisco city prison.

His first story to investigating officers was not his best. As the *Oakland Tribune* reported, "He said he had received a mysterious note from a Chinese [man] in San Francisco, asking him to wait alongside the highway for a package, and then to deliver it, in return for which he would receive $1,000. He held to this story until he was confronted by his mother. Then he broke down and confessed."

Sort of.

In fact, Baker's confession was little more than a self-absorbed, self-serving feature story given to a *Chronicle* reporter seeking a sensational scoop.

"It was my chum, George Beeman, and I who devised the scheme to blackmail Jackling and get $50,000 from him," Baker lied, hoping to protect the real "chum" who had left him holding the bag. "The kidnapping of Mrs. Jackling was just a hoax. All we wanted to do, as far as she was concerned, was to get her out of the way just long enough for her husband to miss her and come to the conclusion that the threats we had made in our note to him were not a joke."

Baker claimed that Beeman, who he said was a book salesman, "planned the whole thing, and I collaborated with him."

Brazenly, or stupidly, he cited his fascination with the Leopold and Loeb case. He and his fantasy partner, George, "followed every step" and "it was our ambition to plan and execute even a more perfect crime than theirs ...."

More perfect was, of course, an oxymoron.

His chronology of the actual crime was, by and large, accurate. The balance of the confession was rubbish.

Although neither was considered a serious suspect, Baker had the decency to clear the cab driver and messenger boy of any involvement.

Then, feeling sorry for himself and seeking public sympathy, he concluded by saying, "I am afraid this thing will break my mother's heart. She has worked hard to try to give me an education .... I have thrown away all I have won ...."

The following day, Baker admitted that he was a creative liar and rescinded his confession. He promptly authored a new one which the *Chronicle* was only too happy to publish. Noting that the second confession was made in the presence of Baker's mother, readers were thus assured of its veracity.

Not only was the George Beeman litany repeated, Baker went out of his way to protect his accomplice. "I do not know where Beeman has gone. He is never at one place more than a short while and it was only when he called unexpectedly that I saw or heard from him."

So much for veracity.

However, Baker's loose regard for the truth became even more emboldened when he told investigators that his previous statements "were given in misapprehension of the consequences resulting from what was in reality a laboratory experiment of the principles of criminology to which I have given extensive attention, under the tutelage of a Mr. George Beeman."

Having spat out that mouthful, he, again, offered a largely accurate chronology of the crime. Then he succumbed to mawkish self-pity.

> I am extremely ashamed of that [ransom] letter. It was crude, and I can only explain my allowance of it as due to a condition of nervous strain brought on by a continuous course

at the university of three years, in addition to work on the outside in the line of teaching.

Let me say again that I sincerely regret doing what I described. In no way did we mean harm to anyone (though I can understand Mr. Jackling's reaction to the cruelty of the letter, and I am sorry for it). It was in the nature of a puerile attempt to apply theories which must have [been] assembled in an irresponsible effort to do something, the consequence of which we did not understand.

Baker's mother told the *Chronicle*, "My boy is a good boy and never gave me a moment's sorrow before this. He overtaxed his mind by studying too much at college. That is why he attempted to do this terrible thing."

While Baker channeled rich fantasies into creative confessions that duped the press, much of the public, and his own mother, the San Francisco police were not so easily bamboozled. Before the ink dried on Baker's first flight of fancy, detectives knew that George Beeman was a figment of Baker's overactive imagination.

Incapable of corralling his narcissistic egotism, Russell Crawford was dropping clues throughout the Bay Area. At a level the gregarious plotter failed to comprehend, it offended him that the fictional Beeman was getting headlines that rightfully were his.

Two days after the foiled extortion attempt, Crawford was taken into custody. "Arrested on the State highway at Palo Alto ... as he was driving his coupe south, Crawford readily submitted to arrest, admitted his identity, and confessed to his part in the plot," reported the *Chronicle*.

Well, almost. The *Chronicle* reported:

"For an hour and a half after being taken to the Redwood City jail, the boy denied any connection with the crime. Then, with a grin, he confessed, saying that he had lied 'just to test the machinery of the law.'"

Early on, it became apparent that Crawford had read Baker's confessions and intended to employ the same strategy.

"Why did you boys select Mr. Jackling for your victim?" he was asked by detectives.

"That's easy," replied Crawford, leaning back and spreading his shoulders. "Jackling is a millionaire. He has the reputation of being a go-getter, and we didn't want to trifle with anybody who would be easy. We were doing things on a big scale and we picked a big man."

"The reason for our crime was not money," he added by way of clarification. "We weren't after money. We wanted to learn more about law and law enforcement."

Crawford was in his element, spinning tales before an audience keenly interested in his performance:

> We entertained theories in our efforts to study criminal law and criminology, that the forces of law enforcement were ineffective. To prove this to our own satisfaction we planned what we thought was the perfect crime. Every detail was to be scientifically mapped and every step was to be carefully planned.
>
> We felt that Mr. Jackling was the proper subject. He was the type of man who would act without hesitation. We allowed him only thirty minutes in which to carry out his part of the scheme, because we thought that this would cause confusion. We depended upon confusion to make our perfect crime a success.
>
> I don't exactly know where our plan failed. Now that I look the case over, I think it was because we handed that messenger boy a dollar. That was too much. It caused him to look us over, and later he was able to provide the police with our descriptions.
>
> We realized that to Mr. Jackling the loss of $50,000 meant nothing. We had no intention of ever harming Mrs. Jackling. To have come into contact with her might have meant violence, and, perhaps, we would have had to take a human life, which would have been inhuman. Neither of us are criminals, and we could do nothing that would brand us as such.
>
> What were we going to do with the $50,000? Well, we had several plans. Bliss' folks are very poor. He always feels sorry

to think that his mother has had to work so hard to put him through college. He was going to use the money to make life more pleasant.

As for myself, I didn't need the money for any specific purpose. I planned to finish my law course, which I took up at the University of Oregon. Then I would go out into the world and be an apostle of better law enforcement.

Late that night, Crawford was taken to San Francisco and lodged with Baker in the city prison. Authorities told the press that charges of extortion would probably be filed early the next week.

Accosted at a small ranch near Sunnyvale, Crawford's mother told a *Chronicle* reporter, "I am simply stupefied by it all. I cannot believe my son did such a thing."

That Crawford's criminal posturing may have been more than scientific experimentation was suggested the day following his arrest. Santa Clara County law enforcement authorities let it be known that the criminology aficionado was a suspect in an attempted extortion the previous May.

John L. Hagelin, a wealthy orchardist and member of the Campbell school board—Crawford attended school in Campbell—was the recipient of an extortion note. It stated that his daughter Mary would be kidnapped and sold into slavery in the Orient should he fail to pay $4,000. Detailed instructions for delivery followed.

Hagelin discovered the extortion note beneath the doormat on his front porch and immediately notified the sheriff's office. The perpetrator was never caught.

Louis Cikuth, a wealthy Watsonville man, came forward with a nearly identical story. In February, he received an extortion note demanding $6,000. If not paid in accordance with detailed instructions, both of his young daughters would be snatched and sold into slavery in the Orient.

The note's writer was still on the loose.

At the same time, J. L. Reed revealed to the *Chronicle* that his son-in-law was something more than a harmless theorist:

> Three weeks ago I influenced my daughter to leave Crawford. He had been mistreating her shamefully, despite the fact that she is about to become a mother. Angered because I stepped into the affair, he came to my home last Sunday night armed with an iron pipe.
>
> "I'm here to get you," he said, rushing at me as I came to the door. I grappled with him, wrested the bar from him and threw him down the stairs. He did not return.
>
> I think Crawford should be punished for the good of society. He is a harmful type.

A *Los Angeles Times* reporter visited the failed criminals at the city prison. Crawford, he wrote, "still found jail an 'extremely interesting place' and was still just a little proud of the 'perfect crime' they concocted."

Baker, on the other hand, "is not so contented." The reporter noted that he was "almost crestfallen."

On June 29, after Jackling appeared at the Hall of Justice and filed formal complaints, the plotters were arraigned in police court. Their cases were continued until July 7, when they were scheduled for a preliminary hearing on charges of attempted kidnapping and attempted extortion.

The same day, authorities intercepted an astonishing letter written by Baker and intended for delivery to Mr. and Mrs. Jackling:

> I hope you will pardon the liberty I assume in telling you directly what were the real motives and purposes of the crime which I, Bliss Baker, and my friend, Russell Crawford, are accused of committing against you both.
>
> In the same light of understanding, all the events of the past few days seem like some unbelievable nightmare.
>
> And that nightmare would never have occurred if its consequences could have been apprehended—shock and disgust on our part, grief and humiliation suffered by our families (our

mothers especially), and the realization on our part that we are considered not as scientific investigators, but merely criminals.

It is easy to understand this confession as a "crawling in the dirt" to escape what we deserve as ordinary felons. But please believe us when we say that the entire plot was due to our lack of common sense and mental balance.

We are both avid readers in criminology. Russell is preparing himself to be a lawyer. I am interested in the subject as a hobby and also because I hope some time to be able to write— and to do this one must know life not only through a study of the righteous but through a keener appreciation of a good man or woman by contrast with his or her less righteous kin.

But mere theory seemed to us for some reason insufficient. And when we were carried away by the spirit of experimentation in desiring to put theory into practice, to test it, we lost reason, it seems, and wronged you—shamefully.

I cannot explain how we lost sight of the inevitable end. It was not money we wished—we were both well enough off not to stoop to such depths for such a selfish consideration. There is no logic at all to the offense. It seemed so clear at the time that we thought only of the execution—we forgot the ends in view. Our fascination led to a total eclipse of all sensible consideration.

And now we both realize that our blind stupidity, in spite of a hard-won education, has brought nothing but misery to us and others.

It is now too late to rectify the wrong done. We are not pleading for leniency on our own accounts. Russell is married, and in a few days will be a father with new responsibilities. His wife is a frail little thing and cannot bear the burden of a dependent child alone. And may I say that if you could meet my mother you would know that no "ideas of crimes for crimes sake" could have arisen in the mind of any son with such a mother.

No crime pays—every criminal is lost before he commits the act that sends him on the long sad path—this is our conclusion, if it can be called such, though we knew that before. It

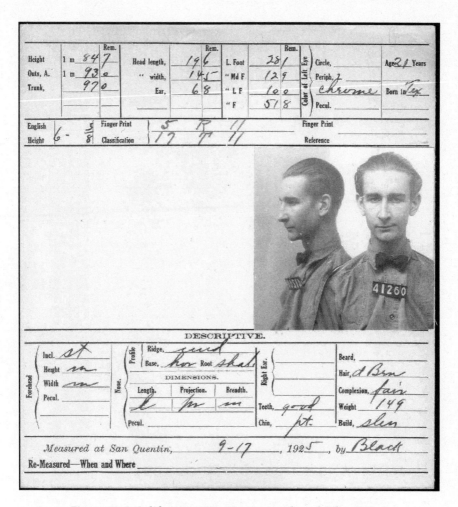

Figure 12.3 California state prison record card, Bliss Baker.
California State Archives

was enthusiasm for scientific investigation on our own accounts that led us on.

Also, we are young. We know little about life. Unfortunately, theories do not furnish a practical basis for action.

We have already paid the penalty in a way that can never be forgotten. Our names, once linked with what every one will consider a crime and not a mere experiment, can never be free

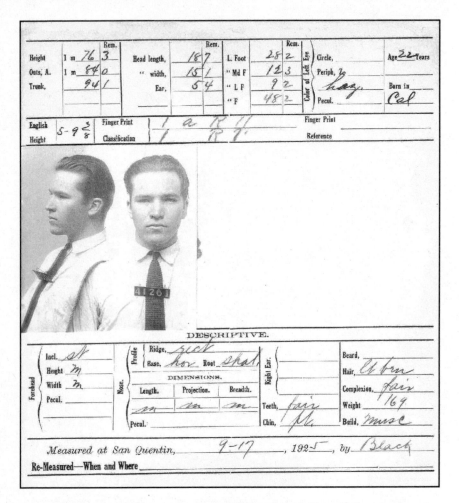

Figure 12.4 California state prison record card, Russell Crawford.
California State Archives

from innuendo. Admitted that the result is the same, still there remains our defense that sneers and disbelief will not consider. There will always be the shadow of crime above us—once suspected. That in itself is a terrible burden for any one to feel hanging above him throughout life.

Let us again assure you that we sincerely repent of the pain we have caused you. We hope your thoughts, in view of this explanation, are not now so harshly disposed towards us.

Bliss Baker

Russell Crawford

If the Jacklings read Baker's magnum opus when it appeared in the northern California press, their reaction went unrecorded.

The young men's preliminary hearing commenced as scheduled, on July 7, in Judge Lyle T. Jacks' police court. Witnesses were mostly police officers involved in the arrests, interrogations, and ongoing investigation.

The *Tribune* attributed the only emotional display to Baker's mother who "broke down when her son was led into the courtroom manacled to his accomplice."

The *Chronicle* noted that "Baker and Crawford smiled frequently throughout the proceedings, particularly when Baker's written confession was read."

The defendants were charged with conspiracy to extort and were bound over for trial in superior court, August 28. No pleas were entered and bail was set at $5,000 each.

Never mind the obvious implications of his deed—striped trousers and a steel bunk in a dreary jail cell—Baker was unable, or unwilling, to grasp the reality of his situation. "Since we didn't injure Mrs. Jackling," he rationalized to a *Bee* reporter, "why should anyone bother further about it? Besides, one of us wishes to finish college and the other is likely to lose his job if he is detained too long."

During the weeks prior to their court date, public defenders agonized over their clients' intractability. Baker and Crawford were convinced that a "harmless scientific experiment" defense would win a jury's sympathy. Defense counsel was emphatic in its belief that such a defense would backfire—badly. It would offend the jurors' intelligence and may even anger a few. Should the defendants be convicted, the jury would have no mercy.

Then, for reasons known only to the accused, the young men did a complete turnabout. "Changing their pleas from not guilty to guilty, Bliss Baker and Russell Crawford today threw themselves on the mercy of the court," reported the *San Mateo Times*, August 28.

Two weeks later, superior court judge Michael J. Roche declared, "The time has come to halt the attempts of the rising generation to commit perfect crimes." With that, he dispatched the would-be extortionists to San Quentin to serve from one to two and a half years behind bars.

The *nouveau* felons were last heard of in November 1925. William H. Nicholl, chief of San Francisco's adult probation department, sought the cooperation of penologists, criminologists, psychiatrists, sociologists, and social workers to establish a psychopathic ward at San Quentin—"for the observation of puzzling mental cases."

He was particularly intrigued by Baker and Crawford. Noted the *Tribune*, "The Jackling plot, Nicholl believes, is stranger from a psychical point of view than the Loeb-Leopold case."

Perhaps it was.

Chapter 13: Escaping the Q

Walter H. Wyeth and Wanda T. Stewart bore proof that convicts came in diverse wrappers. Wyeth was a well-educated insurance broker who dabbled in architecture. However, with the nation twisting in the throes of economic depression, few people purchased insurance, and even fewer needed or could afford an architect. Rather than face a downturn in income, Wyeth reasoned that he could earn a nice living stealing commissions and forging checks.

He was caught.

Stewart, gifted with a mathematical bent, worked as a bookkeeper. He was a bright man who thought he was clever enough to create a system of clandestine profit sharing by manipulating company books in his favor. Apparently, Stewart failed to reckon with the fact that successful businesses were in the habit of hiring equally bright folks to audit their books.

He was caught.

Each man was tried, convicted, and sent to San Quentin. Located some ten miles north of San Francisco, this legendary California institution welcomed criminals newly graduated from the court system, and offered rapid matriculation to graduate- and post-graduate-level instruction in criminality. Wyeth and Stewart were dedicated students who embraced the advanced curriculum with gusto. They shed lingering vestiges of civility, hardened themselves to violence, and adopted a hypothesis that no prison could hold them for any length of time.

On April 26, 1934, they put their theory to the ultimate test.

Among San Quentin's population of 5,500, some 1,000 trusted inmates worked at various tasks outside the penitentiary's walls. Naively, prison authorities extended the trust to Stewart and Wyeth, assigning them to a surveying crew. Not only did the men work outside the prison, the authorities allowed them to dress in civilian clothes.

Assigned to monitor them, veteran guard Charles Green carried a "pocket" pistol with an accurate range of about twenty-five feet. The convicts carried a sharpened axe and a large knife intended to cut surveying stakes.

"Since the men were working fifty feet apart," recalled Green, "I stood between them so that my pistol would reach either of them."

In fact, Green's pistol proved to be an idle ornament.

In a well-orchestrated ruse, Stewart slipped on grass and tumbled toward a clump of brush. Caught in a fool's ploy, Green rushed toward him and ordered the convict to his feet. In so doing, he turned his attention away from Wyeth. In seconds, the other prisoner was behind him and Green felt the cold steel of a knife at his throat.

"They bound me to a scrub oak with some wire that they had smuggled out of the prison, and left me," mused Green. "As soon as I could wiggle loose, I blew my whistle and gave the alarm."

Wiggling loose had required thirty minutes. While the duped guard struggled with his bonds, the escaped convicts were well on their way to parts unknown.

When finally Green blew his whistle, the alarm was sounded at San Quentin. Local authorities were notified of the escape and a bulletin was hastily prepared for transmission on the police teletype.

The teletype system was nearly useless, however. In all of California, just thirty-three law enforcement offices were equipped with teletype receivers. Compounding the problem of communications necessary for a coordinated search effort, few law enforcement agencies were equipped with in-car, two-way radios, and no statewide radio system, by which one agency could contact another, existed.

Sabin Kane, police chief at nearby San Rafael, was among those who received the teletype bulletin. It described the fugitives as "desperados of the most dangerous type." He responded by calling his force together, including off-duty policemen.

Kane's call found officers A. M. Dewey and Phil La Cornec out of uniform and wearing casual clothes. In fact, Dewey was ready to go fishing and was dressed accordingly. Nevertheless, the men joined up and set out to patrol the area in Dewey's steel-gray De Soto police coupe. In the automobile were two revolvers, two 30-30 rifles, a shotgun, and a large store of ammunition.

At about 2:30 in the afternoon, Kenneth Wilburn, a filling station attendant at Irwin and Canal streets in San Rafael, watched two men make their way across a nearby field. As they reached the highway, Dewey's De Soto whizzed by. It stopped, turned around, and approached the men.

Wilburn watched as one of the men leaped onto the vehicle's running board. The other man jumped into the rear seat. "The car stayed on the highway for three or four minutes while those in it apparently talked. Then it moved up the highway. That's all I saw," recalled the attendant.

Within a minute or two, three automobiles carrying prison guards pulled into the gas station and told Wilburn about the escape. He, in turn, told the guards about the odd scene he had witnessed just moments before. Wilburn was certain that something was amiss.

With misplaced confidence in their powers of deductive reasoning, the guards ignored an opportunity for immediate pursuit and possible capture. Instead, they made the erroneous assumption that Dewey and La Cornec had taken the escapees into custody. One of them telephoned the courthouse and asked if the patrolmen and their prisoners had arrived. Learning that authorities there knew nothing about a capture, the guard said, "Oh, I guess they're still on the way over." Then, thinking there was no reason to be on the road, they turned the three cars around and the guards headed back to the penitentiary.

In fact, just as he suspected, the filling station attendant had witnessed a kidnapping. It was amateur day among San Quentin guards, and two of San Rafael's finest were not in the best of form either.

Shortly after the officers' abduction, highway patrolman Jack Agnew passed Dewey's police car just north of San Rafael: "I waved, but Dewey didn't wave back."

He thought it was odd, but there was no reason to think anything was wrong.

Floyd Middagh, a San Rafael police sergeant, was returning from a trip when he passed the gray coupe about three miles out of Napa. He recognized the car by "the red light on the front radiator" and he waved to Dewey. "He looked me right in the eye, but never gave a sign."

Although both lawmen were curious about Dewey's unfriendly behavior, neither officer had the slightest inkling that Dewey and La Cornec were the unwitting traveling companions of fugitive kidnappers.

As time ticked by needlessly, it finally occurred to investigating officers that Wilburn had, indeed, witnessed a kidnapping. At last, word spread among law enforcement agencies that the "desperate" escapees had abducted two San Rafael patrolmen. Fearing for the officer's lives, a massive manhunt—loosely coordinated, badly executed, and reeking of chaos—commenced immediately.

The *Oakland Tribune* reported that "tips" about possible sightings here, there, and everywhere "poured in so fast and in such confusion that authorities were kept working at high pressure."

For reasons unclear—perhaps it was overcompensation for early mistakes made in a disjointed search effort—officers involved in the manhunt were led to believe that a gunfight was a "virtual certainty" when the "showdown" came. Incredibly, they issued a "blanket order" to "shoot on sight."

The order included no magic formula to separate the kidnapped officers from the kidnappers when the shooting began. Apparently, Dewey and La Cornec were expendable.

A "hot tip" placed Dewey's patrol car on a "lonely side road, three miles north of Cloverdale." Declaring that the "quarry was trapped," Sheriff Harry Patteson armed his deputies with rifles, tear gas bombs, and machine guns, and the officers set out to do battle with the fugitives.

The arsenal proved unnecessary. There was no battle.

At 4:10, a truck driver thought he spotted the De Soto on a downtown Napa street. There were, however, just three men in the vehicle.

The trucker was mistaken.

At 6:00 in the evening, an undersheriff at Solano said someone spotted the Dewey automobile in Fairfield, headed west toward Rio Vista. Two hours later, a constable claimed a sighting at Elmira, ten miles north of Fairfield.

If each sighting was accurate, the car was traveling in a circle.

In the East Bay area, the Carquinez Bridge tender reported seeing three "suspicious" men in a Hudson brougham headed toward Oakland just after midnight. A pistol, he claimed, was on the seat beside the driver. Curiously, he kept the information to himself until he spotted a deputy sheriff crossing the bridge at 3:00 A.M.

"It's a cinch those fellows were up to something," he told the deputy three hours after the fact. "They looked suspicious and acted nervous."

Police bought the bridge tender's story. They promptly theorized that the kidnappers had abandoned the De Soto and they had abandoned one of the kidnapped officers as well. Now, so the reasoning went, the remaining officer and two escapees were flitting about the countryside as a threesome in an expensive Hudson brougham.

The theory was speculative nonsense.

Department of Justice agents joined a quartet of prison guards in a nightlong vigil in the Sacramento delta region near Rio Vista and Iselton. Out of sync with the Hudson brougham theorists, Dewey's De Soto was resurrected in another sighting. However, as quickly as it appeared, it disappeared again into the darkness.

Nothing came of the vigil.

Other reports from the Sacramento Valley placed the coupe on a circuitous route to Reno. Convinced that the fugitives were in the vicinity, more than fifty highway patrolmen manned roadblocks in Placer, Nevada, Sutter, Yuba, and Butte counties. They searched all "suspicious" automobiles and questioned their occupants.

What constituted a "suspicious" vehicle was not revealed, and the roadblocks were a waste of time.

Meantime, officers discarded the Hudson brougham theory and San Francisco dispatched lawmen to bridgeheads, ferry terminals, and railway stations. A sharp eye was fixed on busy roads and highways, with officers carrying a description of the commandeered police car.

In the space of a day, De Soto—it was, at best, a lackluster seller—became the most talked about automotive brand in California.

As peace officers scurried about the state's northern reaches, Marin County sheriff Walter B. Sellmer disdained prevailing theories. The kidnapped officers were "hidden in some secluded spot," he boldly insisted, "either tied to trees in some canyon or trussed up in a deserted shack [where] they will not soon be found."

Sellmer believed, also, that Dewey and La Cornec were unharmed. "Those convicts, serving five to life, are smart enough to know that if they harm their prisoners they face the noose."

The sheriff speculated that the escapees were in the vicinity of Napa, "probably traveling in an automobile stolen after abandoning Dewey's police coupe. I think they'll hide out for a while and then head for Reno when they think the coast is clear."

Interesting as Sellmer's scenario was, it, too, differed from reality.

When asked about the sheriff's theory, James B. Holohan, the disgruntled warden of San Quentin, hesitated. "One man's guess is as good as another's," he said. "But I don't think they're anywhere near this place."

Holohan was correct.

In fact, traveling on little frequented backcountry dirt roads and following a circuitous route that covered some 700 miles, the "desperados" were—by direct route—475 miles south of San Quentin. Law enforcement's mad dash about Northern California was all for naught.

Shortly before eight o'clock on the night of April 27, some thirty hours after Stewart and Wyeth tied Green to a tree and wandered away from the penitentiary, the convicts and their captives pulled into San Bernardino. The escapees told Dewey to park the long-sought, steel-gray De Soto coupe curbside on Seventeenth Street between F and G streets. Then, much to the astonishment of the captives, the kidnappers ordered the police officers from the car. The fugitives warned them to "take it easy for ten minutes" before notifying authorities.

Figure 13.1 Officer Dewey tells his story to the chief of the San Bernardino police. *San Francisco History Center, San Francisco Public Library*

"Stewart told me not to make trouble and nobody would get hurt," explained Dewey. "The convicts promised us they would leave our car on the main drag of San Bernardino." The escapees, he said, "circled the block several times to make sure their warning was obeyed."

Abandoning any semblance of police procedure, Dewey and La Cornec did just as they were told. A reporter for the *Oakland Tribune* noted that the sight of two disheveled men "standing motionless at the curb ... aroused the suspicions of a woman in a neighboring house, who called the police." Not until a squad car screeched to a halt in front of them, did the San Rafael officers move a muscle.

Meantime, the penniless convicts visited a drugstore at Marshall Boulevard and E Street. One remained at the wheel of the De Soto, while the other leveled a .45 caliber automatic at the proprietor. Moments later, the holdup man rejoined the driver, after divesting the drug store of $35, a few bars of soap, and a razor—and then they sped northeast.

As the escapees fled San Bernardino, its fast acting police department burned up the telephone wires spreading the alarm. In minutes, the department had dispatched deputies to erect roadblocks on every highway and byway leading in and out of the city. Posses formed and arms were distributed.

When word reached Victorville—a small town on the lip of the Mohave Desert, thirty-one miles north of San Bernardino—that the fugitives might head in that direction, authorities took immediate steps. Deputy Sheriff R. Stanley Snedigar, in charge of the substation at Victorville, immediately summoned special deputies—read civilians—Lou Miller, M. M. Black, and Carl McNew.

"Miller took the wheel with McNew beside him, with a rifle and an automatic pistol," related Snedigar. "Black and I were in the backseat, he with a sawed-off shotgun, and I with a rifle and automatic pistol."

Prepared to intercept the convicts should fate place them in their path, Snedigar later related the ensuing events:

> We sped out of Victorville south on the main highway on the steep grade toward Cajon Pass. As each car approached, we slowed down to see the [license plate] number. Four miles south of town, we saw the coupe with the number we wanted. Miller scattered gravel with a quick turn-around and we were after it. We hit 80 miles an hour and the coupe couldn't do that much. We overhauled it and signaled it to stop. The coupe kept going, so Black leaned out with his shotgun and blew out its left rear tire.
>
> They kept on and we blew the other tire. Then one of the [fugitives] dropped the back window and stuck out his pistol. There was a flash, but we couldn't hear the sound.
>
> McNew and I began shooting with our rifles—we had been told the men had a machine gun.
>
> Pretty soon, after about a mile from where the chase started, the coupe swerved and hit a fence, rolling along for about 60 yards. It came to a stop in a shallow ditch and we stopped on the right side. We didn't see any sign of life in the coupe.
>
> With pistols pointed, we jerked the doors open and Stewart rolled out—dead. Wyeth had huddled forward in the seat, [a] pistol falling out of his hand. He was dead, too.

Figure 13.2 Aftermath of the shootout with escaped San Quentin prisoners.
San Francisco History Center, San Francisco Public Library

> Stewart, the driver, was shot through the chest. Wyeth had a
> bullet in his brain. The car was riddled [with bullet holes] and
> three tires were shot off. We were unhurt.

It was all over, except for the shouting.

San Rafael police chief Sabin Kane was pleased that the manhunt was over, but he was furious with the kidnapped officers. "I
am forming no opinion concerning what took place until I hear
their side of the story," he said disingenuously, all the while wag-
ging a finger at officers Dewey and La Cornec. "But I want to know
why the officers apparently failed to draw their guns when they
approached the escaping convicts. I also want to know what guns
the convicts took from the officers and why the officers, when they

**Figure 13.3 Bystanders inspect
the getaway car.**
*San Francisco History Center,
San Francisco Public Library*

were released, permitted precious minutes to elapse [before] notifying authorities."

When a reporter repeated Kane's statement to the officers, Dewey said, "When you have a .38 poked in your ribs, you're going to do what the man with the .38 tells you."

He was, of course, correct. However, he failed to address Kane's contention that the .38 ought to have been pointed at ribs attached to the escaped convicts, and not the other way around.

Meantime, Dewey wired Kane that he and La Cornec would return to San Rafael as soon as the three blown tires on his bullet-riddled De Soto were replaced. When they did return, both were suspended. A few days later, following an investigation of their abduction, both were fired.

Kane was not alone in his fury. Warden Holohan called guard Charles Green into his San Quentin office and told him he was "through." Green appealed to the warden's sympathetic nature, and Holohan allowed him to resign.

As egg dripped from the collective face of Northern California peace officers, Sheriff Sellmer—the very man who insisted the captive officers were tied to a tree in a lonely canyon or were "trussed up" in a deserted shack—enjoyed a final word with reporters: "It certainly is amazing to find that these fugitives were able to drive a police car and two kidnapped officers all the way to Southern California .... If everybody had cooperated it would have been impossible for these felons to have driven almost the length of the state... without running into police guns sooner than they did."

Certainly, it was true that greater coordination and cooperation among agencies was essential to effective law enforcement. Unwittingly, however, Sellmer's comments revealed yet another problem. It was not a problem endemic only to California, but one that affected police agencies nationwide: the indiscriminate use of deadly force.

Early on in the Wyeth-Stewart drama, a "shoot to kill" order was issued. A sheriff at Cloverdale, caught up in a moment of heat, armed his deputies with machine guns. No doubt, the escapees were dangerous characters. However, their most violent act prior to the shootout was to threaten a prison guard with a knife and tie him to a scrub oak. Machine guns and a "shoot to kill" edict were, in fact, overkill directed at men who had killed no one.

"Running into police guns," to use Sellmer's poignant words, was nasty business. Given the potential bloodbath implicit in the phrase, it invited unintended consequences as well. The point was borne out eight months later, in January 1935, when yet another drama played out between San Quentin convicts and heavily armed officers.

A Second Kidnapping at the Q

In prose as lurid as the incident itself, the *Los Angeles Times* reported, "Roaring guns late today climaxed the most sensational escape attempt in the long and sanguinary history of this prison ...."

It was lunchtime at Warden Holohan's spacious, white house atop a hill overlooking the prison compound. Seated around the dining room table were four important guests: Frank C. Sykes, president of both the California State Prison Board and the State Board of Prison Terms and Pardons; Mark Noon, secretary of the pardons board; and Warren Atherton and Joseph H. Stephens, members of the pardons board.

The luncheon was just breaking up when Holohan glanced up "into gunpoints and four pairs of fierce eyes." Remarkably, a quartet of armed convicts—Rudolph B. Straight, Alex McKay, Joe Kristy, and Fred Landers—swept into the room with "caps yanked over their eyes and with drawn guns."

"Stick up your hands and line up," they barked.

"No time to think now," recalled Holohan. "Nobody knows what he would do in a crisis like that. I didn't reason. Just acted automatically."

In retrospect, reasoning would have proved less traumatic for the warden. In an effort to reach a telephone in the adjoining room and "mobilize San Quentin's machine gunners," he "lunged past the ringleader [Straight] and his long gat."

His leap landed him in the next room where "the heavy butt of the gun crashed squarely across the back of my skull. It dazed me. Like a trip-hammer, he pounded at my head with the gun. I grabbed his arm. That deflected the pistol [and] sent it tearing into the flesh on my face. He wrenched free. A crushing blow dropped me to my knees. He leaped on me like a madman with that trip-hammer arm of his bringing the gun butt down again and again and again. I grappled for the gun to stop the force of the blows. But he crashed my head a dozen times. Blood was blinding me. Then all went blank."

In fact, Landers interfered, shouting, "Hey, we don't want that kind of stuff." Straight backed off and Landers knelt down, took a handkerchief from his pocket, and wiped blood from an open wound on the warden's head.

Then, as Holohan lay unconscious, the convict's attention focused on the luncheon guests. Atherton recalled one of the prisoners saying, "We don't want any trouble now, but we have to get out of here in a hurry."

"If you boys are on the square and promise no shooting," volunteered Atherton, "I'll go as a hostage. But remember, I am the father of four children."

They rejected his offer: "We're going to take all of you with us. Get your clothes off and we'll trade with you."

"At that moment," continued Atherton, "Mrs. Holohan, who had heard the disturbance, came into the room. We could all hear the warden groaning in the next room and she pleaded with the convicts to let her go to her husband:

> "We'll be out of here in five minutes," one of the convicts told her, "and then you can see him."
>
> "But we've always treated you fellows well …. Please, why don't you use your heads and give up this crazy scheme."
>
> "Too late now," said the convict. "We've got to go through with it."

Recalled Sykes, "We were taken so by surprise that we really had no time to think. As they were changing [clothes], we all talked but none of us could think of a plan of escape."

Before they left the warden's home, the convicts forced Noon to call the captain of the guards. Noon explained to the guard that he and other kidnapped board members would accompany the escaping prisoners through the gate. The gate must be opened without delay. There must be no shooting.

The prisoners escorted their captives through the kitchen and out the back door, then ordered them into Holohan's massive, black sedan. Whether by design or accident, the car's siren went off. Two unknowing guards rushed the vehicle. Stopped at gunpoint, they fattened the hostage list to six.

The convicts forced Lieutenant Harry Jones into the automobile and told him he would be its driver, while guard Clarence L. Doose was compelled to ride atop the running board. Moments later, guards attuned to the unfolding drama swung open the rear gate—

it stood adjacent the highway leading to nearby Greenbrae—and the automobile sped through.

The moment the warden's car left the prison compound, "the highway began filling with police cars, their occupants all heavily armed and prepared to shoot it out," wrote the *Times*.

"The convicts were quite calm about the whole thing, astonishingly so," Atherton remembered. "From their conversation, we gathered that they planned to follow the route which took the two escaped convicts, Stewart and Wyeth, to San Bernardino—that is, by cutting across the Blackpoint Road and following little-used secondary roads down the eastern rim of the state, perhaps making for Mexico."

The car headed north through San Rafael "with a fast gathering posse closing in behind it," reported the *San Francisco Chronicle*:

> State highway patrol cars, San Rafael police, fast machines with prison guards, and machine loads of deputy sheriffs trailed behind. Once an ambush blocked the way of the speeding car but when the officers refused to fire, the convicts became elated. They thought they were reasonably safe.
>
> The machine swung over the Blackpoint cutoff and notched to 50, then 60 miles per hour. Ahead was a drawbridge. There was some conversation among the convicts as to whether they would find it open or shut.
>
> It was open and the machine ground to a stop amid a string of curses.

They forced Noon out of the automobile with instructions to tell the posses that parole board members were still in the vehicle. If officers opened fire, warned the convicts, the odds were fifty-fifty that innocent civilians would be killed or wounded.

No great wisdom was necessary to grasp the convict's argument. Nevertheless, some lawmen ignored it.

"The car then doubled back, passing through armed posses of men unable to shoot," penned the *Chronicle*, with undue pathos:

The board members caught glimpses of tense faces in cars with police insignia. Muzzles of shotguns, machine guns, and revolvers pointed their way—all silent, waiting, helpless.

Once there was a rattle of shots. One officer, more daring than the rest, attempted to shoot the tires off the speeding car. He missed, and the escapees roared on, swaying back and forth across the highway.

But as the runaway car gained distance and gave promise of being lost in the mountains to the northwest, several of the posses experimented with firing low, attempting to shoot out the tires of the machine.

At another juncture, while "lead thudded in the rear," the convicts released guards Jones and Doose to lighten the load. "What a cold ride I had," Doose commented to the *San Francisco Call Bulletin*, referring to the twenty miles he rode atop the running board.

With Jones gone, Kristy took the wheel. At breakneck speed, convicts and kidnap victims traveled on.

"Armed posses, many of whom may not have known that officials were in the prison car, started rising on every side," said Atherton. "One tire went flat, and the car began to sway crazily on the highway."

Atherton also noted that law officers were becoming less discriminating: "Things got hotter. A new blast of bullets struck the car, and one of them passed through the rear window and out through the front windshield. I don't think it missed me by more than inches. I ducked, but felt foolish for doing that."

The "air filled with the whine of bullets." Then a second tire blew out and the vehicle swayed drunkenly. As the kidnapped men crouched to elude the "whining sheet of lead" whizzing about the automobile, a bullet crashed into Sykes' hip. Seconds later, a bullet ripped into Stephens' leg.

As if testing the limits of recklessness, lawmen made two captives shooting victims, while the escapees went unscathed.

"We can't make it now, boys," Atherton recalled one of the convicts saying. "We'll have to duck out and fight them somewhere."

The words had just been spoken when, over a small rise, a creamery came into view. "The convicts piled out while the car was still going about 25 miles an hour," said Atherton, "and all four ran for the creamery building. We piled out the other side of the car at the same time and started to scatter for shelter—because from outward appearances, on account of the clothing shift, we looked like convicts and the convicts looked like parole board members."

Atherton's worst nightmare was realized when a deputy leveled a rifle at him. "Stop right there or I'll kill you, you dirty dog!"

Speechless, Atherton stood frozen in his tracks. Just then, he heard his wounded companions, Sykes and Stephens shout, "Don't shoot for God's sake, that's Atherton."

With what the *Chronicle* described as "lightning speed," posse members surrounded the creamery building, located near the tiny village of Valley Ford. Holed up inside, the convicts herded terrified employees at gunpoint into a walk-in refrigerator. Then Straight, for reasons known only to him, left the building through its rear entrance. He stepped into a clearing and leveled his pistol at posse members. In seconds, they perforated his body with bullets.

Officers yelled at the other convicts to come out with their hands up, "threatening to riddle the building if they failed to comply." Fortunately, for the innocent employees lodged inside, to whom posse members did not give a moment's consideration, the escapees came out one by one with their hands in the air.

"They were arrested," noted the *Times*, "and immediately returned to San Quentin."

The incident made plain the hazard of deadly force applied indiscriminately by law enforcement agencies. Firing into an automobile with four kidnap victims held captive inside ranked as sheer stupidity. That the bullet wounds suffered by Sykes and Stephens were not mortal was serendipity, and nothing else. "Running into police guns"—to borrow Sheriff Sellmer's boastful phrase—was an unpleasant experience for folks on either side of the law.

Later that night, the *Chronicle* described "a sudden sortie among the swampy islands of the Sacramento River near Antioch," where one Clyde Stevens was captured in a "burst of gunfire."

The press gave Stevens momentary celebrity when clever reporters named him California's No. 1 Public Enemy and likened him to John Dillinger. In fact, he was a failed bank robber recently released from San Quentin. Nevertheless, Stevens had facilitated the prison break by smuggling guns in the undercarriage of a truck for delivery to Straight and his cohorts.

Perhaps to his chagrin, Stevens promptly lost his Public Enemy title when the State of California determined that he ought to spend the remainder of his life in San Quentin.

Fred Landers, the convict who prevented Straight from murdering Warden Holohan, was sentenced to life in prison.

Tried separately—they were defended by up-and-coming lawyer Melvin Belli—Alex McKay and Joe Kristy were not so lucky. As the *Chronicle* noted, "they were found guilty of all counts on 11 indictments charging them with kidnapping, and kidnapping for the purpose of robbery, of escape, grand theft, and burglary. The first two charges carry the death penalty under the California 'Lindbergh Law'—and no recommendation for mercy was returned."

On April 4, 1935, the court sentenced them to hang.

In fact, there was a recommendation for mercy, and it came from unconventional quarters. On February 16, 1936, Cyril Cane, British consul general in San Francisco, was instructed by the British Foreign Office to ask the governor to grant executive clemency to Alex McKay—a British subject.

A few days later, both McKay and Kristy gained reprieves while the legal community in Sacramento, Washington, D.C., and London—U.S. Secretary of State Cordell Hull and British Foreign Secretary Anthony Eden played roles in this sub-drama—sorted things out. In the end, however, the sorting uncovered nothing helpful in McKay's column.

A second reprieve was granted and when petitioners asked for a third, California governor Frank F. Merriam lost his patience. "I will not sign another reprieve," he stated bluntly. "These men had their day in court. I can no longer interfere."

He did not.

In a mawkish display of self-pity not uncommon among condemned prisoners, McKay and Kristy issued a statement on their execution eve. It bitterly reviled the kidnapped members of the pardons board, two of whom the doomed men had caused to be shot: "It will be magnificent for you to witness the death of men from whom you begged life."

The kidnappers were hanged at San Quentin, on May 22, 1936.

Chapter 14: Snatched from the Peach Bowl

Relaxing in an easy chair beside the console radio, Norma Meeks was examining charges on recent freight bills when she heard a noise. She turned to look. Just then, her husband William entered the room. Astonished, he saw his wife gaping into the barrel of a pistol and two masked men standing just inside the French doors opening onto the front porch.

It was just past midnight, Thursday morning, September 1, 1938.

A swift wave of immobilizing shock passed over the couple. The notion that two gunmen had invaded the sanctity of their home was unthinkable. The Meekses were, after all, middle-class orchardists who made their livelihood in peaches and worked hard for every dollar deposited in their modest bank account. They were decent folks who treated people well and had no enemies.

Incredulity aside, however, the terrifying scene became blunt reality when the gunmen spat out orders. "They told us to lie down on the floor," recalled William. "Then they took rolls of adhesive tape from their pockets and plastered the stuff across our mouths. Next they tied our hands and feet with a rope and some stray pieces of clothing they found in the house."

While one of the intruders stood guard over the helpless couple, the other "ransacked the house, prying into every possible hiding place in a hunt that yielded them no more than seven dollars," reported the *San Francisco Examiner*.

"That took quite a few minutes," said Meeks. "When it was over, the men yanked my wife to her feet, untied the rope around her ankles, and started dragging her out. One of the men said, 'We're going to take your old lady along. You'll get her back when we get $15,000. We know all about kidnapping laws and all about the electric chair—but we want $15,000.'"

When the rancher protested that $15,000 was an impossible sum, one of the men said, "You'd better get it." According to the *Oakland Tribune*, Meeks was told that "if the ransom was not forthcoming, his wife's body would be returned 'piece by piece.'"

The rancher was instructed to "leave the money two miles down the road on a peach loading platform, on Saturday night."

Wrote the *Examiner*, "Meeks told investigators that his wife made no sound as she left the house with her kidnappers—a circumstance open to several interpretations. One—the one favored by Meeks, himself—is that his wife was displaying calmness and courage. Another held that she was gagged. Still a third pointed to a possibility that her abductors may have slugged her into unconsciousness."

Meeks heard the kidnappers drive his car from the garage and waited until the sound of its exhaust faded: "After they'd gone, I squirmed around on the floor trying to get free of the rope. I guess it must have been half an hour before I got loose. Then I yanked the adhesive tape off my mouth and called the sheriff's office at Yuba City."

The violent kidnapping of Norma Meeks was a staggering climax to an otherwise pleasant evening. Earlier, neighbors Will Hudson and his wife dropped by for a round of bridge. Despite sweltering heat, the game progressed cheerfully until well after eleven o'clock when the Hudsons decided to call it a night. The Meekses escorted

Figure 14.1 The Meeks home near Yuba City.
San Francisco History Center, San Francisco Public Library

their guests to the front door of their comfortable six-room bungalow, lingering a few minutes on the porch for a breath of air.

The Meeks ranch, thirty-seven acres planted with mature crop-producing peach trees, was located at Four Corners near Rio Oso, a village of perhaps a hundred people at the southeastern end of Sutter County.

When the couple withdrew into the house, they left the front door ajar to take advantage of a slight breeze. Unbeknownst to them, two men huddled beneath the heavy limbs of a fruit-bearing peach tree directly across the road. From their vantage point, they had watched and waited as the middle-aged ranch couple wiled away an evening of bridge.

At last, the Hudsons bid their hosts goodnight. The men in the orchard watched their automobile disappear in a trail of dust. Then the strangers made their move.

Sutter County Sheriff Bert Ullrey was the first to speak to Meeks. The 58-year-old rancher was so distraught that it was some time before Ullrey could make sense of what had happened. "They have got my wife!" Meeks hollered over and over. "They have got my wife!"

When at last Meeks was sufficiently composed to speak coherently, he gave the sheriff a detailed itinerary of the night's bizarre events. Ullrey scribbled quick notes and put out an all-points bulletin on the police wire. Norma Meeks was described as a slender woman with gray-brown hair, five feet two inches tall, who weighed 110 pounds. She was 55 years old. The kidnap victim was well known in the Sutter area. The Meekses had lived at the Four Points ranch since 1922, and she was an active club woman.

Both abductors were thought to be about 24 years old. One was of medium build with brown eyes and dark brown hair, the other of slight build with light brown hair. They were said to be about five feet nine inches tall and both wore blue denim trousers and jackets.

About 2:30 in the morning, deputies found an abandoned automobile parked between Third and Fourth streets in Marysville, some thirteen miles north. It was a tan, 1938 Chevrolet sedan, which authorities quickly determined was the newly purchased automobile stolen from the Meekses' garage. "The gasoline tank, which held four gallons when it was stolen, was empty," noted the *Fresno Bee*. "The car also contained Mrs. Meeks' glasses and [a] purse, with $5 missing."

Sheriff Ullrey believed that yet a second "machine" was stolen, in which the kidnappers transferred their victim in an effort to "cross up their pursuers."

The *Examiner* elaborated on Ullrey's theory:

> Searchers found tire marks which indicated how the kidnappers and their victim continued on after the Meeks car's gasoline tank ran dry. Beneath a bridge which crosses dry Bear River, some three miles from the Meeks home, searchers located two sets of tire marks which told a fairly clear story.

One set of marks matched those made by the Meeks machine. The other, authorities are convinced, were made by the kidnappers' getaway car. Reading the story of the marks, they said that the kidnappers drove the Meeks machine to this spot, and that one of them then transferred to the getaway machine—possibly taking Mrs. Meeks with him—while the other drove the Meeks car to Marysville.

A measure of credence was given the supposition by Mrs. Burde Ocheltree, a Marysville resident whose home was located near the spot where the Meeks Chevrolet was abandoned. She said she was "awakened sometime after midnight by the racing of a motor; that she listened and heard a car roar away at what seemed to be high speed."

Wisely, the Chevrolet was impounded in a Marysville garage pending further investigation, including a thorough examination for fingerprints.

Governor Frank F. Merriam was awakened by an aide in the middle of the night and told about the abduction. He was furious. A *Los Angeles Times* reporter was in Sacramento when the governor met with reporters:

> "If necessary, every citizen in the State will be called to aid in tracking down these ruthless men so they may be brought to justice and punished for their dastardly crime," Merriam bellowed from the governor's mansion.
>
> "Kidnapping is the most cowardly of all crimes and should immediately be met with fullest cooperation of all law enforcement agencies and citizens of the State. I am determined to see that those responsible for this woman's abduction shall be apprehended immediately and that she is returned unharmed to her family."

By daybreak, law enforcement agencies throughout California were acutely aware of the Meeks kidnapping. As an expression of anger and resolve, Merriam, noted the *Fresno Bee*, "ordered out two companies [about 120 men] of the 184th Infantry, California National Guard, to join forces with 40 California highway patrolmen

... sheriff's officers from Yuba, Sutter, and Sacramento counties, and an armed posse of more than seventy-five farmers."

Nat J. Pieper, chief of the San Francisco division of the FBI, fancied himself in charge of the investigation and dispatched four agents to Sutter County. In fact, Pieper and his men were little more than in-the-way onlookers. Until the kidnapping was seven days old, or unless it was proven that the snatchers had taken their victim across the state line, the FBI had no jurisdiction whatsoever.

However, as a means of freeing up useful deputies, Sheriff Ullrey assigned Pieper and his agents to stand guard at the Meeks ranch. A reporter for the *Bee* acknowledged unhappily that "five G-men kept a growing crowd of newsmen and cameramen" from accosting Meeks, now "being cared for by his two married daughters."

Within a day, the FBI withdrew from guard duty and was not heard from again.

Searchers spread out "fanwise" over a 100 mile area, inspecting river bottoms, culverts, bridges, and the dozens of small feeder roads that led into farms, ranches, and orchards. The *Bee* noted that the search was "centered" five miles southwest of Wheatland, a small farming community fourteen miles south of Marysville, "in the center of California's famous peach bowl."

Wrote the *Bee*, "The possibility the kidnappers may have been among the twenty-five peach pickers employed by Meeks was advanced when a Wheatland branch bank teller recalled he had cashed two checks written by Meeks for two roughly dressed men yesterday who fitted the description given by Meeks."

It was a flimsy clue. It is probable that all twenty-five of Meeks' peach pickers were "roughly dressed," and countless men had brown hair and were about five feet nine inches tall.

"A short-lived flurry of excitement was caused by discovery, by a surveying crew, of a stained strip of white cloth, 15 miles from the Meeks' home," reported the *Examiner*. "Nearby was a similarly stained fragment of rubber with a number of short hairs clotted on the surface. However, the presence nearby of numerous piles of debris and clothing discarded by migratory workers appeared to strip the discovery of any real significance."

Meeks told authorities that the kidnappers spoke with a "drawl." He thought the accent may have had its origin in Oklahoma, and that they were "Okies."

"This, coupled with their reference to the electric chair—the mode of capital punishment employed in Oklahoma—strongly indicated that the two men were migrants from the Dust Bowl, who had worked in harvesting the Yuba-Sutter peach crop, who might possibly have worked at the Meeks ranch, itself," conjectured the *Examiner*.

The *Tribune* advanced the argument to another level when it wrote, "… Some of the Nation's No. 1 gangsters hailed from Oklahoma."

The *Tribune*'s inference of big-time gangster involvement in the Meeks snatching was a fragile stretch of logic. It was nothing more than sensationalism intended to engage naïve readers and sell newspapers. It made no sense that an Oklahoma gangster—whether he was the nation's No. 1 or No. 10 most-sought after hoodlum— would journey to Northern California to kidnap a middle-class ranch wife of modest means.

The *Examiner*, however, made a point worth pondering when it suggested that the culprits might number among the hundreds of migratory workers who picked the peach crop each year. Nevertheless, both Meeks and the newspaper fell into the stereotypical trap of putting Oklahoma accents into the mouths of Dust Bowl refugees who migrated to California.

Beginning in 1930, and extending through the decade, the worst drought in recorded history settled over Oklahoma, Texas, and Arkansas, and throughout much of the Midwest and the Dakotas. It had its genesis in the Homestead Act of 1862, when thousands of settlers plowed up natural prairie grasses and planted millions of acres of dryland wheat. Prairie grasses not destroyed by plows were

devastated by overgrazing cattle. As the drought took hold, over-
farmed and overgrazed land began to blow away. Winds whipped
across the plains, raising billowing clouds of dust, filling the air
with millions of tons of finely plowed top soil, and blackening
the skies for a thousand miles. Drifts twenty feet high marked the
desolation.

Nineteen states hit by this spectacular man-induced ecological
disaster became a vast dust bowl. With crops dead in the field and
cattle starving, Dust Bowl farmers were forced to abandon their
land and seek new homes. As many as 300,000 refugees migrated to
California. In 1937, *Business Week* reported that "the influx is now
averaging one immigrant outfit every ten minutes, and the trek has
only begun …."

Loading as many of their belongings as they could carry in and
on an automobile or truck, this great migration moved steadily
across the land. The migrants' entry into California was not greeted
cordially. For a time, immigrants were turned away at the border—
at gunpoint. Nevertheless, among the first arrivals were families
from Oklahoma. A clever bigot coined the term "Okies," and hostile
Californians applied the name generically. Regardless of his state of
origin, Okie became an immigrant's identifier.

By 1940, slightly less than 11 percent of the state's residents hailed
from "Okie states." In time, Dust Bowl migrants were swallowed
into the belly of California's mainstream population, but throughout the Depression, thousands eked out a living as migrant farm
workers. As *Business Week* noted, in the pocket of many an immigrant could be found an "advertisement painting in glowing terms
the wonderful opportunities to be found in California."

Most migrant workers who picked the Sutter-Yuba County peach
crop lived out of their automobiles or in makeshift river-bottom
hovels. More permanent workers lived in Olivehurst, a shack town
operated loosely by the federal government's Farm Security Administration on the outskirts of Marysville.

Acting on a tip, highway patrol inspector William White led a group of patrolmen in a daybreak raid on an abandoned ranch house, located three miles from Wheatland. Two itinerant Oklahoma orchard workers were said to be holed up there, and their descriptions tallied with the kidnappers'.

The raid yielded no results. From all appearances, the workers had abandoned the house some days prior.

Feeling ran high among officers and volunteer searchers that their efforts would culminate in the discovery of a corpse. When pressed by reporters, Sheriff Ullrey said, "We are hoping against hope that our search does not yield the body of Mrs. Meeks, but there is a distinct possibility that it may. She is in desperate hands."

Governor Merriman ordered the highway patrol to dispatch an additional 100 patrolmen to Sutter County, and volunteers swelled the posse roster to some 300 concerned citizens. Men in the field numbered about 500 when, abruptly, the search was called off.

At 8:00 A.M., Saturday morning, Marion Hunzeker, one of the two Meeks daughters, met with reporters on the ranch house porch. She explained that her father "was in no condition" to appear and read to the press a statement written by him:

> I desire first to thank Federal, State and local authorities and my neighbors for their kind cooperation. I realize everything has been done to bring back my wife and solve the crime that has been perpetrated. Since, however, my wife has not been found, I requested all the authorities to discontinue their efforts to find her.
>
> I have made this request in order that I might try to contact my wife's abductors and to see whether or not I can meet their demands, and see if I can secure some word from my wife.
>
> All of the officers have agreed that for the present, I will not be hindered in my efforts to make contact and should I be able to do so, they will not interfere with me or the parties contacted.

Sheriff Ullrey then spoke to reporters. He told them that daily press briefings would be conducted at 10:00 A.M and 4:00 P.M., and he asked newsmen and neighbors alike to stay away from the Meeks ranch and do nothing that might interfere with possible negotiations.

Meantime, law enforcement officials fielded calls from newspapers across the country. One startled deputy found himself speaking via the transatlantic cable to a reporter from the *London Times*.

Later in the day, Ullrey speculated that the kidnappers may have eluded searchers—that they "might be hundreds of miles away." Had the kidnappers "hidden nearby," some "fresh trace" would have been discovered by now, he asserted.

The Meeks' impounded Chevrolet yielded new clues when Sutter County farm agent Merle D. Collins examined powdery dust on the front fenders and radiator grill. Collins called the fluffy, grayish dust "slickens."

"Patches of the stuff occur in only about five small areas in Yuba County and one in Sutter County," Collins told the *Tribune*. "They are concentrated in the old river bottom lands of the Bear, Feather, and Yuba rivers."

Slickens was the controversial byproduct of hydraulic mining, a system introduced to the California gold country as early as 1853. Put simply, water was shot from hoses under tremendous pressure. Unlike labor-intensive placer mining, in which soil was rinsed to isolate denser gold dust from other elements, hydraulic mining literally blasted soil away. Entire hillsides were leveled. The residue was put through sluices to extract the gold and then dumped indiscriminately into rivers and streams.

River bottoms filled up with tailings and important waterways were clogged. Even San Francisco Bay was affected. However, the most significant damage was done to farmland. When plugged watercourses flooded, otherwise fertile land was rendered useless by silt and debris. More than once, Yuba City-Marysville residents were forced to dig though flood-deposited river bottom mud to reclaim their towns.

As the economic significance of gold mining diminished and the importance of agriculture increased, hydraulic mining was reluctantly discontinued in the face of myriad lawsuits—private, state, and federal—and much delayed legislative action. Slickens was an ever-present reminder of a landscape permanently scarred.

Collins reinforced Sheriff Ullrey's belief that the kidnappers used two cars. "One was their own, which led the way and probably had a driver at the wheel who knew the country well," surmised the *Tribune*. "The other was the stolen Meeks' machine," later recovered in Marysville.

Collins' report continued: "Some time during that wild morning ride, the two cars passed through the old river bottom land where the 'slickens' have been drying into a dust for decades. The lead car powdered Meeks' car."

Slickens found on Meeks' Chevrolet "led Collins to believe that one of the kidnappers knew a route through the bewildering maze of unimproved county roads that wind through the brushy low country.

"It is here that Sheriff Ullrey hopes he will find Mrs. Meeks alive. Her captors will not be far away, he thinks," reported the *Tribune*.

Late Saturday, Meeks issued a plea to the kidnappers through the afternoon editions of Northern California newspapers:

> Appeal to kidnappers—Afraid to contact due to publicity. Arrange new contact. Lines clear. Awaiting.
>
> W. R. Meeks

Acknowledging that the ransom deadline was just hours away, the *Examiner* wrote dramatically that:

> ...the machinery of the vast manhunt stood still to enable the rancher to establish communications with the abductors and arrange for payment.
>
> Thus, the tan frame cottage of the Meeks, which yesterday was the hub of one of Northern California's greatest criminal hunts in history, stood deserted this afternoon save for the

quiet, gray-haired husband of the kidnap victim and a few of their friends and family.

On the heels of Meeks' appeal to the kidnappers, the Sutter County board of supervisors let it be known that arrangements were in the works to post a $500 reward for information leading to the culprits' arrest.

Then something unexpected occurred.

Early Sunday morning—fifty-six hours after her gunpoint abduction—Norma Meeks staggered up the front porch steps of her Four Points ranch house. Husband William dashed out the door yelling and crying, and he threw his arms around her. Norma cried, too, and so did her daughters.

She was lucky to be alive. Her kidnappers were sloppy amateurs, and that made them the most dangerous kind. They planned badly, made no provisions for contingencies, and panicked when the time came to make cogent arrangements for ransom delivery and pickup. Fortunately, they were not cold-blooded killers—just stupid men who blundered their way through a crime they were incapable of executing to completion.

Norma's fate was determined late Saturday afternoon when one of her captors delivered a chilling message. "I've got bad news for you," he told her. "There's been too much publicity. The boss sent word for me to blow your brains out and throw you in the river."

Not surprisingly, the statement terrified his victim.

For reasons known only to him, he returned later with less daunting news: "We're going to leave you for a while. We'll be back when the moon comes up to take you home. But don't try to move. There'll be a lookout and he'll shoot you if you try to go."

In fact, there was no boss, no lookout, and the kidnappers had no intention of returning. Unable to formulate a plan to collect ransom while avoiding police bullets or jail bars, they decided it was an appropriate time to retire from the snatch racket. Or, put succinctly

Figure 14.2 Searching the area where Norma Meeks was held.
San Francisco History Center, San Francisco Public Library

by the *Tribune*, "The magnitude of the search apparently caused the kidnappers to become panic-stricken and flee."

Exposed to the elements and confined to a patch of poison oak, Norma waited for their return. The moon came, but not the kidnappers. She waited. "Eventually, thirst compelled her to cry out," wrote the *Examiner*. "She yelled repeatedly and, receiving no answer, pulled off the blindfold. It was near dawn and Mrs. Meeks, seeing nobody around her, rose to her feet …."

At that juncture, Norma did something remarkable. The *Examiner* reported that before she walked away from the desolate kidnap hideaway:

...she took the precaution, in her weakened and dazed condition, to tie a piece of gauze and a piece of blue chiffon from her dress to the brush to mark the place.

Stumbling over the uneven, hilly terrain, she made her way to a small cottage, obtained a drink of water from its occupant, and—sensing that she was near the town of Sheridan—inquired [about] its distance.

The cottager, Ed Talkington, offered to drive her to Sheridan if she waited two hours, until he was ready to go. She declined and started to walk to town.

In fact, the "cottager" was foreman of the Camp Far West, a sprawling ranch that dominated the landscape as far as the eye could see, and then some. Unbeknownst to Norma, her abductors had chosen an isolated spot on the ranch as their hideout. Given the bustling activity on the Camp Far West, it was pure serendipity that the kidnap lair went undetected.

As Norma walked on, Bud Foster, a ranch hand busy hitching a team of horses to a wagon, glanced at her. Then he looked again. Suddenly, it occurred to him that she was Mrs. Meeks, the kidnap victim. He tied the horses to a rail, jumped behind the wheel of his car, and overtook her as she trudged along the dusty road.

The *Tribune* recorded the encounter: "'I'll give you a lift,' he said, and when the slight woman leaned back in the seat, he added, 'aren't you Mrs. Meeks?' The reply was in the affirmative. And so Foster simply drove up to the Meeks' ranch house and closed the first chapter in the sensational case."

As Norma was weak from hunger and racked by a severe cough, the family put her to bed and summoned her doctor, P. B. Hoffman. Her lungs were congested, she was running a fever, and the physician feared that pneumonia might develop. "The ultimate outcome will be doubtful for the next 24 to 48 hours and anything can happen," he said.

Still, Norma grasped the immediacy of the situation. Against Hoffman's wishes, she welcomed law enforcement officers to her bedside. She answered myriad questions and gave them a detailed statement.

No reporters were present during the questioning, but the resourceful *Examiner* obtained a copy of the victim's statement. No doubt, a rewrite man repaired grammar and syntax and colored the prose with the kind of drama the newspaper's readers expected:

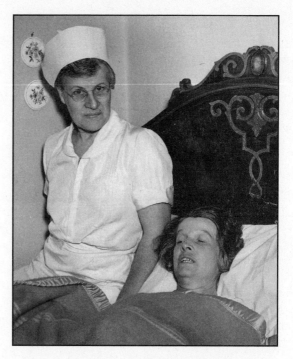

Figure 14.3 Meeks recovering from her ordeal.
San Francisco History Center,
San Francisco Public Library

> I am very hungry and very tired.
>
> For three nights and two days, I have been held a prisoner, out in the open, without shelter from the hot sun during the day, or from the chill at night.
>
> For the first two nights and days, I was forced to go without food. Not until yesterday afternoon did I have anything to eat at all. Then one of the men gave me a small package of cream cheese. Once they offered me some muddy water from a waterhole where cattle had been drinking.
>
> There were three men in the gang that kidnapped me, and from their voices I could tell that they were young men. But I never saw any one of them; at all times the blindfold which was put over my eyes at home was kept there.

She described the men's forced intrusion into the Meeks home, the binding and gagging rendered her and her husband, and her subsequent kidnapping:

> When they drove my car out of the driveway, one of them said he'd shoot me if I didn't keep still. We drove about five minutes or so, and then the car stopped. I heard another car drive up. Someone got out and walked toward my car.
>
> One of the men in my car got out and walked over to meet him, and they talked a few minutes. I couldn't hear what they were saying.
>
> Then the two men in the road walked up to my car, opened the back door, and put something on the floor of the back seat. It felt soft, like clothes or a blanket.
>
> One of the men got back into my car and we drove on. I was pretty sure we headed east, and I thought from the turns we made, we must be going toward Sheridan. We drove a long time. I couldn't tell how long or how far, but was pretty certain we were beyond Sheridan.
>
> I couldn't see and they had to help me out of the car. One man drove away, leaving me with the other. He took my arm and we started to walk. I could see a little out of the bottom of the blindfold. I could just see my feet, but nothing ahead of them, and stumbled frequently.

She described a long trek through rugged country. Then, with no warning, the kidnapper ordered her to stop:

> He told me that we were going to spend the night right there. He said I'd better lie down and get some rest. He gave me a quilt that he must have been carrying, and gave me his coat. Then he sat down on the ground a few feet away and said, "Don't make any noise and don't move around or I'll blow your brains out."
>
> That was a threat that he and the others repeated several times. I lay there on the ground several hours. It wasn't particularly cold, but I didn't sleep.
>
> Sometime before daylight, the man walked over to where I was and told me to get up. We started walking again, up a

little ravine, I thought. We came to a big clump of bushes and he told me to crawl into them. From under my blindfold, the leaves looked like poison oak, but he made me crawl in anyway.

I sat there all day and all night. Part of the time he was away somewhere, but before he'd leave, he'd tell me to keep quiet and not try to escape or he'd shoot me.

More walking, more bushes to crawl under and more threats consumed most of Saturday. Then came late afternoon when the bandits deserted [me]. Not until morning, however, did [I] discard the blindfold and make [my] way out of the thicket.

They didn't speak with any drawl or brogue that I noticed. And although they threatened to shoot me several times, they were never rough or brutal with me.

I'm mighty glad it's over.

Apparently, Norma's abductors were well-schooled in the 1933 revision of the California kidnapping statute. It stipulated that if a kidnap victim suffered bodily harm, the crime became a capital offense. Still, they may have overlooked the fact that if the captive succumbed to an exposure-induced illness, they would face the death penalty as well.

Norma's statement provided law enforcement officers a veritable road map with which to reinstate a vigorous manhunt. While officers tracked down leads, a special contingent set out to find the kidnappers' hideout: Captain E. W. Personius, head of the highway patrol's bureau of investigation; Hugh Hensley, noted tracker and lion hunter; Placer County deputy sheriff L. B. Allen; E. P. Biggs, deputy state forester; Sheriff Ullrey; and the victim's husband searched for the better part of the day before they found the campsite.

"When Meeks, leading the party, sighted the piece of his wife's blue dress flapping from the poison oak clump, he shouted, 'Here it is!'" wrote the *Tribune*.

The kidnappers made no effort to tidy up their camp. Cigarette butts were found stamped into the dust, a portion of a discarded cream cheese wrapper lay nearby, and footprints—of which plaster casts were made—were everywhere.

"The spot was some 300 yards from the banks of Bear River, which separates Placer [County] from Yuba County," reported the *Examiner*:

> It was on the Placer side of the virtually dry river.
>
> In the hideout, searchers found the blanket which the kidnappers had taken from the Meeks home. It was stained with blood—a circumstance which Mrs. Meeks explained by declaring that her nose began bleeding from nervous agitation, coupled with the heat of the day.
>
> On Saturday afternoon—shortly before the kidnappers told Mrs. Meeks they were going to leave her—three searchers traversed the Camp Wild West Ranch, within two miles of the hideout.

The revelation indicated that despite guarantees made to the victim's husband and, consequently, misleading press reports, the search continued after it was said to be discontinued.

It was soon learned that at midnight Saturday, as Norma waited fitfully for the kidnappers' return, Paul Hunzeker, her son-in-law, attempted to make contact with the snatchers at the appointed rendezvous—a fruit loading platform at Jester Station on the road between Sheridan and Wheatland.

When the kidnappers failed to appear, Hunzeker left a note asking that arrangements for a "new contact" be made.

Sheriff Ullrey reiterated his belief that "the crime was the work of novices, and that they were men familiar with the region. If they were not residents of the district, they were itinerant workers who had spent enough time in the locality to familiarize themselves with it."

The *Modesto Bee* confirmed that Ullrey's opinion was embraced by others: "Police officers in Yuba, Sutter, and Placer [counties] said they believed the kidnappers were amateurs in the snatch racket."

On Tuesday, September 6, two days following Norma's return, the *Marysville-Yuba City Appeal Democrat* revealed intriguing information. William Marchi, an orchard worker on the Horst Ranch, located just north of the Placer County hillside where the kidnappers' camp was found, reported seeing three men walking across the fields on Saturday afternoon.

The *Democrat* stated: "The men approached him from the general direction of Camp Far West Ranch and appeared to be nervous and in a hurry. All carried packs. Marchi declared one of the men asked if the water in a nearby irrigation ditch was good to drink. Another, apparently the leader, is quoted as saying: 'Come on, we're in a hurry.'"

A promising lead came from gold prospector Walter Ordway. Elaborating on his story and adding broad assumptions, the *Examiner* wrote that, "For two days he watched two of the kidnappers as they stood guard over their hidden captive; he chatted with them; he inadvertently aided their escape by giving them a ride from the hideout to Marysville."

In fact, Ordway spotted two men he thought were in their mid-twenties fishing along the Bear River on Friday and again on Saturday. He watched them make a campfire atop a hill, which proved to be about 400 yards from the kidnap hideout. On Saturday afternoon, one of the youths told him, "We've got to get back to Marysville in a hurry." They gave no reason for the urgency, but were "in such obvious haste" that the prospector offered to drive them. They gladly accepted.

As the investigation continued, the *Los Angeles Times* vented its spleen against the kidnappers. However, the underlying message was directed at migrants and what the editors considered government coddling of destitute families:

> While some discrepancies appear in the accounts of the reported kidnapping of Mrs. W. R. Meeks of Marysville, the probabilities appear to be that Mrs. Meeks was the victim of a more or less spur-of-the-moment plot concocted by amateurs,

either casual laborers, migrants, or dust-bowl refugees, who became frightened and abandoned their attempt to collect ransom for her.

That all angles of this affair should be investigated thoroughly goes without saying. If the kidnapping took place as described, the criminals, though bunglers, were none-the-less criminals and the escape of Mrs. Meeks from serious illness or injury was due to good fortune and to no good intentions on their part.

Their capture and punishment are imperatively necessary, as well as measures to protect California from criminal activities from the swarm of indigents foisted on the state by the federal government's bungling relief policies.

That afternoon, Norma was up and about and feeling much better. With her doctor's permission, and at her insistence, she accompanied her husband and daughters and a group of officers to the Camp Wild West Ranch.

"Showing surprising activity, Mrs. Meeks led the officers through the brush and over the hilltops, pointing out several landmarks," reported the *Appeal Democrat*:

Although unable to find the spot at which she was taken from the stolen Meeks automobile by the abductors, Mrs. Meeks was able to identify both the shallow ditch, sheltered by a fallen pine, in which she spent the first night as a captive, and the thick clump of poison oak to which the abductors transferred her Friday night.

Mrs. Meeks had personally expressed a desire to visit the remote hideout scene, located beyond the branch of a rocky and winding road about seven miles northeast of Sheridan, and a mile from buildings of the Camp Far West [Ranch].

According to the *Examiner*, the trip "contributed a number of bits of information to the data already under scrutiny of investigators."

However, Sutter County district attorney Lloyd Hewitt was blunt in his appraisal of the investigation's progress: "There is nobody under arrest and there is nobody definitely under suspicion. We have countless bits of information which we must check. There are dozens of persons we want to talk to. But no one of them is a suspect, and none of them will be taken into custody—unless we find he is flagrantly trying to lie to us."

On September 7, Mary Blake, a 28-year-old San Francisco seamstress, was flown by chartered airplane to Yuba City for questioning. She claimed to have accompanied three men she met in a Bay City tavern to Salinas. During the trip, said Blake, the men talked incessantly about the Meeks kidnapping and made highly incriminating statements, such as "We made a mistake by not having one of us stay with her;" "We should have kept her longer;" "Instead of keeping her in the open, we should have put her in a shack;" and "We should have chained her up."

Blake was returned to San Francisco when Salinas sources revealed that the woman was intoxicated—habitually.

Meantime, three men, twice described to Sutter and Yuba county authorities as having been seen in the vicinity of the kidnapping hideout, were taken into custody for questioning. "These men came voluntarily to Marysville … in order to clear themselves of suspicion, and are absolutely not under arrest," Harry C. Hickok, chief of the State Bureau of Identification, told the press.

Photographed, fingerprinted, and put through several hours of grilling, the men—all workers at the LePine Ranch near Wheatland— were taken by deputies to the Meeks ranch house. Norma shook her head. The men were released.

Press attention to the Meeks kidnapping story diminished daily. On September 14, two men wanted by Calaveras County authorities for a San Andreas robbery were taken into custody as suspects in the abduction.

They had nothing to do with it.

By September 24, it appeared that authorities were grasping at straws. A statewide arrest warrant was issued for 27-year-old Pete

Nichols, who had purchased cream cheese in a Wheatland store the day prior to Norma's kidnapping.

Arrested in October 1936, Nichols and his brother Lloyd were charged with the assault and robbery of a Rio Oso rancher. Lloyd was convicted and sent to San Quentin. Pete was released for lack of evidence. Nevertheless, his popularity suffered.

The storekeeper told authorities that Nichols was nervous when he purchased the cream cheese. Pete, who came in voluntarily, told authorities that he was not nervous, but hungry, when he bought the cheese. Hunger won the argument and the man was released.

During the first week of October, an anonymous letter arrived on the desk of C. S. Morrill, chief of the State Division of Criminal Investigation. The letter was mailed from Los Angeles, and the writer claimed to have been involved in the Meeks abduction. He told Morrill that he had been "critically wounded" in an altercation with the kidnapping's "master mind." The unhappy penman suggested, "You can probably find him in San Francisco now.

"I'll turn State's evidence, so help me," the writer declared, "if you pick him up before I die."

The letter was the handiwork of a crackpot.

A few days later, the "hottest break" yet occurred when four suspects were taken into custody in Bakersfield and locked away in the Kern County jail.

Pete Nichols, the supposedly nervous young man partial to cream cheese was one of the suspects.

Wrote the *Examiner*, "The prisoners said they were fruit pickers and admitted that at the time of the Meeks crime they were working on a ranch a half mile from the Meeks place."

Almost immediately, three of the suspects were released for lack of evidence. Nichols, however, was taken to Sutter County for a confrontation with the kidnap victim. Once again, Norma shook her head. Pete was sent on his way.

A similar scene played out at mid-month when two new suspects were brought before Mrs. Meeks. Neither had anything to do with the kidnapping,

After a 45-day run, the Meeks kidnapping story vanished from the California press. Four months passed with nary a word. Nineteen thirty-eight segued into 1939. When it appeared there was little hope of ever solving the crime and bringing its perpetrators to justice, the Marysville-Yuba City newspaper offered a more enlightened view.

"Intensive Hunt for Kidnap Suspects Ends as Brothers Lodged in Sutter Jail," headlined the February 17 issue of the *Appeal Democrat*.

Sutter County sheriff Bert Ullrey, who was right more often than wrong in the investigation prior to Norma's return, announced the arrests. "I feel certain that, when our investigations are complete, we will find that we have the right men," he confidently declared. "Every clue we have been working on and lots of other things that are now being uncovered lead to the Grimes boys."

The "Grimes boys" were brothers Robert and Ollen, twenty-four and twenty-nine-years-old, respectively.

"For the first time," reported the *Appeal Democrat*, "the full scope of an investigation that has gone on without a day's respite since the kidnapping shocked the nation, was revealed."

Ullrey, deputy Dick Kimerer, and district attorney Hewitt had worked "in the strictest of secrecy." A pledge of cooperation was exacted from the press to withhold any news that would expose their hand while they worked "ceaselessly" to tie bits of information together germane to the Grimes brothers. In late fall, the net began to tighten.

"We included the Grimes brothers on our list of suspects less than 48 hours after the kidnapping," said Hewitt. "Efforts to locate them then were not successful, but we learned that they had worked in the Rio Oso district."

Prior to the kidnapping, the brothers were arrested in Placer County. They were tried and placed on probation after being convicted of selling "mortgaged turkeys." However, neither fingerprints nor photographs were on file.

After all the press chatter about Okies and Oklahoma accents, and Dust Bowl refugees, the first viable suspects in the case were migrant farm workers from Louisville, Kentucky. There the "boys" were traced to their mother's home and Louisville authorities were alerted to keep them under surveillance.

Hewitt and Kimerer flew to Kentucky. Ollen had, by then, vanished from Louisville. Robert, however, was picked up by local police and placed in jail to await the California officers. When confronted, the suspect thought the questioning related to his Placer County parole violation.

Asked if he had worked in the Rio Oso area, he said that he had and admitted that he knew William Meeks. He claimed, however, that he learned of the kidnapping from a Texas newspaper he found on a freight train while en route to Louisville. Then, out of the blue, Hewitt asked, "Why did you say you were afraid you would get the electric chair?"

Caught off guard and not thinking, Robert blurted out, "Because I thought that was what the law was." He recognized instantly that he had fallen into a trap and refused to answer further questions.

Meantime, Ollen returned to Louisville and was arrested a few days later. In time, the men were escorted to California by United States marshals acting under federal fugitive warrants. At Sacramento, the suspects were taken before a federal judge who fixed their bail at $10,000 each.

Distance was placed between the brothers when Ollen was incarcerated in the Colusa County jail, while Robert was incarcerated in the Sutter County jail. Norma had tentatively identified the men though photographs. If in-person identification proved consistent,

Hewitt would ask the grand jury to meet at once to return kidnapping indictments.

On the following day, Norma visited the Colusa and Sutter county jails and viewed lineups at each lockup. She singled out the Grimes brothers as the men who kidnapped her.

"We have enough now to go before the grand jury and to ask for indictments, and enough evidence to sustain convictions," Hewitt told the press.

On February 20, the brothers were momentarily reunited when arraigned in justice court. They were charged with kidnapping, and bail was set at $10,000 each. Combined with a like amount set in federal court, bail for each man totaled $20,000.

Retained as counsel for the accused, Erling S. Norby and Richard Fuidge released a statement in which they said, "Both Robert and Ollen Grimes are emphatic and earnest in denying any connection with the Meeks case."

The statement came as no surprise.

Two days following their appearance in justice court, the Grimes brothers were indicted by the Sutter County grand jury. Then, on March 3, they appeared for arraignment in Sutter County superior court. Pleas of not guilty were entered and Judge Arthur Coats scheduled their trial for April 17.

The Grimes trial proved an exception to the rule when it commenced as scheduled with no delays. Jury selection was made with remarkable efficiency and testimony began before the first day was over.

Speaking for the prosecution, District Attorney Hewitt sparked the Grimes brothers' interest when he said, "I will inform counsel for the defense now that we are not going to ask for the death penalty. We do not claim that Mrs. Meeks suffered any bodily injury."

Norby opened for the defense and made clear the direction his arguments would take. He told jurors that the accused brothers were innocent of any wrongdoing. They were, he insisted, clandestine boxcar passengers aboard a freight train en route to Kentucky when the kidnapping occurred.

William Meeks was among the first prosecution witnesses called. He related details—by now well known to most Californians—of his wife's abduction. There were no dramatic revelations or unexpected fireworks.

A light moment occurred during Meeks' testimony when Hewitt asked if he knew the caliber of the kidnappers' gun. The witness drew a laugh from spectators when he replied emphatically, "It looked awfully big."

The trial entered its second day, with a courtroom packed by spectators. Norma Meeks was scheduled to testify and folks came from far and wide to glimpse the woman they had come to know through countless newspaper stories. After all seats will taken, "more [people] filed into the room in a steady stream until standing room along the walls was at a premium," noted the *Appeal Democrat.*

During two hours of testimony, Norma recounted incidents from the moment of her abduction to the time she returned home. A disappointed reporter noted that, "Mrs. Meeks' story revealed few facts not previously told to the authorities and featured in the nation's press."

Hewitt brought his methodical questioning to a sudden climax when he asked the witness if she had seen either of the kidnappers since she walked away from the hillside camp in September.

She replied that she had.

"Do you know now who the man was who acted as the guard at the hideout?" asked Hewitt.

"I do. His name is Robert Grimes," she replied.

"Is that man in this courtroom?"

"Yes, he is seated there at the right, to my right."

The district attorney motioned for Ollen Grimes to rise from his seat at the counsel table. "Is that the man?"

"No," replied Norma.

Hewitt then motioned for the younger brother to stand, and repeated his question.

"That's the man who was in the hideout with me," she said.

The *Appeal Democrat* observed that "neither of the accused men registered the slightest change of expression as they stood. Robert gave absolutely no sign that he had even heard, much less realized the importance, of the damning accusation against him."

Dan Carey, a Rio Oso orchardist, testified that he hired Robert Grimes as a peach picker and paid him by check in January 1938.

C. S. Hite, another Rio Oso orchardist and a neighbor of the Meekses, told the court that the Grimes brothers worked on his ranch during the winter of 1936–1937, and again in August 1938. His account book revealed that the last checks written to the brothers were dated August 20—twelve days prior to the kidnapping.

Hewitt sought to prove that the brothers were residents of the Hotel Humboldt in Sacramento from August 21 through the 31st. Hotel clerk Frank Klein produced the hotel registry and room receipts to support the prosecutor's argument. A third man, said Klein, was with them until the 28th.

The object of the testimony was to refute the defense claim that the brothers were aboard a freight train en route to Louisville when the kidnapping occurred. The third man mentioned by Klein did not become an issue, nor did Norma's claim that there were three kidnappers. In fact, the alleged third man became a moot point throughout the trial.

Ethel Taillefer, who operated a small crossroads store, proved a valuable witness. On the evening of September 2, the day after the kidnapping, a man she identified as Ollen Grimes entered her store. He purchased a pack of cigarettes, bread, canned beans, corned beef, and cream cheese. He drank a bottle of beer, puffed rapidly on a cigarette, and was visibly nervous.

Taillefer testified: "Everyone else who came in the store that day talked about the kidnapping and wondered if Mrs. Meeks would be found. Everyone was excited about it"—except the nervous customer.

Taillefer was so suspicious, she followed the man out of the store and noted the direction he took. Then she telephoned the sheriff's office. It was her call that stimulated initial interest in the elusive Grimes brothers.

On Friday, April 21, the prosecution rested its case. The defense promptly placed Ollen Grimes on the stand. In breathless prose, the *Appeal Democrat* noted that his appearance "marked the first time that the voice of either brother has been heard in the courtroom."

In fact, his voice was barely heard. The witness spoke so quietly that Judge Coats and attorneys for both sides prodded him continuously to speak up. As jurors strained to hear him, Grimes offered a brief history of his Kentucky past and his move to California in 1933.

All at once, Richard Fuidge, the defendants' counsel, abandoned routine questions: "Did you ever, on September 1, or at any other time, kidnap Mrs. Norma Meeks?"

"No, I did not," he replied. For the first time, Ollen's voice was clearly audible.

"Did you ever transport Mrs. Meeks from one part of this county to another and hold her for ransom?"

"No, I never did."

After staunch denials of complicity in the kidnapping, the defendant launched into a detailed account of hopping a freight train at Roseville. He was uncertain, but thought the date was sometime between August 30 and September 1. His destination, he said, was Louisville.

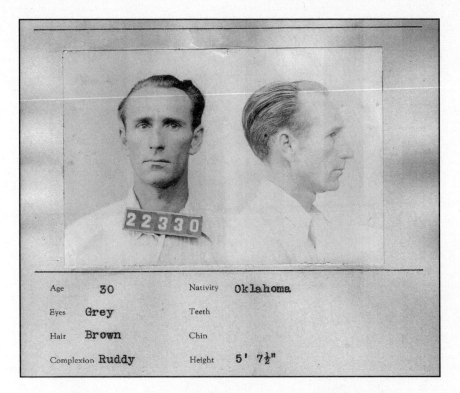

Age	30	Nativity	Oklahoma
Eyes	Grey	Teeth	
Hair	Brown	Chin	
Complexion	Ruddy	Height	5' 7½"

Figure 14.4 California state prison record card, Ollen Grimes.
California State Archives

The trial entered its second week on Monday, April 24, when Robert, the younger Grimes brother, took the stand in his own defense. His testimony largely paralleled that of Ollen. The significant difference was the manner in which it was delivered. Robert spoke in a well-modulated voice that was clearly audible to judge and jury.

Responding to a series of direct questions from his defense counsel, the witness denied playing any part in the Meeks abduction. Asked if the revolver used in the kidnapping was his, he replied that he "had never owned a revolver in his life."

"Did you transport Mrs. Meeks, at any time, to a place in the hills near Camp Far West?"

"No, I never did."

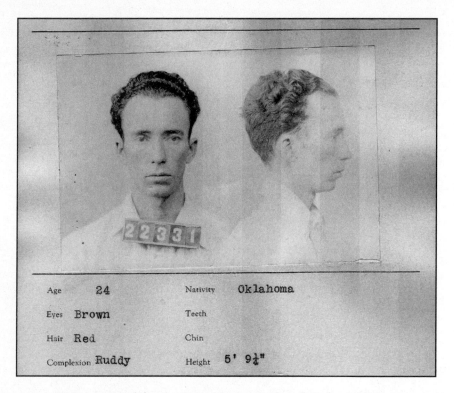

Age	24	Nativity	Oklahoma
Eyes	Brown	Teeth	
Hair	Red	Chin	
Complexion	Ruddy	Height	5' 9¼"

Figure 14.5 California state prison record card, Robert Grimes.
California State Archives

When asked about hopping a freight train to Louisville, he was as unsure about the departure date as his brother had been. He supposed that it was "about the end of August or the first of September."

"He gave approximate times for their arrivals and departures from the numerous towns and cities, but admitted that neither brother carried a watch en route," noted the *Appeal Democrat*:

> Queried by District Attorney Hewitt as to whether he had not "talked over" the route to Louisville with Art E. Griffin, another inmate of the Sutter County jail, Robert replied that he had. He denied, however, that Griffin had helped him prepare his testimony of the route, saying he asked him only regarding the names and the spelling of the names of some of the towns.

Asked if Archie Wenk and Jack Young, two other jail inmates, had not observed him talking the route over with Griffin, Robert said he "supposed that they did."

Much hubbub was made of an alleged "mystery witness." Identified only as a woman, she was slated to appear for the defense the following day. Spectators who arrived early to claim seats were disappointed, and Judge Coats was miffed when the much-touted witness failed to appear.

On that note, the defense rested it case.

Hewitt's closing argument was a ninety-minute summation of evidence against the defendants. When the district attorney resumed his seat, Fuidge rose to his feet and told the court that prosecution testimony "meant nothing" to the case. "There never has been any contention that Mrs. Meeks was not abducted," he said. "Two men did enter the Meeks home and carry her away, but it was not these two boys."

Characterizing the defendants as "poker-faced Kentucky migrants and peach pickers," the *Appeal Democrat* reported that the case was placed in the hands of the jury shortly after 11:30 on the morning of April 25. "Hardly a half hour passed when they were taken to luncheon by two bailiffs."

Anticipating a quick verdict, spectators milled about the courthouse. It was not to be. Disappointed, many went home when the sky darkened and bailiffs escorted the jury to a restaurant for dinner. Then, deliberations continued into the night. Not until 10:45 did the foreman alert the court that jurors had reached a verdict.

"A tense, electric silence filled the packed courtroom when the jurors, after deliberating for six hours and 15 minutes, filed solemnly into the box after having appraised the bailiffs a few moments earlier that they were ready with a verdict," wrote the *Appeal Democrat*: "As they took their seats, Thomas Johnson, the foreman, remained standing with sheets of paper in his hand."

Glancing about, spectators noted that Norma and William Meeks were conspicuously absent.

"Ladies and gentlemen of the jury, have you reached a verdict?" asked the court clerk.

"We have," replied Johnson.

Commented the *Democrat*: "The Spectators, court attaches, newsmen and the two defendants, standing erect and with their eyes fixed on the jury box, seemed to hold their breaths for an instant …."

An instant later, the Grimes brothers were found guilty.

On the final day of April, the brothers were sentenced to life in prison. The next day, May 1—eight months to the day following the kidnapping of Norma Meeks—Robert and Ollen Grimes were taken to Folsom Prison. Their escort was Sheriff Bert Ullrey, the very man who heard William Meeks holler into the telephone, "They have got my wife! They have got my wife!"

Chapter 15: Kidnapped in Place

Henry Bodkin was en route to an evening engagement. He bid goodbye to his wife and son and went to the garage to retrieve his automobile. As he backed slowly out of the driveway, a man crossed the yard and approached the vehicle. Bodkin stopped the car and unrolled the window.

"Are you Mr. Bodkin?" inquired the stranger.

The prominent attorney confirmed his identify and the man told him he was there to deliver a Christmas package. Bodkin would have to sign for it, he said. Just then, a second man emerged from the shadows. Much to Bodkin's astonishment, the new arrival brandished a revolver. "This is a holdup," he announced. His voice was cold, his tone menacing.

He forced Bodkin from his car, and then yet another man materialized. The bandit duo became a trio, and they compelled the lawyer at gunpoint to lead the strangers into his home.

An hour later, the holdup men disappeared into the night. Jewelry belonging to Ruth Bodkin, the lawyer's wife, and valued at some $1,700 disappeared as well. So did $43 in cash taken from Bodkin's pocket.

It was Saturday evening, December 16, 1933.

The holdup men were more brazen than bright, and they left in their wake clues sufficient for Los Angeles police officers to track their whereabouts. In record time, three men—William Tanner, 34; James J. Hill, 41; and Harry C. Brooks, 55—were lodged in the county jail under suspicion of kidnapping and robbery.

Grace Johnson, who rented Harry Brooks a room in the 2900 block of West Ninth Street, had telephoned police about an unusual discovery. In shrubbery beneath Brooks' window, Johnson found a chamois bag. In it was some $1,700 worth of jewelry.

Two days after Christmas, the county grand jury returned indictments charging the men with two counts of kidnapping for the purpose of robbery and two counts of robbery. Trial before superior court judge Charles W. Fricke was scheduled for February 19, 1934.

Almost immediately, Hill, who had no history of criminal activity, confessed his participation in the crime. Perhaps more important, he was separated from the trial and turned state's evidence against Tanner and Brooks.

Fate decreed that this pair of misfits would be the first tried under California's newly revised kidnapping law. The revision stipulated that bodily harm of any kind inflicted on a victim constituted a capital crime. If they found the accused men guilty as charged, the jury was at liberty to impose the death penalty.

The trial commenced as scheduled and the prosecution called Henry Bodkin as its first witness. He identified the accused men as the armed thugs who accosted him in his driveway and forced their way into his home. In lurid detail, he described a drama of stark brutality.

One of the bandits tied Bodkin to a chair and the others forced Ruth and son Grattan into a closet. They locked Amelia Drew, the Bodkin maid, in the closet as well.

With cold efficiency, the kidnappers ransacked the attorney's well-appointed home and collected some $1,700 in jewelry. Bodkin turned over $43, and he told his assailants it was the only cash on hand. Furious, the robbers insisted he was lying. They had it on good authority, they asserted, that hidden away was no less than

$100,000, and probably more. If Bodkin failed to come clean, they would blow his brains away.

To reinforce their deadly intent, one of the hoodlums cocked his revolver and poked it against the lawyer's heart. He held it there some fifteen minutes, all the while repeating the death threat.

When this terrifying ploy failed to turn up additional cash, Tanner put a stick match to a magazine cover and held the flames to the victim's hands. Bodkin cried out in agony and repeated over and over that there was no more money in the house.

At last the bandits conceded that he was telling the truth and the torture ceased. They released Ruth, Grattan, and the maid from the closet. Each was tied to a chair, after which the kidnappers fled the Bodkin home.

Jurors absorbed the ghastliness of Bodkin's ordeal with faces drawn tightly in expressions of revulsion. The testimony did not bode well for the accused.

Hill took the stand as star witness for the prosecution, having earlier pleaded guilty to two counts of robbery—sentence pending. He told the court about meeting Brooks and Tanner in the Frazier Mountains while working as a miner. Brooks had asked him if he "wanted to make some easy money." Brooks then proposed robbing Bodkin. The well-heeled attorney, so said Brooks, kept between $100,000 and $150,000 in his home, as well as jewelry worth $50,000.

Hill testified as follows:

> He asked me if I'd help get it [and] I told him I had never done anything like that in my life. Tanner said, "You're going to help do it!" I said, "no." Tanner said, "if you don't you had better keep your mouth shut for it will take only one bullet to shut it!"

> I said I didn't want to. Then Brooks reached over the table and handed a gun to me and one to Tanner.

After the robbery, the trio went to Brooks' room. According to Hill, they gave him a one-dollar bill as his portion of the spoils.

The prosecution, led by deputy district attorney Grant B. Cooper, intended to prove that Brooks was the kidnapping's mastermind. Tanner was his lackey, Hill his dupe.

When the state rested its case, the defense—led by John Groene and Dan Critchley—put forth a motion asking that charges against the accused men be dismissed for lack of evidence. Judge Fricke denied the motion out of hand.

Called as a defense witness, Tanner shocked no one when he denied any participation in the kidnapping and robbery. He did not hold a flaming magazine cover to Bodkin's hands, he insisted. He was not even there. As a matter of fact, while the holdup was in progress, Tanner was at a dance hall exercising his legs.

The trial was a straightforward affair. There were no fireworks and few surprises. The defense labored at a deficit, while the prosecution sought convictions in a nearly ironclad case. In its closing argument, the state demanded the extreme penalty—death.

On February 28, the court placed the fate of Tanner and Brooks in the hands of seven men and five women. The jury remained sequestered for six hours before returning its verdict—guilty. However, the bulk of deliberation did not focus on a verdict. The jury's debate centered on the death penalty, a choice it ultimately recommended.

A *Los Angeles Times* reporter wrote that "in commenting on the hanging recommendation of the jury, Judge Fricke made it plain that if in his opinion the evidence in the case does not justify the supreme penalty, California law empowers him to set aside the death [sentence] and recommend one of lesser severity."

The reporter noted that "the hanging verdict" was received by District Attorney Buron Fitts "as a definite indication that the citizens of California have ceased to sympathize with kidnappers and will not tolerate such crimes of violence in the future."

The day after the jury rendered its verdict, the *Times* editorialized that Brooks and Tanner were "excellent gallows material." Assuming a tone similar to the district attorney, the editorial suggested, "The only possible service they could be to society would be to illustrate to the criminal world in general that the day of mush-and-milk handling of such criminals in California is past. Their fate could well serve to send a shiver down the spines of gangsters contemplating similar crimes; and by their callous and brutal actions they have forfeited all right to personal consideration."

But public support for the jury's recommendation was not universal even among supporters of the death penalty. Bodkin was not murdered, nor were his injuries life-threatening. Despicable as his treatment was, he survived his ordeal.

In some quarters, it was argued that the lawyer had not been kidnapped at all. Certainly, a brutal robbery had occurred, but the victim was never removed from his own property. How, then, could the crime be defined as kidnapping?

In 1933, stimulated by public indignation over the Lindbergh kidnapping, the legislature amended the California penal code governing the snatch racket. It eliminated asportation, the legal term for "removal" or "carrying off," as a requirement to establish an incidence of kidnapping. Under the amendment, "stationary" kidnapping came within the purview of the statute.

Never mind that Bodkin was not removed from his property. He, his family, and his maid were held against their will, and that fact alone constituted kidnapping. Never mind as well that Bodkin was not murdered. Under the 1933 amendment, jurors could impose the death penalty, or life imprisonment without possibility of parole, if the victim of a kidnapping suffered bodily harm of any kind. There need be no serious injury.

The amendment was so recent that Judge Fricke himself was compelled to study the revised statute. After stating that California law empowered him to set aside the death penalty for lack of compelling evidence, Fricke was forced to reverse himself. He told the

Figure 15.1 Tanner is sentenced to hang.
San Francisco History Center, San Francisco Public Library

press that he could "find no authority for doing so under the provisions set forth in the new kidnapping law."

It was, however, a moot point. "Had I tried the case sitting as judge and jury," noted Fricke after reviewing the evidence, "I would have returned the same verdict." Consequently, on March 5, Brooks and Tanner were sentenced to hang—Brooks at San Quentin on May 11, Tanner at Folsom Prison on the same date.

"Appeals presumably will be taken in both cases and, since they are the first under a new law, probably will delay matters considerably," wrote a *Times* reporter who then digressed into editorial opinion. "Some day such delays will be largely eliminated, and prompt carrying out of sentences will add teeth to a beneficial statute."

Meantime, Fricke dispatched Hill to San Quentin for a term of five years to life on two counts of robbery. "It usually is impossible to convict members of gangs without the testimony of one of the accomplices," he said. "I believe it is only fair and that justice is served better if such witnesses are given special consideration for their assistance."

The judge dismissed two counts of kidnapping pending against Hill.

To no one's surprise, the appeals process commenced in earnest and the May 11 execution date for each kidnapper came and went.

Nine months had passed when Henry Bodkin sought a private meeting with District Attorney Fitts. Bodkin's home had been recently burglarized and word was delivered to him from "underworld sources" that unless Tanner and Brooks were spared the gallows he would be "harassed constantly."

Fitts reopened the investigation, but it plodded along with little enthusiasm. Bodkin, however, was convinced that the condemned men kidnapped and tortured him on orders from "higher-ups."

In May 1935, more than a year after the first execution date passed uneventfully, Bodkin paid visits to San Quentin and Folsom prisons. "I felt that with their doom impending [Brooks and Tanner] might disclose the story behind the [kidnapping] affair."

They did not, but apparently Hill told him an interesting tale. "Hill substantiated my belief that someone higher up was responsible for the three men kidnapping and burning me to obtain money and jewels I was supposed to have," he said after the visit. "Brooks was convicted on the testimony of Hill, who I have no doubt was lying," he declared, "and I want the truth before the men go to their deaths."

Bodkin, who claimed possession of evidence sufficient to implicate another man, was unconvinced that execution was appropriate. Despite the brutality inflicted on him by the kidnappers, the lawyer considered the death penalty excessive punishment. Meanwhile, the new death date set for both men, August 23, approached rapidly.

The *Times* was having none of Bodkin's "tender-heartedness," insisting "appeals should fall on deaf ears." Anxious for the hangman's noose to drop, it editorialized that "the interests of 130,000,000 people in the United States require that the crime of kidnapping be stamped out by rigorous effort, and the sentimental feelings of a few, victims or otherwise, weighs as nothing in the scale against this preponderant interest."

Bodkin met again with Tanner, this time in Fitts' office. Neither lawyer would disclose the nature of the conversation, but each openly expressed their opinion that at least one other man, and possibly three, may have been involved in the kidnapping.

Fitts engineered a subpoena and ordered Tanner to appear before the grand jury on August 9, two weeks prior to his scheduled execution. The day before his appearance, Helen Mendoza—the *Times* characterized her as a "mysterious woman with diamond-studded teeth"—volunteered to corroborate Tanner's statements.

Neither Tanner's nor Mendoza's story—they were tales of three other men manipulating the kidnapping from above—moved the grand jury. Foreman George Rochester told the press that their testimony was not of "sufficient importance to warrant immediate investigation."

While Brooks and Tanner appealed to Governor Frank F. Merriam for commutation of their death sentences to life in prison, Bodkin, Fitts, and others petitioned for a ninety-day stay of execution to enable their on-going investigation. The lawyers were successful, and the court rescheduled the double execution for November 15.

Despite their best efforts, the investigation proved inconclusive. Nevertheless, Fitts and Bodkin, and even Judge Fricke, became convinced that the punishment meted out by the trial jury did not fit the crime. They joined other prominent signatories on a clemency petition to Governor Merriam.

Then, on October 30, William H. Waste, chief justice of the California supreme court, added the high court's weight to the argument for commutation. The death penalty, opined the justices, was cruel and unusual punishment.

They granted yet another stay, but Merriam was in no hurry to make a life-or-death decision. Then, unexpectedly, on January 8, 1936, the governor vacated Brooks' and Tanner's rendezvous with the hangman. He commuted the sentence of each man to life imprisonment without the possibility of parole.

Henry Bodkin got what he wanted. So did the men who kidnapped, robbed, and tortured him. It was an odd ending to an extraordinary tale.

Bibliography

Documents

Fourteenth Census of the United States: 1920—Population. Precinct 36, Bakersfield City, Kern County, California. Department of Commerce—Bureau of the Census.

In the Court of Appeal of the State of California Sixth Appellate District. The People, Plaintiff and Respondent, v. Fernando Dominguez, Defendant and Appellant. HO22727 (San Benito County Super. Ct. No. CRF99-37033). Filed 12/14/04 (opn. On transfer from Supreme Court after grant of review).

O'Laughlin v. Superior Court (1957) 155 CA2d 415.

People v. Bruneman (1935) 4 CA2d 75 [Crim. 2571, Second Appellate District, Division One, January 24, 1935]. *The People, Respondent, v. Les Bruneman, Appellant.*

People v. Pianezzi (1940) 42 CA2d 270) [Crim. 3354, Second Appellate District, Division Two, December 31, 1940]. *The People, Respondent, v. Peter Pianezzi, Appellant.*

People v. Tanner (Cal. 2d 279, 44 P.2d 324 [1935]).

Wickersham, George W. *U.S. National Commission on Law Observance and Enforcement Report.* Washington, D.C.: U.S. Government Printing Office, 1931.

Unpublished Papers

Alexander, Toni Ann. "From Oklahomans to 'Okies': Identity Formation in Rural California." Ph.D. Dissertation, Department of Geography and Anthropology, Louisiana State University, 2004.

Rogers, W. Lane. "When News Was Not News At All: Duplicitous Politicians, Propagandists & Visual Media, from the Early Days of Film to the Eve of World War II." N.d., n.p., University of Arizona, 15 December 2005.

Newspapers

Arizona Daily Star

Arizona Republican

Bisbee (Arizona) Daily Review

Charlotte (North Carolina) News

Chicago Daily Tribune

(Chillicothe) Daily Constitution (Missouri)

Colma Record

Council Bluffs (Iowa) Nonpareil

Daily Californian

Dunkirk (New York) Evening Observer

East Oregonian (Pendleton)

Fresno Bee

Fresno Bee-Republican

Harrisburg (Illinois) Daily Register

Hayward Daily Review

Hayward Review

London Daily Mail

London Sunday Express

London Times

Long Beach Independent

Long Beach Press-Telegram

Los Angeles Daily News

Los Angeles Examiner

Los Angeles Herald

Los Angeles Times

Marysville-Yuba City Appeal-Democrat

Modesto Bee & News-Herald

Modesto News-Herald

New York Herald Tribune

New York Times

Oakland Post Inquirer

Oakland Tribune

Ogden (Utah) Standard-Examiner

Oxnard Daily Courier

Oxnard Press-Courier

Palo Alto Daily News

Pasadena Star-News

Phoenix Gazette

Redding Record-Searchlight

Sacramento Bee

Sacramento Evening Bee

Salt Lake Tribune

San Diego Herald

San Diego Union

San Francisco Call

San Francisco Call-Bulletin

San Francisco Chronicle

San Francisco Examiner

San Jose Mercury Herald

San Jose Mercury News

San Mateo County Times

San Mateo Daily Journal

San Mateo Daily News

San Mateo Times

Santa Rosa Press Democrat

Tombstone (Arizona) Epitaph

Tucson Citizen

Walla Walla (Washington) Union Bulletin

Washington Post

Waterloo (Iowa) Daily Courier

Woodland Daily Democrat

Wire Services

Associated Press

International News Service

United Press

United Press International

Periodicals

Anon. "A Rationale of the Law of Kidnapping." *Columbia Law Review*, vol. 53, no. 4 (April 1953), 540–558.

Anon. "Criminal Law: Kidnapping: California Penal Code § 209." *California Law Review*, vol. 24, no. 2 (January 1936), 220–222.

Anon. "Criminal Law. Kidnapping. Intent to Act Lawfully as a Defense." *Virginia Law Review*, vol. 24, no. 7 (May 1938), 805.

Anon. "Criminal Law. Kidnapping. What Constitutes a Reward?" *Columbia Law Review*, vol. 38, no. 7 (November 1938), 1287–1291.

Anon. "Flee Dust Bowl for California." *Business Week*, vol. 33, no. 404 (3 July 1937), 36–37.

Anon. "Robbery Becomes Kidnapping: Criminal Law, Kidnapping, Armed Robbery Constitutes Kidnapping under California Penal Code Section 209." *Stanford Law Review*, vol. 3, no. 1 (December 1950), 156–162.

Bomar, Horace L. "The Lindbergh Law." *Law and Contemporary Problems*, vol. 1, no. 4, "Extending Federal Powers over Crime" (October 1934), 435–444.

Christiansen, Larry D. "Henceforth and Forever Aimee and Douglas." *Cochise Quarterly*, vol. 8, nos. 3 & 4 (Spring 1979), 3–62.

Collings, Rex A., Jr. "Offences of Violence Against the Person." *Annals of the American Academy of Political and Social Science*, vol. 339, "Crime and the American Penal System" (January 1962), 42–56.

Corn, Joseph J. "Making Flying 'Thinkable': Women Pilots and the Selling of Aviation, 1927–1940." *American Quarterly*, vol. 31, no. 4 (Autumn 1979), 556–571.

Greenspan, Ezra. "George Palmer Putnam: Historical and Cultural Antecedents of an Ex-Yankee Publisher." *New England Quarterly*, vol. 69, no. 4 (December 1996), 605–626.

Kittrie, Nicholas N. "Ransom Kidnapping in America." *Journal of Criminal Law and Criminology*, vol. 71, no. 4 (Winter 1980), 654–657.

Matthews, Burnita Shelton. "The Woman Juror." *Women Lawyers' Journal*, vol. XV, no. 2 (April 1927), 22–28.

Passet, Joanne. "The Nation's Great Library: Herbert Putnam and the Library of Congress, 1899–1939." *Journal of American History*, vol. 81, no. 4 (March 1995), 1770–1771.

Putnam, George Palmer. "A Flyer's Husband." *Forum and Century*, vol. 93, no. 6 (June 1935), 330–332.

Remak, Joachim. "Friends of the New Germany": The Bund and German-American Relations." *Journal of Modern History*, vol. 29, no. 1 (March 1957), 38–41.

Rogers, W. Lane. "Sanitarium of the Southwest: Seeking a Cure in the Arizona Sunshine." *Desert Leaf*, vol. 6, no. 1 (January 1992), 18–19.

Schurer, Ernst. "Der Zweite Weltkrieg und die Exilanten: Eine literarische Antwort." *German Quarterly*, vol. 68, no. 3 (Summer 1995), 345–348.

Sinclair, Upton. "The Evangelist Drowns." *New Republic*, vol. 47 (30 June 1926), 171.

Smith, Arlo E. "Criminal Law: Kidnapping for the Purpose of Robbery." *California Law Review*, vol. 38, no. 5 (December 1950), 920–924.

Steele, Henry Joseph. "Bernhardt of the Sawdust Trail." *Vanity Fair*, vol. 40, no. 1 (March 1933), 38–41.

Books

Alex, Ernest Kahlar. *Ransom Kidnapping in America, 1874–1974: The Creation of a Capital Crime*. Carbondale: Southern Illinois University Press, 1978.

Alexander, Philip W. and Charles P. Hamm. *History of San Mateo County*. Burlingame, California: Press of Burlingame Publishing Co., 1916.

Allen, Frederick Lewis. *Only Yesterday: An Informal History of the Nineteen Twenties*. New York: Harper & Bros., 1931.

Allsop, Kenneth. *The Bootleggers and Their Era*. Garden City, New York: Doubleday, 1961.

Anon. *The Curtiss Standard JN4-D Military Tractor Handbook*. Buffalo, New York: Curtiss Aeroplane and Motor Corporation, 1918.

Asbury, Herbert. *The Great Illusion: An Informal History of Prohibition*. Garden City, New York, 1950.

Block, Eugene B. *The Wizard of Berkeley*. New York: Coward-McCann, 1959.

Butler, Susan. *East of the Dawn: The Life of Amelia Earhart*. Reading, Massachusetts: Addison-Wessley, 1997.

Cashman, Sean Dennis. *America in the Twenties and Thirties*. New York: New York University Press, 1989.

Caughey, John, and Laree Caughey. *Los Angeles: Biography of a City*. Berkeley: University of California Press, 1976.

Chaplin, J. P. *Rumor, Fear and the Madness of Crowds*. New York: Ballantine Books, Inc., 1959.

Collins, Paul F. *Tales of an Old Air-Faring Man: A Half Century of Incidents, Accidents and Providence*. Stevens Point, Wisconsin: University of Wisconsin-Stevens Point Foundation Press, 1983.

Farrell, Harry. *Swift Justice: Murder and Vengeance in a California Town*. New York: St. Martin's Press, 1993.

Fass, Paula S. *Kidnapped: Child Abduction in America*. New York: Oxford University Press, 1997.

Friedman, Lawrence M. *Crime and Punishment in American History*. New York: Basic Books, 1993.

Garraty, John A. and Mark C. Carnes, eds. *The Dictionary of National Biography*. New York: Oxford University Press, 1999.

Goldberg, David J. *Discontented America: The United States in the 1920s*. Baltimore: Johns Hopkins University Press, 1977.

Grun, Bernard. *The Timetables of History: A Horizontal Linkage of People and Events*. New York: Simon & Schuster, 1991.

Gudde, Erwin G., revised by William Bright. *California Place Names: The Origin and Etymology of Current Geographical Names*. Berkeley: University of California Press, 1988.

Guttmacher, Manfred. *The Mind of the Murderer*. New York: Grove Press, 1962.

Halliwell, Leslie, edited by John Walker. *Halliwell's Film Guide*. New York: Harper Collins Publishers, 1991.

Holliday, J. S. *The World Rushed In: The California Gold Rush Experience: An Eyewitness Account of a Nation Heading West.* New York: Simon & Schuster, 1981.

Kennedy, David M. *Freedom from Fear: The American People in Depression and War, 1929–1945.* New York: Oxford University Press, 1999.

Lovell, Mary S. *The Sound of Wings: Amelia Earhart.* New York: St. Martin's Press, 1989.

Malone, Michael P., and Richard W. Etulain. *The American West: A Twentieth-Century History.* Lincoln: University of Nebraska Press, 1989.

Mardsen, George. *Fundamentalism and American Culture: The Shaping of Twentieth Century Evangelism.* New York: Oxford University Press, 1980.

Mavity, Nancy Barr. *Sister Aimee.* Garden City, New York: Doubleday, Doran & Company, 1931.

Mayo, Morrow. *Los Angeles.* New York: Alfred A. Knopf, 1933.

Mink, Gwendolyn, and Alice O'Connor, eds. *Poverty in the United States: An Encyclopedia of History, Politics, and Policy.* Santa Barbara, California: ABC-Clio, 2004.

Murray, Raymond C., and John C. F. Tedrow. *Forensic Geology.* New York: Prentice Hall, 1992.

Nash, Jay Robert. *Bloodletters and Badmen: A Narrative Encyclopedia of American Criminals from the Pilgrims to the Present.* New York: M. Evans and Company, 1973.

Nietzsche, Friedrich, translated and edited by Walter Kaufmann. *On the Genealogy of Morals* and *Ecce Homo*. New York: Vantage Books, 1989.

Niven, John. *Connecticut's Hero: Israel Putnam.* Hartford: American Revolution Bicentennial Commission of Connecticut, 1972.

Powell, Allan Kent, ed. *Utah History Encyclopedia.* Salt Lake City: University of Utah Press, 1994.

Pugliese, Stanislao G. *Carlo Rosselli: Socialist Heretic and Antifascist Exile*. Cambridge: Harvard University Press, 1999.

Rawls, James J., and Richard J. Orsi, eds. *A Golden State: Mining and Economic Development in Gold Rush California*. Berkeley: University of California Press, 1999.

Railey, Hilton Howell. *Touch'd with Madness*. New York: Carrick & Evans, 1938.

Rarick, Eathan. *California Rising: The Life and Times of Pat Brown*. Berkeley: University of California Press, 2005.

Reck, Franklin M. *The Romance of American Transportation*. New York: Thomas Y. Crowell Company, 1962.

Rogers, W. Lane. *Crimes & Misdeeds: Headlines from Arizona's Past*. Flagstaff, Arizona: Northland Publishing, 1995.

Rogers, W. Lane, and Kay Rose Macfarlane. *Ruthless Acts: The Utah Murders*. Baltimore: Publish America, 2007.

Rush, Philip S. *A History of the Californias*. San Diego: Neyenesch Printers, Inc., 1964.

Rutland, Robert. *The Newsmongers: Journalism in the Life of the Nation*. New York: Dial, 1973.

Sifakis, Carl. *The Encyclopedia of American Crime*. New York: Facts on File, Inc., 1982.

Sillitoe, Linda. *A History of Salt Lake County*. Salt Lake City: Utah State Historical Society, 1996.

Smith, James R. *San Francisco's Lost Landmarks*. Sanger, California: Word Dancer Press, 2005.

Sutton, Matthew Avery. *Aimee Semple McPherson and the Resurrection of Christian America*. Cambridge: Harvard University Press, 2007.

Terkel, Studs. *Hard Times: An Oral History of the Great Depression*. New York: Pantheon, 1970.

Thomas, Gordon, and Max Morgan Witts. *The San Francisco Earthquake*. New York: Stein and Day, 1971.

Unger, Irwin, and Debi Unger. *The Guggenheims: A Family History*. New York: Harper Collins Publishers, 2005.

Warren, Earl. *The Memories of Earl Warren*. Garden City, New York: Double Day & Company, 1977.

Watkins, T. H. *The Great Depression: America in the 1930s*. Boston: Little Brown & Company, 1993.

White, G. Edward. *Earl Warren: A Public Life*. New York: Oxford University Press, 1982.

Worster, Donald. *Dust Bowl: The Southern Plains in the 1930s*. New York: Oxford University Press, 1979.

Writers' Program of the Work Projects Administration. *History of Journalism in San Francisco*. San Francisco: Work Projects Administration, 1939–40.

Young, James V. *Hot Type and Pony Wire*. Santa Cruz, California: Western Tangier Press, 1981.

Internet

Anon. "After the Ocean Shore R.R.: Pacifica's Castle of Mystery." Available at http://www.halfmoonbaymemories.com. Accessed 13 June 2007.

Anon. "An early forensic scientist uses sand to solve the mysterious disappearance and murder of a California priest." CSI: California (July 2006). Available at http://www.aggman.com/articles/carved06.htm. Accessed 21 June 2007.

Anon. "Death After Dark." *Time* (27 November 1933). Available at http://www.time.com/time/printout/0,8816,746348,00.html. Accessed 4 April 2007.

Anon. "Disappearance." *Time* (7 June 1926). Available at http://www.time.com/time/printout/0,8816,722025,00.html. Accessed 25 March 2007.

Anon. "Great Depression and World War II, 1929–1945. The Dust Bowl." Library of Congress. Available at http://memory.loc.gov/ammem/ndlpedu/features/timeline/depwwii/dustbowl/onroad.html. Accessed 15 October 2003.

Anon. "History of the Redwood City Courthouse." Local History: Redwood City, CA. Available at http://www.redwoodcity.org/about/local_history/exhibits/courthouse/courthouse_history.htm. Accessed 21 June 2007.

Anon. "Hydraulic Mining and Controversy, 1851–1893." Available at http://www.learncalifornia.org/doc.asp?id=526. Accessed 9 September 2007.

Anon. "Israel Putnam (1718–1790)." Massachusetts Historical Society. Available at www.masshist.org. Accessed 24 November 2006.

Anon. "Keg Sitter Out." *Time* (2 March 1936). Available at http://www.time.com/time/printout/0,8816,847712,00.html. Accessed 27 May 2007.

Anon. "Lindbergh Law and After." *Time* (29 October 1934). Available at http://www.time.com/time/printout/0,8816,882242,00.html. Accessed 21 May 2007.

Anon. "Putnam, Minton & Balch." *Time* (25 August 1930). Available at http://www.time.com/time/printout/0,8816,740155,00.html. Accessed 8 May 2007.

Anon. "Return." *Time* (5 July 1926). Available at http://www.time.com/time/printout/0,8816,722156,00.html. Accessed 25 March 2007.

Anon. "San Quentin Break." *Time* (28 January 1935). Available at http://www.time.com/time/printout/0,8816,748336,00.html. Accessed 27 May 2007

Anon. "Snatch Findings." *Time* (21 May 1934). Available at http://www.time.com/time/printout/0,8816,747420,00.html. Accessed 17 May 2007.

Anon. "The House That Jackling Built." *Almanac* (27 February 2002). Available at http://www.almanacnews.com/morgue/2002/2002_02_27.jackling27.html. Accessed 4 August 2007.

Anon. "The Railroad, Pacifica's Castle, and the Congressman." Available at http://www.halfmoonbaymemories.com. Accessed 13 June 2007.

Anon. "Unprofitable." *Time* (28 May 1934). Available at http://www.time.com/time/printout/0,8816,754136,00.html. Accessed 17 May 2007.

Anon. Untitled. "Died. William F. Gettle...." *Time* (22 December 1941). Available at http://www.time.com/time/printout/0,8816,931998,00.html. Accessed 17 May 2007.

Anon. Untitled. "George Palmer Putnam, husband of...." *Time* (1 May 1939). Available at http://www.time.com/time/printout/0,8816,761187,00.html. Accessed 10 May 2007.

Anon. Untitled. "Publisher George Palmer Putnam, who loves publicity...." *Time* (22 May 1939). Available at http://www.time.com/time/printout/0,8816,761387,00.html. Accessed 10 May 2007.

California Supreme Court Historical Society. History of the California Courts. Chief Justices of California. Available at http://wwwcschs.org/02_history/02_c.html. Accessed 23 July 2007.

Family of Mr. Daniel Cowan Jacklin [sic]. Available at http://www.shucksmith.org/lincolnshire-wolds/all-lincolnshire/14/32062.htm. Accessed 4 August 2007.

Fanslow, Robin A. "The Migrant Experience." American Folklife Center, Library of Congress, 6 April 1998. Available at http://lcweb2.loc.gov.ammem/afctshtml/tsme.html. Accessed 15 October 2003.

Federal Bureau of Investigation. "Short History of the FBI." Available at http://www.fbi.gov/libref/factsfigure/shorthistory.htm. Accessed 10 September 2007.

Gia, Gilbert. "Bakersfield Race Riot, 1893." Historic Bakersfield and Kern County. Available at http://www3.igalaxy.net/~ggia/Articles/1893-BakersfieldRaceRiot/html. Accessed 21 June 2007.

Gold Rush Chronicles. Available at http://comspark.com/chronicles/glossary-d.shtml. Accessed 9 September 2007.

Historical List of Santa Cruz County Sheriffs, 1850–1994. Santa Cruz Public Library. Available at http://www.santacruzpl.org/history/crime/sheriffs.shtml. Accessed 27 May

2007.

Internet Guide to Jazz Age Slang. Available at http://home.earthlink.net/dlarkins/slong-pg.htm. Accessed 19 September 2007.

JoinCalifornia: Election History for the State of California. Available at http://www.joincalifornia.com/candidate/9018. Accessed 18 June 2007.

Los Angeles Almanac. Los Angeles County Sheriffs Past to Present. Available at http://www.laalmanac.com/crime/cr68.htm. Accessed 22 May 2007.

Los Angeles Almanac. Los Angeles Police Department Chiefs Past to Present. Available at http://www.laalmanac.com/crime/cr73.htm. Accessed 4 September 2007.

Open Collections Program: Immigration to the United States, 1789–1930: Chinese Exclusion Act (1882). Harvard University Library. Available at http://ocp.hul.harvard.edu/immigration/themes-exclusion.html. Accessed 5 September 2007.

Oregon Secretary of State Archives Division. Oregon Governors. Available at http://arcweb.sos.state.or.us/banners/governors.htm. Accessed 4 September 2007.

San Mateo County Genealogy—City and County Officials, 1889–1928. Available at http://www.sfgenealogy.com/sanmateo/smoff.htm. Accessed 21 June 2007.

Training Bulletin. Kidnapping. Oakland Police Department. Available at www.oaklandnet.com/government/PolicePubs/TB/Manual%201/1%20L%20%. Accessed 11 September 2007.

Wollenberg, Charles. "Berkeley, A City History." Berkeley Public Library. Available at http://berkeleypubliclibrary.org/community/berkeley_history/a_city_in_history/06boom_and_bust.php. Accessed 19 September 2007.

Index

Hawthorne, Nathaniel 256
Hayward 19
Heck, Franklin 227
Heere, Bertha 37
Heinrich, Edward O. 234
Hensley, Hugh 339
Herron, William F. 227-229, 232-234, 237
Heslin, Father 181-188, 191, 193, 195, 200, 202, 207, 210, 212, 214, 218, 220, 229, 231, 234, 236-238
Hewitt, Lloyd 342, 345, 347, 348, 352, 353
Hickman 52, 54, 55, 58, 59, 61, 62, 64, 65, 69-71, 73, 75-77
Hickman, Alfred 66
Hickman, Eva 52, 59, 66, 68, 70
Hickman, William Edward 51, 53, 56, 67, 72, 79
Hickman, William T. 59, 66
Hickok, Galen 194
Hickok, Harry C. 343
Hickok's Mystery Castle 199, 204
Highland Hospital 9
Highland Park 170, 174
Hightower, William A. 188-241
Hill, James J. 356-358, 360, 361
Hines, William M. 188, 193
Hitchen, Albert 146, 147
Hite, C. S. 349
Hitler, Adolf 260
Hoag, Elizabeth 81
Hobart Building 286, 288
Hoffman, P. B. 336
Hollywood 5, 11, 29, 37, 43, 152, 246, 249, 265, 266
Hollywood Boulevard 29
Hollywood High School 34
Hollywood Savings Bank 30
Holmes, Evelyn 16
Holmes, John M. 11-16, 18, 21, 25

Holmes, Maurice P. 16
Holmes-Thurmond lynching 27
Holohan, James B. 309, 313-316, 320
Holohan, Mrs. 316
Holohan, Warden 75
Holt, Mary 45, 46
Holy Angels Church 181
Homestead Act of 1862 329
Honolulu 276
Hooper Avenue (Hollywood) 33
Hoover, Herbert 28
Hoover, J. Edgar 151
Hopkins, Ernest J. 188, 190, 192-194, 212, 213
Hopper, Hedda 261
Horst Ranch 341
Hotel Humboldt 349
Hotel Marymont 204
Hotel Senate 204, 210
Hotel Sequoia 233
Hotel Whitcomb 5
House of Commons 275
Howard, Leslie 159
Howard, W. D. 170
Howland 277
Howland Island 276
Hudson, Will 324
Hudson, William Henry 256
Hughes, Russell 9
Hull, Cordell 320
Humphreys, Mrs. Walter 171
Huntington Park 32
Hunt, Welby 64, 65, 68, 70, 73
Hunzeker, Marion 331
Hunzeker, Paul 340
Hutton's 154
hydraulic mining 332, 333

I

Idaho 79
Illinois 9, 152
Imperial Cafe 210

ABOUT THE AUTHORS

California historian **James R. Smith** is the author of *San Francisco's Lost Landmarks* as well as a number of historical articles. A well-respected authority in California history, he has spent years chronicling the stories of San Francisco and the California Gold Country. Smith is a frequent lecturer and discussion leader at universities, historical societies, libraries, and bookstores.

A member of the California Historical Society, the San Francisco History Association, the San Francisco Historical Society, and the Library Fund at the University of California, Berkeley, Smith is active in the preservation and promotion of history and historical lore.

Smith is a fourth-generation native of San Francisco and a sixth-generation Californian. He is often found haunting the libraries and archives of his native city and enjoying its social life with his wife Liberty.

Award-winning historian **W. Lane Rogers** is an acknowledged expert in Western American history. He is in his fifteenth year as a Phoenix newspaper columnist, has written hundreds of articles, and has authored a number of books. Titles in the crime genre include *Ruthless Acts: The Utah Murders* and *Crimes & Misdeeds: Headlines from Arizona's Past*. *The California Snatch Racket* is Rogers' third tussle with the felonious underbelly of early twentieth century crime, this time in the Golden State.

The author has spoken before myriad organizations, and he lectures frequently in colleges and universities. His topics reflect the diversity of his writing—World War I, the early film and broadcasting industries, the Great Depression and the 1930s, and the modern Civil Rights Movement.

ADDENDUM

Please Note: My friend and mentor W. Lane Rogers passed away unexpectedly on July 29, 2009. Our next book, *Serious Mischief: Crimes in California* is now complete, so his legacy continues. Lane leaves behind his wife Patricia Rogers, who, as he told me, was the love of his life, and his four children: W. Lane Rogers II (Kim) of Phoenix; Eric Lane Rogers (Teresa) of Ogden, Utah; Rachael Brett Kramer (Drew) of Denver, and Rebecca Tess Congdon (Derek) of Littleton, Colorado. He has eight grandchildren. He is missed by all of us, and by many others.

—James R. Smith